The Poetry of Susan Howe

Modern and Contemporary Poetry and Poetics

Modern and Contemporary Poetry and Poetics promotes and pursues topics in the burgeoning field of twentieth and twenty-first century poetics. Critical and scholarly work on poetry and poetics of interest to the series includes social location in its relationships to subjectivity, to the construction of authorship, to oeuvres, and to careers; poetic reception and dissemination (groups, movements, formations, institutions); the intersection of poetry and theory; questions about language, poetic authority, and the goals of writing; claims in poetics, impacts of social life, and the dynamics of the poetic career as these are staged and debated by poets and inside poems. Topics that are bibliographic, are pedagogic, concern the social field of poetry, and reflect on the history of poetry studies are valued, as well. This series focuses both on individual poets and texts and on larger movements, poetic institutions, and questions about poetic authority, social identifications, and aesthetics.

Language and the Renewal of Society in Walt Whitman, Laura (Riding) Jackson, and Charles Olson
The American Cratylus
Carla Billitteri

Modernism and Poetic Inspiration
The Shadow Mouth
Jed Rasula

The Social Life of Poetry
Appalachia, Race, and Radical Modernism
Chris Green

Procedural Form in Postmodern American Poetry
Berrigan, Antin, Silliman, and Hejinian
David W. Huntsperger

Modernist Writings and Religio-scientific Discourse
H.D., Loy, and Toomer
Lara Vetter

Male Subjectivity and Poetic Form in "New American" Poetry
Male Subjectivity and Poetic Form
Andrew Mossin

The Poetry of Susan Howe
History, Theology, Authority
William Montgomery

The Poetry of Susan Howe
History, Theology, Authority

Will Montgomery

palgrave
macmillan

THE POETRY OF SUSAN HOWE
Copyright © Will Montgomery, 2010.

All rights reserved.

From "Fragment of the Wedding Dress of Sarah Pierpont Edwards" by Susan Howe, in SOULS OF THE LABADIE TRACT, copyright © 2007 by Susan Howe. Reprinted by permission of New Directions Publishing Corp.

First published in 2010 by
PALGRAVE MACMILLAN®
in the United States—a division of St. Martin's Press LLC,
175 Fifth Avenue, New York, NY 10010.

Where this book is distributed in the UK, Europe and the rest of the world, this is by Palgrave Macmillan, a division of Macmillan Publishers Limited, registered in England, company number 785998, of Houndmills, Basingstoke, Hampshire RG21 6XS.

Palgrave Macmillan is the global academic imprint of the above companies and has companies and representatives throughout the world.

Palgrave® and Macmillan® are registered trademarks in the United States, the United Kingdom, Europe and other countries.

ISBN: 978–0–230–62197–8

Library of Congress Cataloging-in-Publication Data

Montgomery, Will.
   The poetry of Susan Howe : history, theology, authority / Will Montgomery.
     p. cm.—(Modern and contemporary poetry and poetics)
   Includes bibliographical references.
   ISBN 978-0-230-62197-8
     1. Howe, Susan, 1937—Criticism and interpretation. 2. Literature and history. I. Title.
PS3558.O893Z77 2010
811'.54—dc22   2010007414

A catalogue record of the book is available from the British Library.

Design by Newgen Imaging Systems (P) Ltd., Chennai, India.

First edition: September 2010

10 9 8 7 6 5 4 3 2 1

Printed in the United States of America.

For NB, AFM, & KVM.

Contents

Introduction	ix
Acknowledgments	xxv
1 The Maternal Disinheritance	1
The Liberties	4
Scare Quotes (The Midnight)	17
2 The Ghost of the Father	27
A Bibliography of the King's Book or, Eikon Basilike	30
The Nonconformist's Memorial	41
3 Susan Howe's Renaissance	55
Pythagorean Silence	57
Defenestration of Prague	68
4 The Poetics of American Space	79
Articulation of Sound Forms in Time	85
Thorow	98
5 Enthusiasm, Telepathy, and Immediacy	113
Melville's Marginalia	117
Arisbe and The Leisure of the Theory Class (Pierce-Arrow)	130
6 The Late Lyric	145
Rückenfigur	148
Bed Hangings	154
Souls of the Labadie Tract	160
Notes	167
Bibliography	197
General Index	211
Index of Works by Susan Howe	217

Introduction

This book gives an account of the unstable, proliferating sets of associative connection that are, for Susan Howe, mobilized in the act of reading. It makes an argument about poetry that embraces lyric representations of war, occluded femininity, Renaissance theatre, the American landscape, religious nonconformism, and visual poetics. Over the course of three and a half decades, Howe has built a body of work that is attentive to the political and ethical infoldings of the minutest utterance and is, in the full range of the word, enthusiastic. The current study aims to pick out a pathway—one among many possible—through this endlessly surprising "word Forest" (*Thorow*, 49).

Howe began publishing poetry with *Hinge Picture* in 1974 and was initially received as part of the amorphous grouping of experimental writers known as the language poets—writers such as Charles Bernstein, Bruce Andrews, Lyn Hejinian, Carla Harryman, Barrett Watten, and Ron Silliman. These authors, now very well known, drew on the classical avant-garde of the early twentieth century, Russian formalism, Marxism, and continental critical theory. They wrote against the expressivist lyric, the illusory coherence of narrative, and the narrow ambitions of confessional and academic verse.[1] The "language" label, like most such tags, is unsatisfactory, as it masks an extremely diverse range of writing. Even given such reservations, however, it was clear from the start that Howe's poetry was out of step with certain general tendencies within language writing. Although Howe was friendly with some of the protagonists of this grouping and was included in their defining early anthology *In the American Tree*, she has never fitted easily under the language banner.[2] Howe shares with many language writers interests in the material text, the political ramifications of radical formal experimentation, and the vexed issue of voice, but her work from the outset contains countervailing investments in mystical thought, American Romanticism, and a reappraisal of lyric.

Howe undeniably valued the radicalism and intellectual commitment of some among the language writers, forming close relationships with two of the protagonists, Lyn Hejinian, on the West Coast, and Charles Bernstein, on the East. Howe's correspondence with Hejinian was one of her most substantial letter-writing relationships of the 1980s. However, she was also closely involved in a correspondence with John Taggart, a poet aligned with Robert Duncan, and one, like Duncan, explicitly in the anti-language camp. Early correspondence with Ian Hamilton Finlay and, a little later, with Norman O. Brown further testifies to the scope of her poetic and intellectual affinities.[3]

Since the late 1980s, her work has been widely anthologized and has drawn a great deal of critical commentary: books by Rachel Tzvia Back and Stephen Collis, and articles or chapters in books by such prominent commentators on American poetry as Michael Davidson, Peter Middleton, Peter Nicholls, Marjorie Perloff, Rachel Blau DuPlessis, Lynn Keller, Susan Schultz and Brian Reed. Howe is typically read as a major voice within the American late modernist tradition—an inheritor of the legacy of Pound, HD, Olson, and others. In the *Cambridge Companion to Ezra Pound*, for example, Nicholls observes that the work bears "eloquent testimony to the continuing role of poet-as-historian."[4] Though her work differs in numerous important ways from that of Pound—not least in its attachment to principles of instability and uncertainty—they share a commitment to an intellectually ambitious mode of poetry that is rooted in close attention to history. Nicholls, one of Howe's most perceptive critical commentators, also notes that Howe's work implies a "fundamental reformulation of Poundian principle" because of its emphasis on the "unreadable" in history.[5] The various implications of that unreadability—whether literal or in the sense of incomprehensible—provide some of the core themes of this book.

Feminist scholars were among the first to respond to Howe's writing. Critics including DuPlessis, Keller, Back, Kathleen Fraser, and Elisabeth Frost have produced valuable discussions of the treatment in Howe's poetry of women as sidelined nonparticipants in history's unfolding. Many have paid particular attention to the issue of silence and to the ways in which Howe's experiments with page space and with an ethics of marginality have led to a poetry in which the effacement of the feminine is rendered. Some have drawn on the poems of *Singularities* and the criticism of *The Birth-mark* to situate Howe as a specifically antinomian voice—a development of a stuttering and marginalized strand of American speech that has its origins in theological disputes among the early settlers of New England. This study is informed by this work but seeks to lead the conversation down new pathways, deriving a sense of permission both from the Nietzschean daring of Howe's portrait of Emily Dickinson in her early critical work *My Emily Dickinson* and from Howe's interest in male writers such as Melville, Edwards, Peirce, and Stevens. Issues of gender and power are, clearly, crucial to Howe's writing, but in this study they are subsumed beneath the overall question of poetic speech.

In recent years, it has become clear that there are numerous contexts in which Howe can be read. Her background as a visual artist with affiliations to American minimalism and to artists such as Agnes Martin and Marcia Hafif, for example, is extremely significant. Marcel Duchamp is a repeated touchstone. She has often acknowledged a debt to Charles Olson, particularly his use of page space (an area discussed by Kathleen Fraser and others). A rarely heard but no less plausible approach would be to point to Howe's Anglo-Irish ancestry and to look to poems such as *The Liberties* and *The Midnight* for motifs of non-belonging, Swiftian wordplay, Yeatsian enchantment, and Gothic unease. Howe's recent work, from *Pierce-Arrow* on, displays an interest in pragmatist thought and makes explicit a genealogy of American letters—Edwards, Emerson, Henry James, William James, Stevens—that is inflected by pragmatist criticism.[6] Although it is clear from the correspondence that Stevens has long been a central interest for Howe, it is only recently, in *Souls of the Labadie Tract* and a 2009 article for *Chicago Review*, that she has explicitly addressed his writing.[7] It is clear that there are multiple vectors of influence and association at work in this writing.

One oblique early marker of Howe's affection for Stevens, however, can be found at the head of her 1990 collection *The Europe of Trusts*. This is in the form of a manifesto-like sequence entitled "THERE ARE NOT LEAVES ENOUGH TO CROWN TO COVER TO CROWN TO COVER."[8] The title is taken from Wallace Stevens' characteristically evasive meditation on the public role of the poet, "United Dames of America." Although no direct reference to Stevens is made in the piece, it advances arguments about the responsibilities of poetry that have affinities with Stevens's famous discussion of sound and the "pressure of reality" in his wartime essay "The Noble Rider and the Sound of Words."

"Leaves" is a textual collage that sketches the considerable extent of Howe's poetic ambition at the time and incorporates many of the formal and thematic elements that define her poems: biblical and literary citation; folk material; autobiography; the censorship or suppression of speech; a pursuit of primeval origins that acknowledges its own impossibility; and, above all, the desire to formulate a poetic response to war and colonial violence. From it, we learn that Howe was born just before the outbreak of the Second World War and that she had an Irish mother and an American father. Howe indicates that her father left home to fight in the war and that his letters home were subject to the editorial attentions of the army censor. She mentions news photographs of the war alongside references to the Bible: Herod's slaughter of the innocents and Rachel, "weeping for her children" ("Leaves," 11). She cites a nursery rhyme ("The hawk with his long claws/ Pulled down the stones./ The dove with her rough bill/ Brought me them home" [Ibid., 12]) and the Greek tragedy *Antigone* (Creon's injunction to Antigone: "Go to the dead and love them" [Ibid., 13]). Interleaved with the prose, which is often catachrestic ("I had so many dead Innocents distance was abolished" [Ibid.,12]), are three sequences of dense and discontinuous poetry. Howe also makes several statements about the nature of her work. She writes, for example, "In my poetry, time and again, questions of assigning *the cause* of history dictate the sound of what is thought" (Ibid.,13). And, "I write to break out into perfect primeval Consent" (Ibid.,14).

The relationship between poetic language and the past is at the heart of her various assertions. "History is the record of winners," she writes ("Leaves," 11), following this *topos* with a stranger formulation: "Poetry brings similitude and representation to configurations waiting from forever to be spoken" (Ibid., 14). Poetry, we might conclude, is a means of following Creon's injunction—a way of recovering some of the experience that history's "winners" might have effaced. Howe's concluding statement to "Leaves" is perhaps her best known pronouncement on her poetry: "I wish I could tenderly lift from the dark side of history, voices that are anonymous, slighted—inarticulate" (14).[9]

How might a poetry rooted in historical particulars incorporate the "perfect" and the "primeval"? How is it possible to illuminate the "dark side of history," to give voice to the "inarticulate," to represent that which has been "forever" unspoken? These are the tasks that Howe sets herself. The difficulty of her poetry of this period is a necessary difficulty that has its origins in the problems that confront a poetry of witness when what it seeks to memorialize has vanished.[10]

There is in "Leaves," moreover, an unresolved tension between a poetry of redress and a poetry of grace—the demands of the temporal order and the spiritual. This tension is a fundamental characteristic of Howe's work. The growing body of critical writing on Howe's poetry has had much to say about its ethical imperatives, tending to find in its formal freedoms the poetic realization of an anticanonical and antiauthoritarian literary and political radicalism. This book is skeptical about some of these claims, although they can, indeed, be found in Howe's poetry and literary criticism. Accounts of Howe's work have often tended to elide the presence of a theological impulse in her poetry. The poetry's frequent use of language of spiritual immediacy sits uneasily with late-twentieth-century and early twenty-first-century progressive politics. The mystical current in the writing, present from its beginnings in the 1970s to the present day, is not always compatible with the elements of Marxian, psychoanalytic, and poststructuralist thought that provide the intellectual context for those who write on her.[11] The theory boom of the 1980s and 1990s is, of course, the context in which Howe herself was writing some of her best known works. Yet the poems are not quite as amenable to contemporary theoretical toolkits as some have implied.

When Howe writes, as she has recently, that "poetry flows into prayer" ("Choir Answers to Choir: Notes on Jonathan Edwards and Wallace Stevens," 61), she seems explicitly to be problematizing the status of the poetic and its relation to the critical discourses that surround it, insisting on some sort of special status for poetic speech but at the same time perceiving the poetic in genres other than poetry. This study is secular in nature and has no investment in religious belief. However, it seeks to explore the significance of this provocative feature of Howe's writing, which, I argue, extends through considerations of political authority and unconscious experience into a theory of reading. Although I often refer to writers and philosophers whose work can be read in productive parallel with Howe's, I suppress neither the poetry's engagement with older, metaphysical vocabularies nor the uncomfortable fit between this aspect of the work and a broadly progressive politics.

Howe writes in *My Emily Dickinson* (a book that often reads as a thinking-through of Howe's own poetics; hereafter, *MED*) that Dickinson "explored the implications of breaking the law just short of breaking off communication with a reader" (*MED*, 11). A quasi-religious enthusiasm is, for Howe, a way of returning poetic language to its founding and incoercible strangeness. A quality of outsideness—telepathy, the enigmatic message, citation, the violence of the linebreak—allows the poetry, like Mr. Dick's kite in *Eikon*, to drift beyond the control of either writer or reader. The figure of the itinerant—Hope Atherton in *Articulation of Sound Forms in Time*; the "scout" of *Thorow*, Mangan/Bartleby or Peirce—exemplifies the intellectual nonconformism of this outsideness.

The contract between temporal and atemporal registers—history and grace—in the work is unstable, and it puts the poetry's competing ambitions under enormous pressure. The intractable problems that Howe sets herself in "Leaves" are discernible throughout a complex body of work that makes the resistance of interpretative endeavor almost a condition of its existence. The writing's greatest resource is its ability to tap into an "understory" (*Thorow*, 50)—a form of linguistic unconscious that permits literary communication of the kind that Howe calls telepathy.

In Howe's poetry, religious experience and the experience of poetic language continually fold into one another. The peculiarly volatile pact between sound and history that her poetry proposes causes her work to be shot through with uncertainty and indeterminacy. Yet, at the same time, it aspires to a degree of purchase on the workings of worldly injustice. The generative paradox at the center of the work lies in the poetry's capacity to retain a quality of uncoercible otherness while at the same time articulating narratives of usurpation and exclusion. As Howe recognizes in *Birth-mark*, such narratives tread a fine line between illumination and obscurity: "The Lord is the Word. He scatters short fragments. Jonah cried out to the Word when floods encompassed him. A Sound Believer hears old Chaos as in a deep sea. A narrative refuses to conform to its project" (*Birth-mark*, 61). This question of a specifically poetic mode of utterance is central to my account of Howe. There has been a tendency among critics to read Howe's poems as the realization of their prefaces, as if they performed a number of intellectual tasks that might just as easily have been carried out in other discursive modes. But these narratives do not conform to their projects. Although I pay attention—sometimes, as in this introduction, a good deal of attention—to these prefaces, the focus of my book is on the obdurate strangeness of the language in the body of the poems, a form of poetry that is refractory to critical discussion (as "Chaos cast cold intellect back" ["Leaves," 14] suggests). Lines such as the following present enormous problems to the critic:

> Summary of fleeting summary
> Pseudonym cast across empty
>
> Peak proud heart
> Majestic caparisoned cloud cumuli
> East sweeps hewn flank ("Leaves," 13)

It is impossible to put such sequences through the mills of conventional prosody or exegesis. The three words "Peak proud heart," for example, appear to stand in isolation, making a unit neither of sense nor of syntax. Nor does the line appear to communicate with the lines that precede or follow it. Yet, even in an excerpt of less than 20 words, the diction (Howe's poetry draws on carefully delimited lexical fields) and the handling of sound lend the lines a vestigial coherence. A description of the interplay between such patterns of lyric coherence and the poetry's more broken qualities forms part of the argument of this book.

Although this book contributes to the work of sketching in Howe's sources, makes frequent reference to her own statements about her poetry, and finds various critical theorists and philosophers to be helpful when describing her poems, it also seeks to articulate—or be articulate about—the poetry's impenetrability. It is notable, for example, that the poem *Articulation of Sound Forms in Time* is usually discussed with reference to the wandering protagonist of the first section, Hope Atherton; the poem's longest section, however, "Taking the Forest," ranges far beyond the physical and temporal environment that dominates the earlier sections of the poem. The poetry in such passages is immensely accomplished and suggestive, but its resistant quality poses problems for the exegete, as if, by default, he or she is assimilated to the censorious band of "scholars, lawyers, investigators, judges" that troubles the speaker of "Leaves" (10).

Those who write on Howe have often, with good reason, noted her poetry's allegiance to silenced social groupings: women, the marginalized, and nonconformists of various sorts. This aspect of the poetry has frequently been aligned with arguments about the revision of the canon that point to Howe's intervention in disputes about the editing of Emily Dickinson, for example, or her important research on early American captivity narratives. However, although much of this critical work is valuable, I do not want to lose sight of Howe's commitment to texts that are central to the canon—Shakespeare, Milton, the Bible, Yeats, Eliot, and Stevens. Howe's writing does not have a straightforwardly agonistic relation to either social or literary authority (although her prose sometimes encourages such a view). Her positions are more complex; the powerful anti-authoritarian currents in the work are accompanied by an ambivalent investment in notions such as voice, literary tradition, autobiography, and lyric.[12] This interpretation of her work certainly does not come from the perspective of a conservative recuperation of Howe's unsettling voice. On the contrary, I argue that Howe's revisionary approach to such features of the literary allow her to speak, as it were, both from the inside and the outside. This is a poetry in which the lure of sanctified authority and its political descendants is not simply negated; it is shown to be a part of the wider culture, imbricated within social experience and inescapable. The puzzle of authority animates this writing. I read the work as productive of combustible antinomies rather than as antinomian per se.

There are, in my view, two basic configurations of authority in Howe's writing. One is monolithic, vengeful, and overbearing. This can be found in such statements as "Behind the facade of Harvard University is a scaffold and a regicide" (Foster interview, 176); in the discussion of patriarchy, colonialism, and grammar that precedes *Thorow*; and in some of Howe's comments on the editing of Emily Dickinson's texts. Another is presented more ambivalently, in a way that acknowledges the pervasive reach and subtle workings of power. This is a power that is productive as well as coercive. It is the version of authority we find in Howe's discussions of Emily Dickinson's Master Letters, in her feminized representations of Charles I in *Eikon*, Melville in *Melville's Marginalia* (and elsewhere), and the Christ of John's gospel in *The Nonconformist's Memorial*. The latter is the version of authority that I find most persuasive and challenging.

* * *

A key point of departure for this book, less often discussed than "Leaves," is Howe's substantial preface to her *Frame Structures: Early Poems 1974–1979* (hereafter cited as *FS*), which was published in 1996. In this text, the idea of relations, both familial and lexical, is explored at length. The preface is clearly—and revealingly—an attempt to impose retrospectively the coherence of Howe's mature poetics on the earlier work. It also touches on the prominence of Howe's American ancestors—the DeWolfe Howes, the Quincys, and the Adams—in New England history. The ways in which past and present interfere with one other through the medium of language—as they certainly do in the preface to *Frame Structures*—is a theme to which my book will often return.

The preface both describes and embodies a process of "lexical drift" (*FS*, 22). It functions as a kind of framing device, by means of which a poet much concerned with the movement between past and present considers her own past as a writer and chooses to sketch in certain autobiographical details that inform the early poems. The privileged site for the play of reciprocal determination between past and present is linguistic. In asserting the embeddedness of her family history in New England history, Howe uses a succession of puns to draw speculative links between discrete narratives. It soon becomes clear that these links verge on the arbitrary: they are sustained by the claims Howe makes for a mode of cognition that is proper to poetry, one that follows linguistic trails to offer an associative counter to more linear literary and political histories. This identifies language as the driving force of history and its repressed aspects—puns, sounding, visual appearance, materialization in the book—as the vessel through which history can in some sense be re-encountered.

Poetic thought, then, is given an enormous burden: to trace lines of energy through linguistic similitudes—coincidences that might appear to be mere epiphenomena of expression. As she formulates it in "Leaves," "Poetry brings similitude and representation to configurations waiting from forever to be spoken" (14).[13] This form of response to the past pursues threads of inquiry that are so deeply woven into the narrative texture of personal and collective history as to be almost imperceptible: "Historical imagination gathers in the missing," writes Howe on the first page of the 1996 preface (*FS*, 3).

The place of the poet, for Howe, is at a point intersected by such strands. The poetic voice engaged in this lexical drift is felt to be private but knows itself to be public. This conception of poetic composition has both passive and active faces: the poet can appear as a medium through whom the past speaks or as a figure performing ambitious acts of historical imagination through language. "The struggles of dead wills *do* speak through survivors," Howe says in an early interview. "How can we approach the dead ones deep in time's silence?"[14]

The answer to her question may come through the unexpected conjunctions and unsettling disjunctions that characterize her understanding of poetic language. One might object, of course, that her similitudes—in the preface to *Frame Structures*, for example, the links between such words as *daughter* and *slaughter*, or *Niagara* and *Nigeria*—are arbitrary alignments whose claim to facilitate a form of historical knowledge is tendentious. One might also object that statements such as "Telepsychology. We have always been in contact with one another" (*FS*, 25) offer the poet the hieratic privilege of access to a form of mystical knowledge. The earlier assertion, in "Leaves," that poetry can bring "representation and similitude to configurations waiting from for ever to be spoken" is not only unequivocal but untestable. An evaluation of Howe's arguments around poetic form and its relation to history will be a central preoccupation of parts of this book.

Similitude for Howe is a means of gaining access to material that lies outside the written record. An extreme example of this method of imposing a counter-rational grid on an incident is the anecdote at the opening of the preface to *Frame Structures*. This event, which assured Howe's vocation as a poet, is also central to "Leaves," and to the "Pearl Harbor" section of *Pythagorean Silence*. In syntactically stretched prose, Howe tells of a visit to the zoo at Buffalo with her father in 1941, when she was four. The animals are acting strangely, and she and her father later learn that the Japanese had just attacked Pearl Harbor, provoking the entry of the United States into the Second World War and the prolonged absence of Howe's father, who immediately joined up.

> Daddy held on tightly to my hand because animals do communicate in a state resembling dissociation so a prepared people will rid the settlement of ice deities identified with rivers they cause animism. Everyone talking of war in those days. Enough to weigh against love. Animals sense something about ruin I think he said our human spirits being partly immaterial

at that prefigured time though we didn't know then how free will carries us past to be distance waiting for another meeting a true relation. (*FS*, 3).

In an interview with Charles Bernstein, Howe is explicit about this incident: the polar bears "knew" something had happened, she says, adding "I am a poet of war but I am a woman."[15] Howe, then, not only links a major world-historical event to her own vocation as a poet, but she imputes a telepathic sensitivity to the bears, who become an emblem of an otherness hemmed in and abused by modernity: "Three bears running around rocks as if to show how modern rationalism springs from barbarism and with such noise to show how boldly ventured is half won" (*FS*, 3).[16] Howe's poetry counters, or perhaps complements, history with "historical imagination," which is the setting for the transaction between the "immaterial" and everyday experience. Moreover, there is, at the dense and syntactically broken end of the paragraph, a speculation on prophecy, predestination ("prefigured"), and "free will," which proceeds to the wordplay of "true relation" (i.e., her father).[17] Here, "we didn't know then" wryly undoes the logic of predestination by suggesting that one could know better and so move outside its embrace.

Howe's ostensible assertion, which plugs the polar bears into a kind of Reuters network of the animal world, filters the decisive pairing of public (war) and private (paternal abandonment) calamities through the sensibility of a child: "I was a deep and nervous child with the north wind of the fairy story ringing in my ears as well as direct perception" (*FS*, 3). The apparent absurdity of her—or her father's—speculation about the bears dissolves when it is considered as a motif for the associative logic that Howe considers proper to poetic language.

Howe's poetry works, at various levels, through a questioning of sequence. The multidirectional logic of collage replaces that of narrative. At their most fundamental level, the sequences of letters that spell words are subject to the torsion of history. In her preface to *Frame Structures*, Howe offers a form of writing that is dense with secondary associations and finely tuned to the precarious dependence of sound and sense on the basic unit of the letter. Describing the movements of herself and her sister Fanny as children, taking shortcuts between home and school across public and private land, Howe writes,

> Between Berkeley Street and Brattle some meticulous gardens still remained among lawns abandoned to children some even wilder patches of weed and brush.... Boundaries interlinking public and private are very well, precaution and policy, thought is arranged over this, the property

of *h* (breath without sound) comes between *g* and *t* (sound without breath) in daughter slaughter laughter. Letters launched into space rush one child to the next, more or less at large, acting wolves and tigers, colliding with landowners (by subterfuge). (*FS*, 10)

Poetic speech is impelled by the apparent happenstance of linguistic similitudes. The movements of Howe and her sister are reconceived as lexical wandering: changing a letter within a word directs thought—and the child's mind—down avenues as distinct as "daughter" and "slaughter." For Howe, who as a girl played Astyanax in *Trojan Women*, the conjunction is not random.[18] Howe's method in this preface is to use punning as a kind of forced coincidence, an intervention in the arrangement of accidentals. Punning is a moment that allows language to get the upper hand, but it is also something that Howe forces through her exploitation of such contiguities.

The wandering attention of Howe's prose in her *Frame Structures* preface draws "lines of association" between her childhood and the lives of relatives and ancestors and literary and political history (in this I am adapting a phrase used by Marjorie Perloff in her discussion of *Frame Structures*: "the text's war space is crisscrossed by 'life-lines,' lines of descent, connection, and association").[19] Howe's polemical forcing of circumstances verges on a literary fantasy of omnipotence, as if she were ascribing to her linguistic resources magical powers to force the world to do her bidding. Yet for Howe inside and outside, private and public interpenetrate. Her omnipotence, a childhood delusion recalled in a memoir of childhood, continually flips into its opposite—determination by the public medium of language—as "Letters launched into space rush one child to the next" (*FS*, 10).

An exemplary forced coincidence colors the account given of Howe's American family history. Her paternal grandfather's "immediate family constellation" was based in a large farmhouse named Weetamoe by the sea in Bristol, Massachusetts. When Howe was researching her essay on Mary Rowlandson, who was taken captive by Native Americans during King Philip's War (1675–77), she "ran across" the figure of Weetamoo, Queen of Pocasset and sister-in-law to King Philip (or Metacomet).[20] Weetamoo was eventually drowned while escaping the "Christian soldiers," and her body was washed up on land that became part of the DeWolfe Howe farm (*FS*, 21–22). The family's background is thus linked, in a near admission of guilt by association, by the word Weetamoe to the near destruction of the Native Americans in early American history.

What do these similitudes amount to? How can Howe, at the end of the twentieth century, not the nineteenth, write, "Telepsychology. We have always been in contact with one another" (*FS*, 25)? She does not make it clear whether such assertions are merely part of a polemical expression of the force of poetic language, or whether they amounts to a genuine conviction that, for example, Weetamoo's death, mediated by Weetamoe, implicates Howe by linguistic and actual genealogy in America's colonial past. Is her method, in other words, a self-aware arrogation of magical powers to the poet (who knows this to be a device) or the expression of a belief in an unconscious of language from which word-constellations—Weetamoo/ Weetamoe, daughter/ slaughter—erupt as symptoms indicative of trauma? Once again, the flow of determination appears to run in both directions.

Howe's opening account of the polar bears in Delaware Park, entitled "Flanders," is answered by the closing section of the preface, "Flinders": "The brute force is Buffalo because of its position as a way station whose primary function is the movement of goods from east to west and vice versa in dark reaches before soldiers come foraging. Close by lies a great forest approaching Modernism my early poems project aggression" (*FS*, 29).

The departure of Howe's father to war is a personal loss that marked the intrusion of what Howe calls the "geopolitical chain of violence" on Howe's early life.[21] Buffalo (where Howe taught for many years at SUNY) comes to represent a brutalized and exploited nature, encircled, like the early New England settlements, by 'wilderness'. It is this wilderness, under the sign of "Modernism," that Howe claims her poems begin to explore. The preface to *Frame Structures*, although intended to serve as an introduction to her 1970s poems, might serve as an introduction to the major long poems surveyed in this book. Punning, telepathy, and the question of a writer's relation to her words and those of others are themes that occur throughout the work. "Lexical drift" as a means of accommodating history within poetry is a fundamental characteristic of Howe's ambitions. The poems of the 1980s and 1990s are inhabited by the voices of the dead and by ghostly representations of authority such as Joseph Ellicott, the founder of Buffalo, whom she compares in her preface to *Frame Structures* to Hamlet's father (*FS*, 29). Howe's allusion to the dead Weetamoo and, toward the end of the preface, to Ophelia, form part of a meditation on the relation between gender and literary form that extends throughout her writing career.

In "Leaves," as we have seen, Howe cites Creon's words to Antigone before he orders her to be buried alive: "Go to the dead and love them." In her writing, Howe often implicitly assumes a destiny akin to that of Antigone (who explicitly features in the late 1990s poem "Rückenfigur"), consigned to a place from which speech is impossible. The corpse of Antigone's brother

Polynices is torn apart by wild dogs. Howe seeks to achieve through the presentation of such brokenness a kind of coherence. The image in "Leaves" of "Rachel weeping for her children" ("Leaves," 11) communicates a distress at violence which fills the poetry with death, mourning and dispossession. Nonetheless, Howe remains committed to the transformative estrangements of the reading experience.

* * *

This book aims to be a comprehensive survey of Howe's poetry. However, given the breadth of the oeuvre and the need for extended discussion of core texts, the book necessarily brings its own exclusions. I have reluctantly decided not to give close attention to the early poems collected in *Frame Structures*: *Hinge Picture*, *Chanting at the Crystal Sea*, *Cabbage Gardens*, and *Secret History of the Dividing Line*.[22] I exclude three brief poems from detailed discussion: "Scattering as Behavior Toward Risk," "Silence Wager Stories," and "Kidnapped" (collected in *Singularities*, *The Nonconformist's Memorial* and *The Midnight* respectively).[23] Although these poems are significant works in their own right, my book is oriented toward the larger historical and formal ambitions evident in the longer poems. Of Howe's recent collection *Souls of the Labadie Tract*, I discuss at length only its longest and most substantial poem, the title poem. Another exclusion is a very early work, an 'Irish' poem that Howe has chosen not to republish: *The Western Borders* (1976).[24] In this case, detailed discussion of the poem would not have added to the treatment of Ireland I give elsewhere.

My argument proceeds thematically. These themes only sometimes (as in chapters 3 and 4) coincide with the organization of poems in Howe's books. I begin with chapter-long discussions of the poetry's maternal and paternal axes, which structure the writing's relationship to tropes of displacement and authority in numerous ways. I then discuss the mechanisms of metamorphosis that Howe explores in the 1980s work that anchors itself in the Renaissance imagination. My fourth chapter examines the meeting of Europe and America in her *Singularities* poems, particularly as registered in issues of language and landscape. I then discuss the linked themes of telepathy and enthusiasm, particularly as these affect the relationship between print and manuscripts. My final chapter discusses the category of lyric in Howe's recent work.

This book is often informed, explicitly and implicitly, by Howe's extraordinary critical writing, though it sometimes takes issue with some of her positions. *My Emily Dickinson* and *Birth-mark*, following in the wake of Williams's *In the American Grain* and Olson's *Call Me Ishmael*, are unusual and provocative books, deliberately placing themselves to one side of conventional academic prose. Indeed, many of the texts gathered in *Birth-mark* can be read as provocative cross-genre collages that embrace poetry, historical enquiry, polemical literary criticism, and textual scholarship. However, my book is specifically oriented toward a discussion of poetic speech. Howe's critical writing, even where it questions the nature and status of such writing, makes itself felt as a background presence, rather than as the focus of a particular chapter. Howe's use of prose in her poems is discussed in my accounts of *Thorow*, *Melville's Marginalia*, and *The Midnight*. For extended treatment of Howe's critical work, the reader is referred to Stephen Collis's *Through Words of Others: Susan Howe and Anarcho-Scholasticism*, in which a useful discussion of power and freedom is conducted.

I cite from the extant editions of Howe's work. For example, I discuss *Pythagorean Silence*, *Defenestration of Prague*, and *The Liberties*, first published in small press editions in 1982, 1983, and 1980 respectively, in the versions in which they appear in the current reprint of 1990's *The Europe of Trusts*, rather than the original small-press editions in which they appeared. Similarly, I discuss *The Midnight*, rather than the earlier book versions of the texts published by Granary Books and the Coracle Press. Although in some cases—the visual material in the Kulchur Foundation edition of *The Liberties*, for example—there is much to be gained in discussion of the small-press editions, I have sought to discuss works that are available to a wide readership. It seems likely that future editions (and related critical discussion) will follow the versions of the texts in the current New Directions and Wesleyan editions.

It is worth noting, however, that in some cases early, small-press editions of the poems are superior in one way or another. The Awede edition of *Articulation of Sound Forms in Time*, for example, gives much more page space to the poetry (although it lacks most of the later version's prefatory prose section, "The Falls Fight"). Howe is extremely interested in the book as physical artifact, and this dimension of the work is often better appreciated in the less condensed small press versions. However, although the material dimensions of Howe's work has received useful discussion in the writing of Michael Davidson and others, my book is principally concerned with the conceptual arena of Howe's poetry and poetics.

A Note on Referencing

I have italicized both the titles of books by Susan Howe and the titles of individual long poems (as many of these have seen separate publication in book form).

When giving references to works by Howe I have either shortened titles to one or two significant words (*Articulation* for *Articulation of Sound Forms in Time*, for example) or used the following abbreviations:

FS—*"Preface: Frame Structures"*
PS—*Pythagorean Silence*
MED—*My Emily Dickinson*
NCM—*The Nonconformist's Memorial* (i.e., the poem, not the collection of the same title)
MM—*Melville's Marginalia*
P-A—*Pierce-Arrow*
TM—*The Midnight*
SLT—*Souls of the Labadie Tract*

For purposes of referencing, I have treated the books up to and including *The Nonconformist's Memorial* as collections of discrete poems, each referenced by title (*Defenestration*, 12, for example). References to *Pierce-Arrow*, *The Midnight* and *Souls of the Labadie Tract* point the reader to the book rather than to the particular poem (*TM*, 12, for example). References to texts by Howe are given parenthetically in the main text, as are many of my references to key interviews. I have, as indicated in my introduction, used the editions published by New Directions and Wesleyan.

When citing Howe's interviews and dialogues with other writers, rather than reproduce the titles under which they were published, I have generally used the name of the interlocutor: "Keller interview," for example.

Unless otherwise stated, all italicized emphases within quotations derive from the source citation.

I have referred to the Alexander text of Shakespeare and the Authorized Version of the Bible.

Acknowledgments

My thanks to Susan Howe for granting permission for me to cite freely from her books, correspondence, journals and working notes. She has been generous with her permission and in answering the occasional query but appropriately rigorous in keeping a distance from my work. I am grateful to New Directions Publishing Corporation and to Wesleyan University Press for permission to cite from their publications. Thanks are also due to the staff of Special Collections, University of California, San Diego, who were extremely helpful when I visited, and of University of California, Santa Cruz, with whom I communicated at a distance. Research trips to the United States were funded by the Central Research Fund of the University of London and the United Kingdom's Arts and Humanities Research Board (as it then was). Many individuals have read all or part of this in earlier form and commented; particular thanks go to Clair Wills, Rachel Potter, Peter Nicholls, Robert Hampson, Peter Middleton and Palgrave's series editor, Rachel Blau DuPlessis. Earlier versions of my discussions of *Pythagorean Silence*, *Defenestration of Prague*, *Thorow* and *Melville's Marginalia* appeared in the *Journal of American Studies*, *Textual Practice* and *Paragraph*. A very brief passages from shorter articles in *Parataxis* and *Poetry Review* have survived in altered form.

Excerpts from *Singularities*, and *Birth-mark: Unsettling the Wilderness in American Literary History* © 1990 and 1993 by Susan Howe, and reprinted by permission of Wesleyan University Press.

Excerpts from *Frame Structures: Early Poems 1974–1979* © 1996; *My Emily Dickinson* © 1985; *The Europe of Trusts* © 1990; *The Nonconformist's Memorial* © 1993; *Pierce-Arrow* © 1999; *The Midnight* © 2003; *Souls of the Labadie Tract* © 2007; by Susan Howe, reprinted by permission of New Directions Publishing Corp.

CHAPTER 1

The Maternal Disinheritance

Susan Howe has said that she finds the split in her between Irish and American to be the respective pulls of mother and father—a "civil war in the soul."[1] One way, indeed, of approaching her works is to step back for a moment from their broader historical and theoretical engagements and consider the ways in which affective attachments to the mother and the father are marked within them. Although this will not foreclose the larger ambitions of these texts, it provides a way of separating maternal and paternal impulses in the work—impulses that have ready implications for Howe's treatment of language, for example, or of social authority.

Howe's mother, Mary Manning Howe, was an Anglo-Irish actress, playwright, and director. She was active in the literary and theatrical scenes in Dublin in the 1920s and 1930s and was directed by Yeats when she was a student at the Abbey Theatre.[2] In the United States, she ran the Poets' Theatre in Boston, while Howe's father taught law at Harvard. Those with whom Mary Manning Howe worked included Frank O'Hara, John Ashbery, Bunny Lang, Edward Gorey, and Robert Lowell.[3] Faber published her theatrical adaptation of *Finnegans Wake* in 1958; *The Last Chronicles of Ballyfungus*, a comic novel, was published in 1978.

What is essential to any reflection on Howe's relationship to Ireland is a consideration that an Anglo-Irish—not an Irish—sensibility is at issue. My reading therefore differs in emphasis from Lynn Keller's suggestion that, in Howe's poems, an oppressed "'feminine' figure (or entity such as Ireland)" is set against the "repressive operation of the hegemonic/colonizing system, which is both manifest and reinforced through conventional language use."[4] The relationship between authority and language is complicated, in my view, both by Anglo-Irishness and by ambivalence (not straightforward antipathy) toward the paternal and its various symbolic corollaries. Neither Back's discussion of *The Liberties* nor Golding's discussion of Howe and Ireland—each of which, like Keller's work on Howe, has much to offer—probes the question of Anglo-Irishness.[5] Howe's relationship with Ireland is not simply one of sympathy for a colonized people that can be assimilated to what Golding calls, referring to early work such as *The Liberties*, "the poetic, the marginal, the 'uncodifiable' [and] the female."[6]

Instead, Howe works from an awareness of the doubly displaced status of the Anglo-Irish, the descendants of the early English settlers in the sixteenth and seventeenth centuries and the main channel through which Anglophone Irish literature was voiced—Swift, Irish Gothic, Yeats, Synge, and Beckett all share this background. It is an inheritance that reflects a small but privileged grouping who are considered un-English by the English and un-Irish by the Irish. Indeed, inheritance seems a questionable term, as the Anglo-Irish 'big house'—itself a prime locus of literary atmosphere, from Gothic to Bowen—became a target of republican violence, particularly in the Irish Civil War of 1922–23. Although, as with Yeats, a vigorous involvement with native cultural traditions has sometimes been shown by the Anglo-Irish, a quality of not-belonging has characterized this form of cultural identity, which has often sought to disavow itself. It is this sense of rootlessness, perhaps, that provokes Howe to assert in *The Midnight* (2003), after listing a variety of minority religious sects, outsiders, and misfits, "I cling to you with all my divided attention. Itinerantly. It's the maternal Anglo-Irish disinheritance" (*TM*, 66). As Howe's work unfolds, attributes that are ambivalently associated with both her mother and Anglo-Irishness can be seen to assert themselves: homelessness, division, doubleness, wandering, and the border between early emotional bonds and their sublimation in the public medium of the artwork.

Cabbage Gardens, published in 1979 but written before *Secret History of the Dividing Line* (1978) contains an epigraphs from Boswell's *Life of Samuel Johnson*. The Johnson quotation announces a key Howe theme, as Johnson muses on whether one might be able to write "The Cabbage-garden, a Poem": "The poem might begin with the advantages of civilized society over a rude state, exemplified by the Scotch, who had no cabbages till Oliver Cromwell's soldiers introduced them; and one might thus shew how arts are propagated by conquest, as they were by the Roman arms" (*Cabbage Gardens*, 74). Howe returns again and again in her poetry to the mutual implication of culture and conquest. In later work, especially in *Singularities*, she is concerned with the settling of New England, but here she is particularly interested in Ireland. Although a more nuanced reflection on the ambivalences of Anglo-Irishness will mark later work, *Cabbage Gardens* is formally self-conscious about the double bind of an Anglophone culture that is anxious about the violence of its origins.

Although it is hard to ignore the poem's occasional but troubling romanticization of Ireland's fertile store of Celtic myth, there is a level of political allusion too: the reference to Cromwell at the head of the poem cannot but place these tales in the context of Johnson's words on the conquest of the rude by the civilized:

> The enemy coming on roads
> and clouds
> aeons.
> Cashel has fallen
> trees are turf (*Cabbage Gardens*, 75)

These lines refer to the capture of Cashel by Cromwell's troops, which was the occasion of a massacre of the townsfolk. The line "trees are turf" allude to the deforestation that was carried out under Cromwell.[7] However, the book's Irishness is not reflected in a straightforward identification with the victims of colonial aggression. Even at this early stage in her writing, Howe is too aware of the ironies of colonial domination. However obliquely she addresses Johnson's Cabbage-garden fancy, her own art is similarly traversed by conquest. When, in the preface to *The Europe of Trusts*, Howe writes that "history is the record of winners" ("Leaves," 11), she is close to Johnson's "arts are propagated by conquest." The indirectness and difficulty of *Cabbage Gardens* suggests an acknowledgement that it, too, is party to the culture of conquest but that it is seeking to disrupt that culture's forms of expression. Increasingly in her work, the quality of hesitancy that an awareness of this dilemma provokes becomes an integral stylistic feature of that resistance.

In *The Midnight*, it is through the maternal gift of Yeats, an affect-laden bridge between her mother and the world, that Howe offers a revised description of the formation of her own voice, as a "Separatist" (Liberties, 204):

> She clung to William's words by speaking them aloud. So there were always three dimensions visual textual auditory at once. Waves of sound connected us, by associational syllabic magic to an original but imaginary place existing somewhere across the ocean between the emphasis of sound and the emphasis of sense. I loved listening to her voice. I felt my own vocabulary as something hopelessly mixed and at the same time hardened into glass. (*TM*, 75)

The constituent elements of this passage—cultural displacement, the mother's voice, poetry—emphasize the maternal component of Howe's poetic identity. Yet the continuity between this and the paternal, American elements with which it is mixed in Howe's work is powerfully evident. The words "visual textual auditory" and "associational syllabic magic" indicate that the poetry's animating energy is the capacity to exploit the hidden lines of association, bearers of power and affect alike, that cathect language: what Howe elsewhere calls "Pilings of thought under spoken" (*Articulation*, 30).

The Liberties

The Liberties is a poem of exile and estrangement that is built around the relationship between Jonathan Swift and Esther Johnson, the principal addressee of Swift's *Journal to Stella*.[8] At one level, it concerns Howe's relationship, through her mother, with Ireland. At another level, it uses the figure of Swift as an emblem of a paternally coded law.

The poem, initially published in 1980, predates both *Pythagorean Silence* and *Defenestration of Prague*, but it is placed at the end of *The Europe of Trusts*. Howe weaves into the poem strands of *King Lear* (notably the disinherited Cordelia), Ibsen's *The Wild Duck*, fairy tales, and myth. On the title page is a picture of an Irish airmail stamp displaying the figure of the Angel Victor (Saint Patrick's messenger) carrying the voice of the Irish (Vox Hiberniae) out across Lough Derg. The stamp has personal significance for Howe: it was attached to the last letter sent to the family by the poem's dedicatee, her Irish maternal grandmother, Susan Manning. The image is an emblem that represents the transmissibility of speech across temporal and geographical borders and that captures some of Howe's own concerns about displacement and cross-cultural communication.

In structure, *The Liberties* shares the tripartite form of the other poems collected in *The Europe of Trusts*. In this case, however, the sequence contains several subdivisions: section I has three parts, section II is a drama in seven parts unfolding over the days of the week,[9] and section III is a succession of visually oriented poems.[10] The form is mixed, and nowhere does the poem sequence use the series of single lines and couplets ranged left that dominate the central sections of the other *Europe of Trusts* poems. As with the earlier *Hinge Picture*, the visual aspects of the text are integral to the writing. Many poems are organized in bird shapes, and much use is made of word-grids. As with *Pythagorean Silence* and *Defenestration of Prague*, a relatively disarranged first section is followed by the appearance of greater order in the second part, and then again by more typographically disordered work.

The poem's title suggests the freedom-captivity dyad that is so important to Howe's writing, but more concretely it refers to the area to the west of St Patrick's Cathedral in Dublin—so named in the medieval period because it was one of several districts not subject to the jurisdiction of either the Crown or the city authorities. Part of the dramatized middle section of *The Liberties*, "God's Spies," is explicitly set in St Patrick's Cathedral. Elsewhere, there are several references to Viking Dublin (the Liberties district was built on the site of an earlier Viking settlement), and the poem sequence ends with an old map of Ireland's Eye, an islet at the mouth of Howth harbor, near Dublin. The geography of Dublin appears early in the poem, where page 159's second word-grid contains the words "poddle" and "Thingmount."[11] Howe is attempting, through the accumulation of small details, to build a historically layered picture of this part of the city:

> when I began writing this time, I was really trying to paint that part of the landscape of Dublin in words. I was trying to get the place, a foreign place that was home to my mother, on paper. I thought I could understand my mother that way—I might go back to my grandmother, who I am named after and who I loved though I never saw her that often, separated as we were by first war and always the ocean. (Foster interview, 166)

Although the analogy is with painting, Howe's visual poetic is neither directly representational nor abstract. Using a method akin to collage, Howe brings together fragments that, taken together, do not amount to a whole. What remains is a disconcertingly open-ended and provisional text. Dublin's Scandinavian beginnings are as visible as the subterranean River Poddle, and the city's past is recoverable only in piecemeal, indirect ways.

As in Joyce's *The Dead*, there is a preoccupation in the poem sequence with the weight of this past, with exile figured in the image of wild geese, and with a movement "west-the-sea." This westward trajectory is that taken by Howe herself just before the outbreak of the Second World War, when her mother crossed with her from Ireland to the United States (Howe was 16 months old).

The Liberties is the first of Howe's works explicitly to link her writing with the Anglo-Irish literary line. Swift is invoked as the point of departure for an already displaced tradition that still sounds a note of not-belonging in Howe's own work. Yeats is the continuation of that tradition, trading on the curious lyrical mysticism of the once unofficial Celtic-Catholic version of Irish history, but only as that version is endorsed by the very Anglo-Irish presence that had once done so much to suppress it.[12]

In *The Liberties*, Howe for the first time uses an explanatory preface, an important innovation in her work, which would become a common feature of her later poems.[13] It is written in an ironically sober expository style and sketches the historical background of Swift and Stella's relationship. The introduction is interspersed with fragments of poetry and correspondence, although it does not approximate the hybrid verse/ prose form of some later prefaces.[14] Howe writes only of the Swift/ Stella relationship, not developing other key themes in the work. Moreover, the accumulation of documentary detail in the preface suggests that Howe views historical narratives as a kind of intermediate stage in the pursuit of what falls outside them; her own work might be said to complement such writing, offering the voice of what she terms: "Iwho/ crawl/ between thwarts" (*Liberties*, 177, 179).

* * *

Of the Anglo-Irishness of her mother, Mary Manning Howe, Howe writes, "[h]er three daughters became aware of Ireland and New England either concurrently or as the obverse and reverse of the same thing at once" ("Ether/ Either," 119). Howe situates herself at the crux of a horizontal, geographical disjunction and a vertical, historical one. Surrounded by the desirable and undesirable burdens of cultural and familial inheritance, the "homeward rush of exile" in *The Liberties* works as a paradoxical twinning of refuge and displacement at the level of the personal (the relation of Howe's poetic vocation to her father and her mother), of populations (the Irish diaspora), and of lyric (the formal consequences of seeking to address a notion of absence in poetic language).

The key to the maternal preoccupations of *The Liberties* can be found in *The Midnight*'s equivocal invocation of "maternal disinheritance." In these and other texts, Howe offers a matrilineal genealogy of expression that is predicated on absence—"*disinheritance.*" At these points, Howe seems to be setting up Anglo-Irishness as a marker of resistance to fully conceived social identities—and, indeed, to identity politics. Rather than succumb to the romanticized dispossession and bardic associations of certain narratives of Irish history, Howe recognizes her affiliations with an invader culture—a grouping that came to be perceived as alien by the English as well as by the Irish. This identification corresponds with the acknowledgement of her family's implication in New England history in Howe's preface to *Frame Structures*. Moreover, an inheritance that is coded as patrilineal will always place women in a peripheral position. In gender terms, Howe's relationship to her literary inheritance is similarly troubled by differing allegiances and by a paucity of female antecedents.

These ideas are captured in the numerous bird motifs scattered throughout the poem series. The poem contains many references to crossing water, and the governing metaphor for this is flight. The theme of crossing over—whether of exile, transfiguration or death—find its most frequent expression in the figure of birds, particularly swans or geese. This motif stretches across familial and historical borders. It is frequently realized in the actual shape of the poems: most of the pages in the first part of *The Liberties* contain a poem in the shape of a bird. Many of these examples, such as that on page 165, are strongly marked:

>   she raised her hand
>   a girl
>   it was sand
>   a horse
>   green there
>   a spear (*Liberties*, 165)

The bird shapes that Howe brings into *The Liberties* are a means of reinforcing the dense layering of bird references in the text and lending homogeneity to a poem sequence that often appears fragmented to the point of unintelligibility. However, Howe's use of shape poems, unusual in her work, is only one aspect of her treatment of birds. *The Liberties* gathers together disparate narratives of birds in order to assemble an ambitious collection of threads that runs from medieval Ireland through the early years of the Anglo-Irish ascendancy to Howe's own late-twentieth-century anxieties about origins. Howe's maternal disinheritance confers on her a restiveness that both desires and shuns national identifications. Exile becomes a metaphor for the condition of the poet, and its counterpart—home—a dream of an unachievable communicative transparency.

Stella is first linked through birds to Ireland by means of a trivial detail in the *Journal* itself that Howe makes the epigraph to the first section of *The Liberties* proper: "As for Patrick's bird, he brought him for his tameness, and now he is grown the wildest I ever saw. His wings have been quilled thrice and are now up again: he will be able to fly after us to Ireland, if he be willing—Yes, Mrs. Stella..."[15] This epigraph announces the themes of flight, migration, freedom, and captivity that are to be developed in the poem.

The opposition of wildness and tameness prepares us for motifs that will coalesce around the poem's glancing allusions to Ibsen's *The Wild Duck*. The movement of Swift and his servant to and fro between Ireland and London is comparable, but distinct from, Stella's once-and-for-all removal from England (she settled in Ireland on Swift's advice). The bird's imagined voyage across the Irish sea is a precursor of both Howe's own journey across the Atlantic and that of the letter bearing the Vox Hiberniae. When Howe writes "bird migration, story migration" (*Liberties*, 178), therefore, she is writing of a movement of displaced peoples and literatures that begins in her own experience.

Bird imagery is also drawn from the Irish myth of Lir. "Lir was an ocean God whose children turned into swans" (*Liberties*, 172), writes Howe early in the Book of Cordelia section of the poem sequence. (Lir was a distant model for Shakespeare's Lear.) In the Irish myth, three children were turned into swans by their stepmother and compelled to fly over the seas around Ireland for 900 years. Again, an idea of restless wandering, or itinerancy in exile, is asserted.

Like the swans, the poem's wild geese have a particular cultural resonance. "Wild geese" was the name given to the Earls of Tyrone and Tyrconnell, who fled the country in 1607 when the English were consolidating their presence in Ireland; the term wild geese then became a more general metaphor for subsequent generations who left Ireland. The flight of the wild geese, or earls, which was the precursor of the depopulation of Ireland under the English, is connected in the poem to the wild swans of the children of Lir myth. If the geese that Gabriel Conroy wishes to put to the knife in Joyce's *The Dead* announce a skepticism about tradition, wild swans can perhaps escape the defeats of the past.[16] In 1888, Yeats, as part of his folkloric endeavor, edited a collection of Irish fairy tales that contained the story *The Twelve Wild Geese*, a variant of the popular tale also found in Grimm and Hans Christian Andersen. In the tale a princess finds herself obliged to take a vow of silence and knit jackets for her twelve brothers, who have been turned into geese by a witch. As with the figures of Daphne and Ophelia (discussed in my chapter 3), the metamorphosis is an occasion for estrangement from human form, a kind of corporeal exile.

The birth of the princess in the tale follows from her mother's wish: "oh, had I only a daughter with her skin as white as that snow, her cheeks as red as that blood, and her hair as black as that raven, I'd give away every one of my twelve sons for her."[17] Howe brings the Yeatsian narrative into contact with Swift when she cites Swift's "On the Death of Mrs Johnson": "Her hair was blacker than a raven and every feature of her face in perfection."[18] Through the raven and the geese, Howe aligns the silent, self-sacrificing fairy-tale princess with Stella. She does so through indirect use of the Anglo-Irish literary tradition. The swan princes, like the children of Lir and Cordelia, are removed from their inheritance. The princess's vow of silence in the tale adds to the poem's accumulation of anxiety about the relationship of women to public speech.

In Stella, Howe finds a figure for an elided femininity that is in the shadow of a ghostly or absent paternity. Stella, by Howe's account, is a vestigial character and, by Swift's, she only eats "an ounce a week" (*Liberties*, 152).[19] Swift does not preserve her side of their correspondence and there is not even, Howe writes, a portrait of her on whose authenticity people can agree (*Liberties*, 152). Stella died young, in her late 40s, much disturbed by Swift's relationship with Esther Vanhomrigh (who he nicknamed Vanessa), yet "[n]othing is known of Stella's feelings or what she suffered from" (*Liberties*, 154).[20] Swift and Stella never married and, as Howe notes, their friendship has been surrounded by rumor and speculation. Although Stella looked after Swift's household, she lived elsewhere. Beside Swift, in short, Stella was a shadow. As so often in Howe, femininity is threatened with silencing.[21] In *The Liberties*, the tables are turned as Swift, not Stella, becomes a ghost.

Swift's divided cultural loyalties and his interest in punning form a bridge between Howe's writing and his. A letter to Lyn Hejinian suggests the genesis of *The Liberties*:

> Recently I have been reading lots about Jonathan Swift. Not so much Gulliver, but shorter works and his Journal to Stella.... They had a code—the whole thing is fascinating.... Also his essay A Modest Defense of Punning and A Discourse to Prove the Antiquity of the English Tongue. Oh, words, words, words, how he loved and believed in the life of words... I am beginning to work around with some ideas on that score and will see where they take me.[22]

Swift's wordplay takes Howe, via her mother, to another interrogator of Irish identity, Joyce. Joyce, of course, was not Anglo-Irish, but he was so important to Mary Manning Howe that she adapted *Finnegans Wake* for the stage in the 1950s. In an interview, Howe describes her mother's relation to Joyce's final masterpiece: "my mother just reads it and knows it because she *thinks* like that" (Falon interview, 41).

For Howe herself, there is clearly an identification with Swift that brings in its wake an association between cultural displacement and linguistic innovation: "It was interesting to find that Swift was constantly wrenched between England and Ireland when he was a small child. It helps to explain the fracturing of language in his writing" (Foster interview, 166). The preface attributes a culpable neglect to Swift in his relationship with Stella. Yet, against this, another aspect of Swift—Swift the punster—is brought into play to give Stella's soul the attributes of swiftness. Thus, an emblem of patriarchal authority is treated with some equivocation. The word "Swift" itself has a strange and mobile life in the poem: one of the refrains is "Swift, you are Swift" (*Liberties*, 188; 199) and "Swift, they were Swift" (*Liberties*, 185). Stella is "known for the swiftness of her soul" (*Liberties*, 163), and Stella's swiftness seems, in Howe's hands, to become an ironic rebuke to the paternalistic and legislating aspects of Swift (Swift tutored Stella when she was a girl). Her "swiftness" is associated with the painful liberty of exile and her liminality. In the figure of the "swift" Stella, therefore, ideas of neglect and disinheritance on the one hand, and linguistic freedom and marginality on the other, are simultaneously rehearsed.

Silence is the prerogative of Cordelia as well as Stella.[23] Her appearance in the poem constantly circles around her "Nothing, my lord." At one point, she says the word "nothing" four times on one page (*Liberties*, 197). Also, she describes herself as "leafy" (*Liberties*, 195), echoing Stella's "her snowy flesh was all in leaf" (*Liberties*, 187) and prefiguring the Daphne imagery used in *Pythagorean Silence*. Cordelia expresses a double-bind that consigns femininity to the margins:

> But crucial words outside the book
> those words are bullets.
> Lodged in the ebbing actual
> women in the flight of time stand framed. (*Liberties*, 178)

Whereas male speech enters the flux of history as written record, all Stella can boast is to be buried next to Swift, under his epitaph.[24] If "in history people are all dead" (*Liberties*, 187), the written record is the only permanence: "How did we happen—because we were written" (*Liberties*, 197), says Cordelia. In her not-thereness, Stella shares Cordelia's disinheritance. The fairy tale of the twelve wild geese and the myth of the children of Lir are also stories of disinheritance set in motion by a break in familial continuity in the shape of a stepmother. In each case, it is royal flesh—the point at which inheritance is sanctioned by heaven—that grows feathers and takes flight. In Howe's poem, the usurpation of women's speech can be reversed by finding, in a poetics of collage, the freedom of flight that belongs to the birds in the tales that she cites.

One of the traumatizing secrets of history, Howe's poem implies, is the secret of women's experience. The "homeward rush of exile" expresses a community of silence that places living women among the dead. One way of wresting intelligibility from the fragmented narratives of Howe's poetry, therefore, might be to attempt to seek in it evidence of a stifled speech that communicates through associative, rather than denotative, means. The broken and hybrid nature of the third section of the poem is the point at which the poem most approximates this enigmatic incoherence. There are several word-grids, such as the following, positioned under the letter *C*, that suggest tangential communication between diverse words:

3.	bare	cube		arm	white
glass	weary			medium	verge
physic	stone			pane	golden
thin	swallow			concept	nor
dower	darker	ha		hue	yell
crisscross	luminate			wheel	a
up	wild	crown		flame	sa
tom	sa	nero		mum	mum
exeunt	fool			vault	tucket
clap	no	machination		fum	3

(*Liberties*, 207)

Such patterns almost defy readerly resolution. The grid follows another shape poem under the letter *S*, so we can assume that Stella and Cordelia are invoked. In Cordelia's poem, there are words imported from *Lear*: dower, glass, fum, exeunt, physic, machination, and so on. There are also sound associations— mum/ fum; ha/ hue; dower/ darker—and connections based on meaning— glass/ pane; golden/ luminate/ flame; yell/ hue (in the sense of outcry). The patterning of the words obliges the reader to scan the text in crisscross fashion. The making of oblique and unexpected associations is implicitly encouraged. The figure three, which begins and ends the grid (if a left-to-right and top-to-bottom approach is followed) suggests the trio of Swift, Cordelia, and Stella; the trinity; and the Oedipal triangle.[25] At the same time, the grid resists assimilation into a meaningful pattern. The words do not cohere in the presence of an interpretative key, and the relationships between them remain obscure.

Kathleen Fraser, in *Translating the Unspeakable*, mounts an important discussion of the adaptation of Olsonian visual poetics by women poets including Howe, Hannah Weiner, Norma Cole and Barbara Guest. She cites "The Fire," a word-grid from Duncan's *Passages* serial poem and relates it, via Duncan's own commentary, to Olson and further back to Pound's use of Fenollosa's *The Chinese Written Character as a Medium for Poetry*. Fraser writes that, from Duncan's use of the grid as a means of imposing the rhythm of the heartbeat on the poem,

> We can imply Duncan's profound connection to Olson's *page* as a graphically energetic site in which to manifest one's *physical* alignment with the

arrival of language in the mind. This empathic visual concurrence generated a kind of lithographic 'stone', inscribed over the next thirty-year interval, discharging both the Duncan/ Olson ghost print *and* a variety of original documentation, claiming the magnetic formal shape of the Agnes Martin grid for entirely new translations of formerly 'unspeakable' material unearthed by a number of women poets in the last two decades.[26]

These analogies seem entirely apposite: Howe has written of Duncan and (ambivalently) of Olson, and she has also cited Martin as a key influence (see my chapter 5). Yet for Howe translatability itself seems to be at issue. Rather than Duncan's aim with his word-grid—*"evocation of a presence"*[27]—Howe is seeking to indicate an absence. Her grids in *The Liberties* are a verbal means of representing aspects of literary and historical inquiry that resist interpretation. Cordelia's fate—disinheritance—is typical for women. However, the narratives of such dispossession are scarce: how does the poet-researcher embark on the imaginative feat required to disentangle that experience from a faulty historical record? *The Liberties* is an example of such necessarily compromised poetic research, communicating nothing so forcefully as the intransigence of its historical object.[28]

* * *

The treatment of the maternal in *The Liberties* coincides with representations of paternal authority and of familial bonds. I will discuss the paternal in some detail in my next chapter. However, it is worth saying at this point that law is represented through an insubstantial paternal figure—the ghost of Swift in the "God's Spies" section of the poem—that is set against images of feminine speech and liberating flight. Further in the background lies Howe's own father, absent during the Second World War and sometimes aligned with institutional authority in Howe's work.[29] In this way, a fundamental Howe motif is explored: that of an absent origin of authority.[30] Through this figure, as I will suggest in the following chapter, Howe's poetry can address themes as diverse as social authority, regicide, paternity, negative theology, and deconstructive thought.

In *Liberties* the representations of the paternal are bound into reflections on familial relationships that continually cross over into the field of literary relations. The ghost of Hamlet's father is a central figure for Howe. She wrote to John Taggart, "To this day I feel my father is like the ghost [in *Hamlet*]. Always with me, always smiling in that sad way and waiting to be avenged!!"[31] In "God's Spies," Swift appears as a ghost, recalling Hamlet's father. The ghost "walks through" Stella and "preaches a silent sermon" (*Liberties*, 193); he appears Lear-like and "fantastically dressed with wildflowers" (*Liberties*, 189); he sobs and "cries to heaven" (*Liberties*, 192).[32] It is at one level a representation of Swift's long senescence, but the salient aspect of the scene is a reversal of familial power, a transfer of authority from father to daughter: Stella speaks and Swift is a phantom. Stella reads one of her poems (Howe gives the full text in "God's Spies") and even quotes back at Swift's ghost his chiding comment about her spelling: "say Stella when you copy next,/ will you keep strictly to the text?"[33] (*Liberties*, 193). Swift's ghost finally exits, "distracted" (*Liberties*, 193). Part of what Howe achieves, therefore, in her treatment of Stella is the exorcism of a baleful paternal presence.[34]

The familial threads in *The Liberties* are drawn together in the poem's incorporation of Ibsen's *The Wild Duck*. In her correspondence with Taggart, Howe mentions that at age fourteen she played the part of Hedvig, whom she describes as a "sacrificial victim," in *The Wild Duck*.[35] Hedvig, whose family have given sanctuary to a wild duck to which she has become particularly attached, feels betrayed by her father and shoots herself with a pistol. The duck had been shot and injured by the merchant Werle, who, we learn toward the end of the play, is probably Hedvig's father. For Howe, as she writes in a letter to Taggart, a knot of attitudes toward both sides of her own family is filtered through the play:

> I have known what it is to dislike a mother. When she nearly died I was overwhelmed by guilt and regret but now she is healthy and back to her old tricks—hate remains, and that is a fearful thing to feel towards your parent. There is no forgiveness by the anxious conscience for that sin, Ibsen once said about *The Wild Duck* in a little note—this influenced me in *The Liberties* more than one could ever guess....
>
> When they [i.e., wild ducks] are wounded—they go to the bottom, the stubborn devils, and bite on fast—but if you have a good dog, and it is in shallow water? then Hedvig like the wild duck—Gregor's knowledge of children's first and deepest sorrows. They are not about love; no, they are family sorrow—painful home circumstances.[36]

The Wild Duck's Hedvig is, like Cordelia, a daughter who is sacrificed. In her letter Howe appears to identify with Hedvig. Cordelia, Stella, Hedvig and Howe herself are different facets of the poem's probing of the theme of disinheritance.[37] Howe's choice of cover for her *Pierce-Arrow*—herself as a girl playing Astyanax, a sacrificed daughter, in *The Trojan Women*—develops, needless to say, a similar theme, presenting Howe as "sacrificial victim."

It is worth noting that in the letter cited above Howe discusses Ibsen's play in the context of *maternal* rather than paternal neglect. It is the latter, of course, that is at the heart of Ibsen's play.[38] There are no mothers in Howe's poem, but both maternal and paternal presences are important to it. On one hand, it seems reasonable to deduce a combination of aggression and guilt that colors Howe's relationship both to her mother and to Ireland. On the other, the paternal representation of law is continually fading to an invisibility that does not appear to weaken its hold. While the poem addresses the inadequate representation of female experience in the archive, its relationship with what might be termed a matrilineal literary inheritance is highly equivocal. Rather than a straightforward endorsement of an elided femininity against an overbearing patriarchy, then, a more complex entanglement—one of greater psychoanalytic plausibility—of guilt, fantasy, and desire toward both the maternal and paternal imagoes emerges. Instead of a neat and agreeably decipherable Oedipal triangle, *The Liberties* presents a tangle that defies legibility.

The most striking allusions to *The Wild Duck* are in the "God's Spies" section of *The Liberties*: a gun is fired at some wild geese (*Liberties*, 197); the last sound in the playlet is a gunshot; and, crucially, during the cathedral sequence, Stella follows a recital of her poem by shooting herself in the heart with a pistol. In the seventh and final section of "God's Spies," moreover, *The Wild Duck* is linked directly to *King Lear*. Cordelia says,

> King Lear asleep
> King Lear awakened by his daughter Cordelia.
>   (*Softly with flashing eyes*):
> Don't be afraid. Don't be afraid.
> We will leave the stage as prisoners (*Pause*)
> In the bonds of—(*Pause*)
> childhood. (*Pause*)
> Let those who are gone rest—let them rest.
> Haphazardly they lie—there—on the bottom—
> tangle and seaweed—grinding their teeth. (*Liberties*, 198)

The connection between the two plays can be made through Howe's reference, in the letter to Taggart cited above, to the injured wild duck going to the bottom and "biting on fast." A few lines further on, Cordelia says, "They bite themselves fast in the tangle—grinding their teeth—listening in dread—the seamark (*Pause*) blotted out—shoved away" (*Liberties*, 199). *Lear* and *The Wild Duck* are linked, in these compressed lines, through the intensity of the father-daughter bond and a suggestion of severe emotional damage. It is imprisonment, in this view, that is stressed in the "birds i'the cage" image of *King Lear*'s final scene (V, iii, 9). Howe's reading of *Lear*, then, emphasizes not the brief reconciliation of father and daughter but the immense violence that is set in train by the opening scene of paternal disavowal.

The apocalyptic end of *Lear*, a cementing of the abandonment that immediately follows Cordelia's reconciliation with her father, sets the scene for an image of the unquiet dead. These ghosts do not "rest"—they grind their teeth uneasily underwater. The lines offer a metaphor for an imperfectly repressed trauma and the aftershocks it presents in the life of the individual. From the perspective of collective rather than private history, this imperfect repression describes a larger historical process at which the fragmentary matter of *The Liberties* can do no more than gesture.[39]

The image of the injured wild duck going to the bottom refers to a realm of children's experience that is a kind of refuge from trauma or "painful home circumstances." In these lines, Howe addresses a clotted nexus of guilt, sacrifice, revenge, neglect, and constraint. The refrain "they murder each other," often spoken in "God's Spies," refers as much to familial loathing as to Lear and Cordelia or Swift and Stella—especially if read in conjunction with Howe's remarks to Taggart about the "hate" she sometimes felt for her mother.

In *The Liberties*, these questions of violence and abandonment are intimately linked with birds, which become figures of cultural displacement. Yet, at the same time, birds represent, against this violence, a kind of freedom—a linguistic displacement. Howe places this freedom in the orbit of the metamorphoses and the passage from life to death that she would soon approach in *Pythagorean Silence* and *Defenestration of Prague*. In *The Liberties*, developing the angel image of the postage stamp, Howe writes: "Her spirit flew in feathers" (*Liberties*, 187). A few pages further into "God's Spies," a flock of wild geese fly overhead. Cordelia says,

> Transfigured cries. The cries of souls transfigured.
> Beating their wings—making great circles—
> upward—evermore—*free*—
>   Silence.
> A swan. White swans—seven. (*Pause*): Nothing. (*Liberties*, 197)

The geese and the swans refer, via fairy tale, myth, and Yeats, to a metamorphosis,[40] but Howe brings ambivalence to her treatment of her subject, linking the metamorphoses to the idea of liberty. In Cordelia's speeches (such as the apophatic declaration: "Nothing is our own!"; *Liberties*, 197) darkness, fear, death, freedom, and exile coincide. The dark, primal space in which the wild duck bites hard onto the tangled seaweed is a place of banishment, but it is, in a way that successfully resists formulation, uncolonized. Howe is writing of a volatile conjunction of loss and freedom. With "Her spirit flew in feathers" (*Liberties,* 187), the lyric impulse is given wings, but on condition of a painful metamorphosis. The transfiguration into a bird—goose or swan—that haunts Irish history and myth is also a translation into death that, like Ophelia's swan song, makes a form of poetic speech possible (see my chapter 3). Lyric is, in this view, a kind of refuge. Hedvig's death is, echoing Ibsen, the "revenge" of the forest, and the wild duck's "stubborn" clinging to underwater vegetation suggests a potential for the embattled poetry of what Howe, in a letter to Taggart, describes as a "destitute time."[41]

This underwater space is explicitly linked to a paternal absence by Cordelia, who comes to a visionary identification of homing, exile and freedom:

> I learned in leafy woods hmmm—depths of the sea
> that Noone in first father—so soon a terror
> of feathery wings—soft and tremblingly swift—
> How did we happen—because we were written.
>
> *She tears off her blindfold. Blinks in the light. Then,*
> *as if searching her memory*
>
> Come to the surface again, true love, True.
> You with your cradlegrave cords. Nothing can
> estrange the tattling deep of summer hummed
> in honeyed trees hmmm—a hush of homing—
> homeward rush of exile—flight—Liberty. (*Radiant*) (*Liberties,* 197)[42]

The "homeward rush of exile" is the poem's central paradox, linking the flight of political exile with the estrangement and abandonment Howe herself describes when she writes about her father's departure for the war. It encompasses her own mixture of Anglo-Irishness and Americanness. She, her father, and her mother are underwater, trapped in the "cradlegrave cords" of inheritance. The "wild geese in a stammered place" (*Liberties,* 158) that scud graphically across Howe's pages represent the embattled freedom of a voice half-strangled by these "cords." In Cordelia's "Noone in first father," Howe presents an experience of abandonment and "terror" that is also liberating.[43] At the same time, the phrase gestures at the psychic underpinnings of social authority. The scene at the Buffalo zoo, as she has said, formed her as a poet, but it is impossible to disentangle the poetic liberty it inaugurates from suffering. This painful ambivalence in the poem involves turning away from the maternal example, as Howe tries to "understand" her mother through writing about Dublin—the move toward understanding suggests a rationalizing shift away from the "sin" of hatred.[44] This ambivalent encounter extends to both an embrace and a rejection of the "irish susans" that she does and does not resemble (*Liberties*, 213).

Ultimately, the image of Ireland's Eye on the poem's last page is also "Ireland's I," punning on Donalbain's phrase in *Macbeth* when opting for exile: "to Ireland, I."[45] The heading to page 204, "Formation of a Separatist, I" both cements the Shakespearean echo and prepares us for the lines "Across the Atlantic, I/ inherit myself" on page 213. Howe's own movement was in the opposite direction to that of Donalbain—she is one of the wild geese, even if the geese represent the dispossession of the Catholic population. Although she is not claiming direct experience of the immense traumas of the displacement of populations in the twentieth century, she, like the Anglo-Irish, is not at home in her own country America. Despite this doubled removal, she at the same time "inherits" herself (*Liberties*, 213). Separation and disinheritance in the poem tend to collapse into their opposites, much as paternal and maternal motifs are entangled, in a paradoxical movement that is central to her understanding of the unstable border territory inhabited by lyric poetry.

Scare Quotes (The Midnight)

The Midnight (2003) is a rather ambivalent elegy for Howe's mother, who died in 1999. The book continues the drift away from the themes of colonial violence that had dominated the 1980s and 1990s work with which Howe made her name. *The Midnight*'s immediate concerns are domestic: familial ties, embroidered fabrics, and reading for private pleasure.[46] However, the work fans out from these starting points to explore the transmission, through often-obscure lines of connection, of cultural motifs across generations and geographical boundaries.

The Midnight's prose sections, entitled *Scare Quotes I* and *II*, are a realization of the intricate, associative prose style that Howe had anticipated in her introduction to *Frame Structures*. Using fabrics and books as her guiding motifs, Howe arrives at an innovative form of collage that combines both integrative and disintegrative impulses. The titular phrase "Scare Quotes" itself plays with the menacing affective energies set in motion by Howe's practice of citation. *The Midnight* also develops Howe's longstanding interest in the points of transition between word and image, and between the material and the immaterial.

The Midnight is Howe's fullest engagement with a problem with which she had been working since *The Liberties*: the relationship between prose and poetry. In the intervening period, serial poems such as *Melville's Marginalia* and the critical text *The Birth-mark* had made a point of blurring this generic distinction. In the case of *The Midnight*, the two modes are clearly demarcated, with two sections entitled *Scare Quotes* devoted to prose, two entitled *Bed Hangings* devoted to poetry, and a further short sequence of poetry entitled *Kidnapped*.[47] The particular style of prose that Howe has developed in her later writing, however, might equally be read as a kind of poetry and can be viewed in relation to a tradition of prose work by poets such as Williams, Ashbery, and Hejinian.[48] Apparently casual in tone, Howe's prose in *Scare Quotes* reveals itself to be layered and complex as the book progresses, with its key motifs—doubleness, fabrics, and relationships—revoiced in many different ways. Although the *Scare Quotes* and *Bed Hangings* sections contain common themes, I will discuss them separately (see chapter 6 for my account of *Bed Hangings*).

The Midnight is a book about books—books cited, inscribed, inherited, and loved. It is stylistically diverse, combining literary speculations, memoir, lyric poetry, and photography. This last is the most striking of its innovations: there are more than fifty illustrations, most of them photographs of books that had belonged to Howe's mother or her uncle or reproductions of photographs from the Howe family album.

The *Scare Quotes* sections are built around the editions of Yeats, Stevenson, and others that Howe inherited from her mother and her mother's brother. Howe treats these heirlooms, with their annotations, bookmarks, and pasted-in newspaper cuttings, as the material bearers of affect.[49] She uses the psychoanalyst D. W. Winnicott's term "transitional object" to describe the precarious psychic terrain, somewhere between private and public selves, that the books inhabit (*TM*, 60). As soon as she opens their covers she is propelled along eccentric trajectories that mingle references to the books' former owners with highly personal literary conjunctions. Beneath the deceptively urbane prose of these sections of the book are intricate patterns of association that span such diverse authors as Michael Drayton, Milton, Sheridan, Dickinson, William Allingham, Eliot, and Hart Crane.

Howe's reflections on her mother's Anglo-Irishness drive the book's intellectual restlessness. Anglo-Irishness, she has suggested in an interview, is a condition of "fundamental estrangement."[50] She offers a matrilineal style of expression that is founded on lack—again, "disinheritance" (*TM*, 66). The culturally displaced quality of Anglo-Irishness—doubly displaced in Howe's case by re-plantation in the United States—becomes a token of the book's unceasing associative movement.

In the epigraph to *The Midnight* Howe announces, "There was a time when bookbinders placed a tissue interleaf between frontispiece and title page in order to prevent illustration and text from rubbing together. Although a sign is understood to be consubstantial with the thing or being it represents, word and picture are essentially rivals. The transitional space between image and scripture is often a zone of contention" (*TM*, xi). That "zone of contention" is where I will begin my discussion of *Scare Quotes*. This transitional space represents territory analogous to the boundaries of *Secret History of the Dividing Line*, the borderlands explored by Hope Atherton, the New England of *My Emily Dickinson* ("Contradiction is the book of this place"; *MED*, 45), the precarious page-space of *Eikon Basilike*, or *Birth-mark*'s "Antinomy. A conflict of authority. A contradiction between conclusions that seem equally logical reasonable correct sealed natural necessary" (*Birthmark*, 141). Whereas these earlier examples turn on the experience of division, *The Midnight* pursues a trajectory that assigns particularly productive, associative energies to contention and transition. The book contains many examples of paradox, contradiction, doubleness, and duplicity. These motifs of contention are Howe's platform for a series of reflections, filtered at times through Winnicottian object relations, on the entanglement of affect and representation in the act of literary consumption.

The interleaf, or a variation on the theme, occurs in many places in *The Midnight*.[51] Its first appearance is on the front cover, John Singer Sargeant's portrait of Ellen Terry as Lady Macbeth, taken from the second volume of Bram Stoker's book on the actor Henry Irving.[52] The image is partially obscured by a diaphanous interleaf, and the facing page, a few centimeters of which are visible to its left, contains discernible text. Words are often broken up by the right-hand margin and by the crop of the picture. The viewer can see fragments of Shakespearean play titles: *Macbeth*, *The Mer-*, *-ut Nothing*, even an *H-* that appears to preface a *Hamlet* that is obscured by the backward-folding interleaf.

The cover, in other words, shows a rivalrous meeting of image and text. Both are partially obscured by the interleaf; the cropping of the image serves to present us with a found poem drawn from Stoker's words. The interleaf represents a porous barrier. Through it, both text and illustration assume a hazy, indefinite quality. Word and image are separated from one another, yet the permeable boundary is itself a third term, introducing an element of visual distortion that modifies both image and text.

Howe describes the interleaf in her Uncle John's (i.e. her mother's brother's) copy of a book by Robert Louis Stevenson (both the author and his protagonist are among the key literary wanderers in *The Midnight*):

> When I grasp the interleaf in Uncle John's copy of *Ballantrae* between my thumb and forefinger, in one position the filmy fabric takes on the

properties of the title page, in another the properties of the frontispiece. Added to this change in particulars, what I see has the sense of touch. The tissue's impalpable nature is uncannily perverse. It's in a position of house arrest—arrest by throwing the curtain open to a certain wild license. For and against. (*TM*, 144)

The figure of the interleaf fosters a peculiar atmosphere of literary interconnection. This allows Howe to draw unexpected lines between, say, Michael Drayton and Hart Crane, or between her mother's wit and counterfactuals in logic. A relationship between word and image is announced, but the intractability of this relationship makes it representative of a range of associative relations that are explored throughout the book: "The relational space," writes Howe, "is the thing that's alive with something from somewhere else" (*TM*, 58).

In writing of the modernist tradition, the technique of pursuing relations between the apparently dissimilar is exemplified by collage. *The Midnight* is a kind of scrapbook, dependent on what Howe calls "scissor work" (*TM*, 60)—itself a refinement of the cutting and pasting performed by her relatives as they add material to their books. The book thus deprives the technique of collage of some of its mystique, bringing it into contact with the everyday interleaving of texts—cuttings, annotations, mementoes, and so on—by Howe's book-owning ancestors (a custom that was once widespread). Early in *Scare Quotes II*, a phrase from Emerson on the subject of citation indicates the extent of Howe's commitment to this technique: "Every book is a quotation; and every house is a quotation out of all forests and mines and stone quarries; and every man is a quotation from all his ancestors" (*TM*, 116). At the back of Howe's mind, too, perhaps, is her description of Emily Dickinson's ability to fuse disparate discourses: "She built a new poetic form from her fractured sense of being eternally on intellectual borders.... Pulling pieces of geometry, geology, alchemy, philosophy, politics, biography, biology, mythology, and philology from alien territory, a 'sheltered' woman audaciously invented a new grammar grounded in humility and hesitation" (*MED*, 21). The fact that Howe's quotations are brought together as "scare quotes" further underscores the unsettling quality of multiple citation as a method. *The Midnight*, however, is a work of collage in which meaning is produced not—or not chiefly—through the friction generated by juxtaposition, but through a larger, more integrative process that builds associations along thematic, auditory and visual lines. The many references to fabric, then, are not merely thematic; they provide the book with a guiding structural metaphor.

The use of collage is mediated, as I have noted, by psychoanalytic theory, which complicates Howe's treatment of the role of the maternal in her writing. *Scare Quotes I* is preceded by a facsimile of a Charles Peirce manuscript that reads as follows:

> Some mother loves her child
> Every mother loves her child
> Something loves everything of which it is mother (*TM*, 42)

A short way further into the book, Howe develops this into a way of thinking about books within the framework of maternal attachment: "My mother's close relations treated their books as transitional objects (judged by a few survivors remaining in my possession) to be held, loved, carried around, meddled with, abandoned, sometimes mutilated. They contain dedications, private messages, marginal annotations, hints, snapshots, press cuttings, warnings" (*TM*, 60). Howe's inherited books, sheltering all this material, become "a space children used to play in" (ibid., 60). For Winnicott, the transitional object marks the point at which the infant begins the process of acknowledgment of a world that is not it or that part of it occupied by the introjected mother's breast. The blanket (or other object) to which the child develops a powerful attachment provides a space that is neither subjective nor objective. It neither fully corresponds to the introjected breast nor to the final recognition that the breast is external to the child. As the transitional object is progressively decathected, the force of that attachment can be felt in other aspects of human experience. Winnicott writes, "This intermediate area of experience, unchallenged in respect of its belonging to inner or external (shared) reality, constitutes the greater part of the infant's experience, and throughout life is retained in the intense experiencing that belongs to the arts and to religion and to imaginative living, and to creative scientific work."[53]

The Midnight treats books as repositories of the intense affective relationship that belongs to Winnicott's larger idea of transitional objects. The book is seen as the point at which currents of private emotion come into contact with broader cultural investments. Encountered as an heirloom, the book is both material and affective in nature—it is not merely a textual phenomenon. Such books, rooted in a maternal embrace that might be compared to the reassuring enclosure of bed-hangings, become the nodal points for obscure paths of association that stray across the verbal and visual fields. As Howe writes in *Birth-mark*, "Strond strund stronde strand. The margin submerges phonic substance. A mother's thread or line is ringed about with silence so poems are" (37). In this way, the powerful tableau that depicts Howe's mother reading to her from Yeats—"Waves of sound connected us, by associational syllabic magic to an original but imaginary place existing somewhere across the ocean between the emphasis of sound and the emphasis of sense. I loved listening to her voice"—can be viewed as both a point of departure for Howe's art and a maternally inflected model for an associative poetics.

This confluence of the maternal and collage-like assemblies is developed in one of the passages in *Scare Quotes* that discusses the landscape architect Frederick Law Olmsted:

> I am assembling materials for a recurrent return somewhere. Familiar sound textures, deliverances, vagabond quotations, preservations, wilderness shrubs, little resuscitated patterns. Historical or miraculous. Thousands of correlations have to be sliced and spliced. In the analytic hour that is night in which Olmsted, not being able to see what has happened in his mind with regard to his mother, sleeplessly exists, perhaps there is surety that after a silence she will contact him again in bits. (*TM*, 85)

Here, at the "analytic hour," a specific poetics is advanced within the ambit of maternal affection. Olmsted designed the park in Buffalo in which Howe had her revelatory childhood experience on the day of Pearl Harbor. In *The Midnight*, the Olmsted narrative begins with the death of Olmsted's mother when he was six. While Olmsted was staying with a minister in Guilford, home to Howe since the 1970s, a sick child died. Howe cites Olmsted's recollection of praying by the new grave that God might wake the child so he could lead her to her mother.[54] Again, the link to Howe's own bereavement is clear. Olmsted, she writes, composed this autobiographical fragment as a remedy for insomnia—itself a key preoccupation of Howe in these texts. Nighttime—"when I should be unconscious in my closet" (*TM*, 85)—is a time of potentially mediumistic encounter with the past. Both the insomniac and the book lover hover on the borders of the "recurrent return" of unconscious processes, longing to be delivered into an experience in which "historical or miraculous" slicing and splicing can take place. The prose style of *The Midnight* captures this mode of uncertain reverie, poised between waking and dreaming.

* * *

Scare Quotes I begins with a passage in which Howe describes her difficulties sleeping with a levity that had hitherto been unusual in her writing: "I am an insomniac who goes to bed in a closet" (*TM*, 43). The bed is one of the key settings of this text of nocturnal experience. Howe links her wakefulness to the Great Awakening—an eighteenth-century outburst of religious enthusiasm—and then introduces the theme of bed hangings, the embroidered cloth curtains that once commonly surrounded bedsteads: "In an American Dictionary of the English language a curtain is a cloth hanging used in theaters to conceal the stage from the spectators, while an itinerant is someone who travels from place to place and is unsettled; particularly a preacher" (*TM*, 43). There is scarcely a passage in the book that cannot be linked in one way or another to this central network of motifs. Themes addressed in this fashion include culture and wilderness, doubleness, counterfeiting, the dead mother, kidnapped children, fabrics, books as material bearers of affect, memory, and the relationship between word and world.

Also on the first page of *Scare Quotes I* is the observation that English preachers were instrumental in the Great Awakening. Howe uses this fact to pull some of her threads together:

> When Europe enters the space of its margin, the "Kingdom of God in America" receives European memory into itself. In thin places bedsteads confront their own edges. English actors and ministers play key roles in eighteenth century Revivalism. Sometimes charismatic itinerant preachers have no doctrinal or institutional affiliations. Field beds have canopies at the top resembling tents. (*TM*, 43)

In these few lines, the public world of warfare and religious revivalism is bound up with private domestic space. A bed can be a field bed, surrounded by hangings as if it were a tent. The embroidered bed hangings become a means of describing the transmission of cultural motifs. Such hangings were made by people whose uncelebrated labor is part of the work through which a culture is renewed and perpetuated. Eighteenth-century America, in this version, remains a precarious place. Its memory is European. The cultural space defined by the English language has uncertain borders, and the communication of that culture is often bound up with warfare.

A page further into the book, Howe relates the legend of an early producer of bed hangings, a Scots seamstress of the eleventh century named Thorgunna. When she moved from the Outer Hebrides to England, her "fantastically embroidered needlework" (*TM*, 44) exposed her to the risk of being branded a witch—"ownership of her hangings could mean curtains" (*TM*, 45). She destroys her work. "It's an aesthetics of erasure," writes Howe of the labor that produces bed hangings—traditionally women's work (ibid.).

The figure of Thorgunna continues the exploration of femininity, spinning, and aesthetic activity that appears in 1989's *Eikon*.[55] This motif is treated differently, however, as questions of gender are given a relatively muted role in this text in comparison to other concerns. Bed hangings and curtains are part of a matrix of ways at looking at the intricately knotted nature of human textual experience. The theme of fabric recurs throughout the book. In successive pages, for example, it appears in relation to the Renaissance poet Michael Drayton's verses (*TM*, 45); to Elizabeth I's fascination with lace and ruffs (ibid.); to an eighteenth-century Boston widow's industry (ibid., 46—here Howe might be drawing a parallel with her own bereavement); and to the young Emerson, who, in the first of several appearances in the book, is quoted as hoping to "put on eloquence, like a robe" (ibid., 46).

Later in the book, fabric is linked to another key theme, duplicity, in the following description of Howe's mother: "She loved to *embroider* facts. Facts were *cloth* to her. Maybe lying is how she knew she was alive because she felt trapped by something ruthless in her environment and had to beat the odds" (*TM*, 76, my emphases). Bed hangings thus represent a kind of border, or boundary, and, hence, witness two realities. In Howe's mother's case, fictiveness is inextricably linked to representation: "she believed with evangelical fervor in the literal truth of the theatre" (*TM*, 134).[56]

In the presentation of these themes, curtains and doubleness are emphatically brought together. If Olmsted's parkland acts as a kind of bridge between nature and culture, the interleaf becomes for Howe a point at which contending ideas can be thought simultaneously. The book contains many such paradoxical pairings—word and image, fact and fiction, palpable and impalpable.

The Master of Ballantrae, one of the books Howe inherited from her uncle John, provides one of the anchors for these ideas. Late in *Scare Quotes II*, for example, Howe reproduces the frontispiece of this book, showing the aftermath of the fateful coin-toss from which the novel's action unfolds. The interleaf in this edition is one of those that fascinates Howe:

> The tissue interleaf in *Ballantrae* serves as a whisper and a stage direction. Kinship—sensationally, not linked as each would be if overscored. Folie à deux? Perhaps. A sentence is but one unit but inside there are two separate syntactic units.... The interleaf shelters the frontispiece though it's flimsy and somewhat slippery, like self-deceit. (TM, 57)

The tossing of the coin determines which of the two Durie brothers will support the Jacobite cause and which the English (thus securing the familial succession whatever the outcome of the conflict). The brothers are two sides of the same coin, continually opposed, but always drawn together, even in their death and burial. "Oh! There are double words, for everything," says the Master, "the word that swells, the word that belittles; you cannot fight me with a word!"[57] The "double words" phrase is cited by Howe, who observes, with teasing opacity, "The aspect of James Durie that functions as his true self is a relational space of unconscious negative counter-transference. All the excitement is in the nebulous space that is relational" (*TM*, 77–78). The word "relational" now combines familial affective bonds with wider forms of associative connection through a poetics of collage.

In *Ballantrae*, the coin is thrown through the family shield in a splendid stained window. When it is retrieved, the guinea piece is described as "the root of all the evil."[58] Ballantrae adopts it as a personal compass, often spinning a coin to decide which direction to go when, toward the end of the book, he is wandering. He even uses this chance operation to decide, when faced with a band of possibly hostile Indians, to "lay down with his face in the dust"[59]—a presage of his approaching death.

For Howe, however, the combination of doubleness and chance embodied by the coin has productive poetic possibilities: it becomes the "nebulous space" that accommodates a specifically poetic mode of thought. When she throws bookmarks onto a page of her mother's edition of Yeats, she is using a chance procedure to produce poetry from the words left uncovered in much the same way that the Master uses a coin (his downfall) to determine his next move (*TM*, 78). The intrinsically fictive quality of poetic speech is further associated for Howe with her mother's duplicity and wit: "She tossed her words like coins. If two systems of value, the exchange of money and language, are a unified entity, the thrill is two sides tossed at once for theatrical emphasis. On the devil's side or on either side, the closer you come the more protean" (*TM*, 63). Coins, therefore, become in *Scare Quotes* representatives of an exemplary doubleness—that is, for good *and* for ill, maternal in origin for Howe.

The sheer diversity and strangeness of the interlocked constellations of ideas in *Scare Quotes* should by now be apparent. The conclusion to *Scare Quotes II* weaves together some of these threads:

> Are the children asleep? All who read must cross the divide—one from the other. Towards whom am I floating? I'll tie a rope around your waist if you say who you are. Remember we are travelling as relations.
> Well, it's the way of the world. (*TM*, 146)

The borderline time of midnight, then, represents the potential of the act of reading. This spans private, domestic, and public spheres; conscious and unconscious experience. The word "relations"—the most important word in *The Midnight* as a whole—might refer to relatives, textual associations, social relations, or the relationship between author and reader. The concluding passage makes a large claim for the ability of reading to re-present human experience. Reading, in the world of *The Midnight*, is at once hallucinatory, transformative and ecstatic.

CHAPTER 2

The Ghost of the Father

Alongside the maternal associations of identity, speech, and inheritance discussed in the previous chapter, there runs in Howe's work an appraisal of ideas of law, authority, and patriarchy. Often the two currents are intertwined, and I do not wish to suggest a schematic division of the work along maternal and paternal lines any more than I would wish to separate the writing into discrete clusters of 'Irish' and 'American' work. Alongside the exploration of the marginalized feminine in *The Liberties*, for example, law is represented through an insubstantial paternal figure, a composite that superimposes Swift on Lear and the ghost of Hamlet's father. Further in the background lies Howe's own father. In this chapter, I explore some of the poems in which a paternally coded set of associations is strongly evident. In this work, Howe explores the notion of an aporetic origin of authority. Through this motif, which is central to her work, Howe addresses concepts including social authority, regicide, paternity, negative theology, and deconstructive thought.

Everywhere in Howe's writing, paternity is a vexed or doubtful issue. On one hand, this might be autobiographical, as for example in a 1982 letter to Ron Silliman on *Pythagorean Silence*: "When you are 4 and your father vanishes like that and you don't see him again until you are 8, something has been lost forever."[1] On the other hand, the ghostly father that haunts Howe's writing is the memorialization of a divine lawgiver, which Cordelia characterizes as "Noone in first father" (*Liberties*, 197). Here, Howe's poetry appears to address an evasive or even absent divinity. In a letter to Taggart, she makes more explicit the link between paternity, divinity, and her own poetics:

> Lyric "I" is both guard of sacred vision, guard of the holy unseen, guard of what must remain unmutilated—Truth, beauty, tenderness, charity; and

a hunter of the words to say the vision. Like Heidegger's shield in his essay on Hölderlin and Rilke. *Absence is what has not been said or spoken, the place to where our imagination keeps returning.* So poets admire and desire this absence.... Who did Christ cry for on the cross? Where was his absent Father?[2]

Although the lyric "I" was anathema to many of Howe's contemporaries among language writers—the "guard", if anything, of the specious claim to coherence of the poem's speaking subject—for Howe, despite the polyphony of her writing, the I appears to guarantee an ethics of poetic "vision". The I is, in this view, not identical with the speaking subject. It is a notional, quasi-divine absence that serves to underwrite the poem by preserving the strangeness of poetic speech. Both the origin—the speaker—and the referent of this speech are inaccessible. "Vision" is organized around absence and, moreover, overseen by the paternal imago, which appears to guard the perimeters of symbolization. The ghostly fathers of Howe's writing represent an absence, an identificatory chasm, that is both traumatic and enabling. Howe appears to link paternal absence, an absent divinity, and lyric poetry. It is as if, in her understanding of the event at Buffalo in 1941, the wound of paternal absence clears "the place to where our imagination keeps returning."

Issues of paternal authority are powerfully evident in 1978's *Secret History of the Dividing Line*, the poem in which Howe's mature style begins to make itself felt. Formally speaking, it is a hybrid series, combining word-grids, prose, upside-down writing, and blocks of direct quotation. There are many instances, moreover, of the page-long sequences of short single lines and couplets that dominate most of her poems of the 1980s and 1990s. The title comes from William Byrd's *The Secret History of the Line*, his private, initially suppressed, version of his *History of the Dividing Line*, which narrated the establishment of the boundary between North Carolina and Virginia in 1728.[3] Byrd and a party of surveyors travelled westward through the wilderness, marking the dividing line.[4] The "secret" version abounds in puns and also contains many accounts of the sexual exploits of the surveyors as they "hunted" women "wherever they went—white, black, and red."[5] The marking out of the territory is accompanied by rapacious sexual behavior, both toward the indigenous population and other settlers; the authoritative text, then, conceals an illicit parallel account of the line-drawing exercise in which violence, male sexual aggression, and linguistic play are present.

One of the poem's acknowledged sources is *Touched with Fire: Civil War Letters and Diary of Oliver Wendell Holmes Jr., 1861–64*, edited by Howe's father, Mark DeWolfe Howe. Mark is also Howe's son's name, and the name of her paternal grandfather and great-grandfather.[6] However, the word "Mark" has two key meanings within the poem: the physical act of making marks on a page and the notion of the mark as something that delineates a border or dividing line. The poem's exploration of mark-making thus prefigures the overmapping of text and landscape in *Thorow*.

Although the suspension of any legislating paternal function seems to be one of the goals of Howe's poetics in the 1980s and early 1990s, there is a more literal engagement with the issue of paternity, as well. Paternal absence has biographical resonance for Howe. In interviews and in other of Howe's prose texts, a picture emerges of a Harvard scholar who was a diligent and conscientious professor of law.[7] From the outset, Howe's relationship with the archive seems to have been connected in complex ways with her relationship to her father. She writes, "During the 1950s, although I was only a high school student, I was already a library cormorant. I needed out-of-the-way volumes from Widener Library. My father said it would be trespassing if I went into the stacks to find them" (*Birth-mark*, 18).[8] For Howe, this idea of authority is closely associated with the regulation of knowledge by academic institutions: "If you are a woman, archives hold perpetual ironies. Because the gaps and silences are where you find yourself" (Foster interview, 158).[9] There is, then, a profound ambivalence toward an institutional acquisition of knowledge that is thought to be aligned with patriarchy (particularly in Howe's reading of the editing of Emily Dickinson's manuscripts). On one hand, archives are considered to prolong the hegemony of those who guard America's cultural heritage; on the other, they are places in which to get ecstatically lost, the sources of wild, "out-of-the-way" knowledge that might undermine that patrimony.

Fiona Green's account of *Secret History* draws suggestively on Howe's journals to link her text's sources—Oliver Wendell Holmes Jr., Dickens, Beckett, Webster's dictionary—with a working through of the process of mourning for her dead father. Although her rejection of attempts to seek "political correlatives" for what some writers see as Howe's avoidance of linguistic "closure" is relatively unusual in critical readings of Howe, Green's account of *Secret History* as a therapeutic narrative of mourning that "works towards a point of rest" and "makes the subject who speaks it whole" is, perhaps, insufficiently alive to the energies in the poem that point toward violence and dispersal.[10] Moreover, although Green is right to link the motif of the absent father in Howe's poetry with the episode at the Buffalo zoo and his sudden death in 1967, a more productive critical reading can be made *outward* from these events in Howe's life to her rich explorations of the idea of an absent authority in her writing than *inward* toward Howe's personal experience of pain.[11]

Secret History fuses local and private meanings with their wider public contexts. Howe's mode of citation is elastic in form and, through elision and close attention to sound, she channels the various voices into a form of poetic speech that is neither a single voice nor a mere agglomeration of diverse significant utterances. The brevity and concision of her lines, the sharp editing, and the consistent treatment of themes such as darkness, power, speech, and violence lend her work a distinctive stylistic signature. An immediately recognizable voice emerges, paradoxically, from a poetic practice that appears to suggest that a truly private utterance is an impossibility. Mourning is but one feature of a battery of more or less explicit effects that address the notion of paternity, from the 'law' of signification to the mapmaking corollaries of military conquest. Two poems from her 1993 collection *The Nonconformist's Memorial* are the strongest exemplars of this pattern in her thought: the title poem and *Eikon Basilike*.

A Bibliography of the King's Book or, Eikon Basilike

A Bibliography of the King's Book or, Eikon Basilike is explicitly organized around the motifs of absence and authority. In *Eikon,* Howe explores these themes by bringing together the textual debris generated by the death of Charles I and the literary-critical theory of the death of the author—widely current among Anglophone writers and academics influenced by poststructuralist thought in the late 1980s and early 1990s. Howe's poem is haunted by "the ghost of a king" (*Eikon*, 50), a flexible and, of course, typically paternal figure who represents the psychic legacy of the regicide, the absent origin of social authority, and the spectral return of the author in the affective contours of the literary text.

The execution of Charles I and the Christological interpretation of the event propagated by his supporters are central to the poem.[12] However, Howe's poem is a response to the texts that circulate around the event more than to the actual regicide. The interpenetration of reality and representation, as with the earlier *Defenestration*, is a key theme, both for her and for seventeenth-century commentators to whom she alludes or whom she cites. (Indeed, in its treatment of authority, performance, and the feminine, the poem can be read as an extension of issues explored in *Defenestration*, as Howe's attention shifts from the Elizabethan and Jacobean courts to the English Civil War.) Howe's poem builds on various documents surrounding the regicide and links them in a sequence of "fragmentary narrative enclaves" (*Eikon*, 69). The poem is especially concerned with the *Eikon Basilike*, a compendium of prayers and meditations thought by many to have been written by Charles I, and with *Eikonoklastes*, Milton's thoroughgoing, point-by-point riposte to the booklet's claims. Uncertainty about the authorship of the *Eikon Basilike*—now generally considered to have been written by either Bishop John Gauden or both Gauden and the king—continues to the present day. As Howe points out in her introduction, however, more important even than the *Eikon Basilike* or its Miltonic rebuttal is her reading of the Victorian study *A Bibliography of the King's Book; or, Eikon Basilike*, by Edward Almack. This book, from which much of Howe's found textual material is drawn, lists and describes each of the editions of the *Eikon Basilike*, which was issued in thirty-five English and twenty-five foreign editions in 1649 alone. Almack's book acts as a mediating frame, interposing an antiquarian filter between the warring texts that Howe discusses and her own readers. The question of the authorship of the *Eikon Basilike* in the poem is thus already at one remove, approached as it is through Almack's bibliography.[13]

Eikon is the first of Howe's major long poems since *Secret History of the Dividing Line* not to have a tripartite structure. Like *The Liberties* and the poems of *Singularities*, and unlike *The Nonconformist's Memorial*, it has a prose preface, "MAKING THE GHOST WALK ABOUT AGAIN AND AGAIN," although this is not demarcated from the rest of the poem. The main body of the poem contains visual poems, short lyrics, and blocks of text taken from other authors. It is Howe's most typographically disarranged work and, with its themes of sacrifice, authorship, paternity, marginalized femininity, and political and religious conflict, it is the most condensed single example of her methods and interests in the 1980s and 1990s.

The regicide has, for Howe, Shakespearean pre-echoes: "The real King's last word 'Remember' recalls the fictive Ghost-king's admonition to his son [i.e. in *Hamlet*]. The ghost of a king certainly haunted the Puritans and the years of the Protectorate. Charles I became the ghost of Hamlet's father, Caesar's ghost, Banquo's ghost, the ghost of Richard II" (*Eikon*, 48). The execution of the king, then, throws a shadow both over subsequent events and backward over prior literary texts. "Remember" is a prophecy that has retrospective agency. Howe is working with a temporality that shuttles backward and forward between past and present. Embedded in the historicity of language, the regicide cannot be disentangled from later readers' experiences of the stage dramas that preceded it. Howe also appears to be conjecturing, when she writes that Charles's "performance on the scaffold was worthy of that author-actor who played the part of the Ghost in *Hamlet*" (ibid.), that the problem of sovereignty demanded both fictive and real enactment. In this case, life was imitating art in the performance of a crisis of legitimacy that had been present in English culture since the Elizabethan period.[14] The regicide, in this view, is the fulfillment of a literary prophecy.

The poem approaches authorship and authority in history by means of a matted web of allusions and overlaid texts deriving from Howe's work in the archives: contemporary accounts of the execution are cited; there are quotations from the Bible, mythology, Sir Thomas More's *The History of King Richard the Third*, and Dickens's *David Copperfield*.[15] Howe confects a kind of provisional history from the various textual elements that feed into the poem. This history is represented in a manner that voices the vexed and recursive problem of literary origins around which her poem circles around. Howe understands the regicide as an event of sacrificial violence with consequences that echoed in the subsequent history of the language community, down to the literature and politics of present-day America.

In her letter of 29 August 1988 to Norman O. Brown, Howe asserts the importance of the regicide to American cultural identity:

> It's all connected to the old *Eikon*. Everything connects. Because I think we (in America) are haunted by a primal sin—I do believe in sin—I know no one else does any more. Apart from rabid Born Again people. But maybe for the Puritans the primal sin was not only land robbery from the Indians (to say the least) but that primal murder of the Father on their heads. Regicide—what a word.[16]

However casual this remark, Howe is making a speculative assertion about patricide as a primal psycho-social motif. For her, this has profound implications for the relationship between form and representation in her writing. Peter Nicholls argues that her writing's relationship to originary trauma—such as her putative "primal murder of the father"—informs her understanding of the overarching category of history: "Howe's history... is always uncertain: it will not quite become what Jean-François Lyotard has called 'memorial history,' it will not allow us to forget the original traumatic event by the psychic defense of a normalizing narrative. 'One forgets,' says Lyotard, 'as soon as one believes, draws conclusions, and holds for certain.'"[17] Howe's text is in accord with this imputation of a kind of forgetfulness to historical narrative, which her work suggests is characterized by stasis and certitude. Her history aspires to give voice to memory through a drifting and uncertain form of non-narrative, rather than the memorial.[18] Howe's broken, center-less text—or collection of texts—is an attempt to accommodate the "original traumatic event" by other means. Lyotard goes on to write: "The entire web of influences, contexts, conditions, causalities (and the respective, reciprocal hierarchies), woven by the historian, is certainly not completely compromised. It holds the past in suspension. It itself exists only in expectation of its complements, supplements, corrections, additions, contributions."[19] Such supplementation might be said to occur in poetry such as Howe's. However, notwithstanding Nicholls' elegant analogy with Lyotard, readers of Howe should be wary of an unreflective dismissal of normalizing narratives—the implication that such narratives are somehow inherently conservative (or psychically timid) is an example of an undialectical endorsement of the asystemic that has marked much Howe criticism.[20]

Read from a slightly different perspective, the array of historical fragments in *Eikon* also points to the theoretical question of the death of the author. Howe cements the association in her introduction with a quotation from Pierre Macherey's *A Theory of Literary Production* that describes fictional discourse as "sealed and interminably completed or endlessly beginning again, diffuse and dense, coiled about an absent centre, which it can neither conceal nor reveal" (*Eikon*, 50).[21] She brings her various threads together immediately after this quotation by concluding the introduction, "The absent center is the ghost of a king."

In her interview with Edward Foster, Howe expands on the various impulses that fed into *Eikon*, citing an unfinished essay on the Mathers that was overshadowed by the ghosts of her father and Perry Miller; the illness of her friend George Butterick, editor of Olson's poems; Olson himself; and her interest in typography.[22] "Somehow," she concludes, "all my thinking about the misediting of Dickinson's texts, George's careful editing of Charles Olson's poems, all the forgotten little captivity narratives, the now-forgotten *Eikon*, the words *Eikon, Eikonoklastes*, and *regicide*—all sharp vertical sounds, all came together and then split open."[23] This splitting causes the autobiographical material to be distributed in such a way that it is, on the whole, beneath the threshold of visibility. Nonetheless, it may contribute significantly to the hard-to-define quality of coherence that characterizes Howe's texts.

At a theoretical level, the paternal is represented as the origin of law and identified with both authorial and divine creativity. In a key book for Howe, *Call Me Ishmael*, Olson drew on the narrative of origins in Freud's "Moses and Monotheism." Howe similarly has recourse to a notion of founding parricide in her thinking about the links between the regicide and the 'dead' author. The social order established in the wake of this founding sacrifice, as Freud's speculation in "Moses and Monotheism" and other texts goes, remains haunted by this inaugural act of violence. Writing, too, for Howe, represses a destructuring, "wild interiority".[24] When Howe writes "A First didn't write it" (*Eikon*, 63), she is drawing such an analogy. The dead paternal figure serves as an emblem that can link the death of Charles, putative author of the *Eikon Basilike*, to the theory of the death of the author. The analogy is made more explicit further down the same page, when Howe writes of "The Author and Finisher/ The Author of the Fact." The status of this "Author" becomes inaccessible with the sacrifice of Charles, the doubts over the authorship of the *Eikon Basilike*, and the questions about Howe's father that lie in the background of the poem.

Howe's concept of the workings of authority in poetic language in the late 1980s and early 1990s is rooted in the intertwining of absence and the sacred. This is apparent in *Eikon*'s treatment of the themes of divine sacrifice and authorial absence. In my discussion of *The Nonconformist's Memorial*, I will describe the theological content in Howe's writing in terms of the absent divinity of negative theology. In this respect, the writing of Michel de Certeau, the radical historiographer, is helpful in theorizing Howe's methods.[25] Howe's notion of the sacred depends on the legitimating function of sovereignty.[26] The resistance to figuration around which mystical writing is organized becomes, in the thought of Certeau, a point of departure for writing that is specifically poetic and which, for that very reason, proceeds from a notion of authority. To clarify, in a discussion of seventeenth-century mysticism, Certeau writes:

> the name of God is placed in the position of being *unthinkable* and *authorizing* at one and the same time. It is all the more authorizing precisely because it is itself authorized by no reason or system of thought. Therefore, it is not the experience that guarantees the existence of God: God, on the contrary, guarantees the experience. The name is authorized by nothing. For that reason, its status is *poetic*—if Edmond Jabès is correct in saying that poetry is what nothing authorizes.[27]

Howe's poetry circles in similar fashion around the sacred, which makes itself felt as an unsayable non-presence that provides a kind of extra-textual guarantee for the poetry. In Howe's case, this point of origin is a place of wildness and violence, as is evidenced in lines such as "wrath at fierce center" (*Defenestration*, 137) or "slipping back to primordial/ We go through the word Forest" (*Thorow*, 49). It is also an encounter with the law. The very act of ascribing meaning is seen as a legislating act; Howe's poetry seeks to evade such limits, authorizing its indiscipline by appealing to a chaotic understanding of the sacred. This sacred is, then, at once inside the law—an authorizing force—and outside it—the radical disruption of authority. It is what Howe means by the term "Lawless center" (*Articulation*, 22), paradoxically authorizing because, in the terms advanced by de Certeau, subject to no law.[28]

The execution of Charles is an exemplary moment for Howe. Her poem, far from being a consideration of the real event, is a treatment of the various qualities of fictiveness—myth, prophecy, and masque—that surround both the regicide and the possibly forged *Eikon Basilike*. Most important, the regicide is a figure around which a constellation of thoughts that both question and endorse sovereignty and the law can congregate. The death of the divinely sanctioned monarch enacts the very problematization of legitimacy that haunts Howe's work: the law-giver, authorized by nothing, vanishes, and poetry emerges in that lawless center.

In the preceding survey of Howe's descriptions of poetic origins, there is, it must be acknowledged, a degree of inconsistency between the ideas of a "wild interiority"," a "lawless center", and an "absent center"—distinct but partially coinciding ideas that have guided my discussion of her poems. Each of these formulations attempts, in a different way, to formulate a space posited as incommensurable. The first—a broadly psychoanalytic perspective—might be understood as a psychic region of unvoiced drives. The second—a recovery of Romanticism—imagines a similar domain from a more abstract perspective, a fertile originary point beyond the reach of law. The third—a variant of deconstruction with a debt to negative theology—governs the conceptual environment of *Eikon* and stresses the void at the point that might underpin or guarantee meaning or law. Rather than seek to weld these into an elaborate non-contradictory poetics, I think it more useful to observe that each is a version of Howe's fascination with a transcendent outsideness. This aspect of her thought can be filtered through the spiritual urgency of antinomianism, the rhetoric of American romanticism (with Hawthorne, Thoreau, Olson and Duncan in the background), or the literary-critical preoccupations of the late twentieth century. Her poetry is so populated with the voices of others that it is more appropriate to characterize it as a mobile structure of overlapping tendencies than to impose a univocal critical narrative.

* * *

The poem's various responses to authoritarian discourses, whether these discourses are explicitly political or modes of conceiving authorship, can be understood through Howe's notion of scattering. This is especially apparent in the final pages of *Eikon*, which contain a treatment of ideological 'drift' and two metaphors for Howe's poetry: the first as a kite on a long string, the second as an arrangement of threads. The first of these three instances, a brief poem, compresses some of *Eikon*'s key themes:

> Dominant ideologies drift
> Charles I who is "Caesar"
> Restless Cromwell who is "Caesar"
> Disembodied beyond language
> in those copies are copies (*Eikon*, 80)

The verse appears to suggest that political domination is a constant and that, despite the succession of hegemonic "ideologies," there are analogies to be drawn between successive sovereign figures of authority and their respective configurations of political domination. Charles I and Cromwell are anticipated both by Shakespeare's Caesar and by Caesar himself. Royalist iconography—a mystification of authority—is locked in battle with Miltonic iconoclasm, but each is similarly structured around an authorizing central presence. The "scattering" that Howe celebrates in her Arachne and Ariadne pages, also at the end of the poem, replaces certainty with contingency, and authenticity with forgery: "in those copies are copies" (*Eikon*, 80). Belief in authority and faith in the author are confronted with a mode of literary work that can never be satisfactorily moored to an authorial subject.

At a 1988 reading, Howe described a passage from Dickens that she cites on the penultimate page of *Eikon*—a description of Mr. Dick's kite in *David Copperfield*—as "a perfect definition" of her poetry.[29] The kite, "covered with manuscript" (*Eikon*, 81) alluding to the death of Charles I, corresponds to the associative movement of her poetry and her work's removal from the author on publication. Howe's talk of drifting and scattering, in addition to its visual realization, refers to this quality of happenstance and the poetry's dependence on the associations that readers bring to it: "'There's plenty of string,' said Mr. Dick, 'and when it flies high, it takes the facts a long way. That's my manner of diffusing 'em. I don't know where they may come down. It's according to circumstances, and the wind, and so forth; but I take my chance of that'" (*Eikon*, 81). What is Howe doing when she suggests that her poetry, like Mr. Dick's kite, "takes the facts a long way"? This should not be read as a denial of the availability of historical fact per se. Rather, it describes the ability of her poetry to transpose such material into an entirely different mode of expression. Far from Lyotard's characterization of a forgetful "memorial history" of certainties and conclusions, Howe's writing seeks a rememorialization of the past that draws communicative power from her oblique and disjunctive methods. The poetry, in this view, speaks a truth that lies to one side, both in terms of what and how it communicates, of that sanctioned by institutional authority. Not only are the more typographically innovative pages emblematic of a process of scattering, but even the more conventional poems are apt to be blown by the winds of readerly interpretation.[30]

At the visual level, Milton's iconoclasm is registered in the violent "splitting open" that is translated into the extraordinarily broken texts of *Eikon*.[31] There are nine strongly visual poems in *Eikon*.[32] The theologically inflected social crisis surrounding the regicide produces a visual echo in the text. Following the 1988 reading already mentioned, Howe said that she considered the "icon smashing and the vertical lines" (see *Eikon* 54, 56–57) to be "a certain kind of dictatorship." She, on the other hand, in a restatement of the Lyotardian thrust of *Thorow,* favors a "drifting" or "scattering" movement, evident in the Ariadne and Arachne pages of the poem (*Eikon,* 79; 82).³³

Each of these pages develops the subject of the threading of narratives implicit in Howe's engagement with her various documentary sources.³⁴ The closing Arachne page is a final enactment of the poem's movement from a crisis of authority toward a gendered third term associated with drifting. The strands and threads pursued by the scholar-poet hang down inconclusively, offering the reader various means of negotiating the scattered words.

Yet the thread in *Eikon* is always apt to give out: if *Eikon,* like the royalist pamphlet, has its "beginnings in a breach" (*Eikon,* 49) the poem at the end returns to an absence. The reader's attention is directed toward the figure of Pamela, who is imported from Sidney's *Arcadia,* rather than toward the contending ideologies exemplified by *Eikon Basilike* and *Eikonoklastes.* One of Milton's principal levers in his attack on the King's Book was the inclusion in many editions of a prayer that, Milton pointed out, was "stol'n word for word from the mouth of a Heathen fiction praying to a heathen God; and that in no serious book, but the vain amatorious Poem of *Sir Philip Sidneys Arcadia.*"³⁵ Some have since argued that, in an act of propagandist skullduggery, Milton himself arranged to have the prayer inserted into the anthology so he could more easily attack it.³⁶

In her introductory section, Howe writes, "A captive Shepherdess has entered through a gap in ideology. 'Pammela in the Countesses Arcadia,' confronts the inauthentic literary work with its beginnings in a breach" (*Eikon,* 49). As Back plausibly argues, Pamela's prayer, words from which are placed at the head of the poem, immediately after the introduction ("Oh Lord, oh lord" *Eikon,* 51), amounts to a "challenge" to "print culture," as it insists that "even the printed text is, at all times, pulling from and relating to works that preceded it, and that no word, poem or prayer is 'the possession' of an isolated writer."³⁷ Pamela appears to stand for something close to Howe's comments on the "gaps and silences" (Foster interview, 158) that the archive offers the woman scholar—an expressive void that is the potential site of a speculative commentary on marginality. This idea of the feminine within the poem is the repressed aspect of the dispute over legitimate authority being conducted between Puritans and Royalists. In this case, it is perhaps one of Howe's "perpetual ironies" (Foster interview, 158) that the cornerstone of the dispute is a representation of femininity that both functions as an emblem of inauthenticity and represents, for Milton, an image of pagan impropriety—a scapegoating vessel for his animus against the monarchy.

The figure of Pamela, Milton's "Heathen fiction," appears only briefly in the body of the poem-sequence, in a poem that places her alongside the issue of authenticity:

> Heathen woman
> out of heathen legend
> in a little scrip
> the First's own hand
> Counterfeit piece
> published to undeceive
> the world
> In his reply Pseudomisus
> shifts the balance
> of emphasis (*Eikon*, 67)[38]

Pamela's fleeting appearance in a "Counterfeit piece" alerts the reader to what Milton considered the bogus piety of *Eikon Basilike*. For Howe, however, Pamela's "religious supplications" (*Eikon*, 49) represent a way out of the battle between contending views of authority. Pamela, from a "pagan" poem, belongs outside the Christian paradigm, but her presence inserts a principle of uncertainty that threatens to overturn the terms of the dispute between Royalists and Puritans. Her appearance is followed by lines that pit a metonym serving for both divine creation and authorship—"the First's own hand"—against the denial of authenticity—"Counterfeit piece/ published to undeceive/ the world." Read alongside Howe's introductory section, the lines suggest that the riddle of authenticity surrounding the prayer serves to expose the propagandist ends of both Milton and the Royalists. Pamela functions as a gendered third term that frustrates the claims to truth of both sides of the opposition. Moreover, as a token of inauthenticity and religious nonconformism, she can be understood to short-circuit the paradigm that depends on the author-creator as a guarantor of a text's integrity. The character of Pamela is a means of rescuing the linking of femininity with deception (one that, as I will argue in my next chapter, can be found in 'Pythagorean' oppositions) from its pejorative associations. *Defenestration* and *The Midnight* similarly explore the implications of dissimulation.

Howe is asserting a conception of poetry that is dependent on its performative and fictive status. In her interview with Foster she remarks:

Behind the facade of Harvard University is a scaffold and a regicide. Under the ivy and civility there is the instinct for murder, erasure, and authoritarianism. Behind Milton's beautiful words borrowed from other traditions is a rage to destroy and tear down. He hoped his *Eikonoklastes* would erase the *Eikon Basilike* or at least would show it to be a forgery. But *Comus* is a masque and theatrical performance too. An elaborate facade, a forgery. A poem is an icon.[39]

Both literary artifacts and the institutions whose duty it is to validate and uphold their cultural status conceal, in this view, an atavistic urge toward violence.[40] The Milton of *Eikonoklastes*, for Howe, suppresses both its own violence and its reliance on rhetorical strategies: its performance of rationality is as much a performance as *Comus*. She accuses Milton of suppressing the forgery and dissimulation involved in all authorship. Poetic language, Howe suggests, is iconic and, like the masquing of *Comus* or of her own *Defenestration*, is a form of speech that is aware of its own artificiality. Poetry, in this view, exceeds logical argumentation such as that of *Eikonoklastes* and has the communicative potential of an "icon."[41] The demythologizing rigor of *Eikonoklastes*, for all its rhetorical beauty, is a reasoned facade that conceals a censorious violence.

Against *Eikon*'s various attacks on authenticity and authorship, it should be noted that, although Howe has written that Foucault's influential essay "What Is an Author?" "directly inspired and informed" (*Birth-mark*, 37) her writing on New England cultural history, she has asked,

> How can "the subject (and its substitutes)...be stripped of its creative role and analyzed as a complex and variable function of discourse" before we have been allowed to even see what *she, Emily Dickinson*, reveals of her most profound self in the multiple multilayered scripts, sets, notes, and scraps she left us? I cannot murmur indifferently: "What matter who's speaking?" I emphatically insist it does matter who's speaking.[42]

Howe, writing of Dickinson's manuscripts, is raising issues of the control exercised over archival material by institutions such as Harvard University, where Dickinson's fascicles are held. For Howe, these questions of power bring to the fore the issue of personal agency, as evidenced in Dickinson's manuscripts and other papers. She resists reading Dickinson without reference to the author Emily Dickinson, choosing, instead, to pay attention to those aspects of a fully constituted nineteenth-century subjectivity—however much they are effects of discursive or historical agency—that might be available to later readers. Although the prominence of found texts and ghostly authors in Howe's poetry clearly displays an interest in dismantling, or at least reorienting, the idea of the author, there is nonetheless an accompanying concern both with the exercise of authorial control and with the ways in which a sedimented selfhood emerges in poetic language.

At this point, it might be useful to complicate Howe's endorsement of drifting as a means of resistance to such ideas of authority with her assertion, "I emphatically insist it does matter who's speaking" (*Birth-mark*, 20). The wandering threads of Ariadne and Arachne and Mr. Dick's errant kite are, as we have seen, a means of eluding authority conceived as a rigid system. Yet they risk denying themselves any purchase on the material at hand. *Eikon* has an ethical case to answer in that the edifice of associations that develops around the beheading of Charles beckons, though scattering, toward an anarchistic dispersal of political agency that threatens to undermine Howe's oft-asserted intolerance of oppression. The twin sites of putative freedom, text and politics, once again interfere with one another rather than coinciding. Although the gesture toward a theory of sovereignty is elegantly framed, it might be observed that Milton's iconoclasm is more attuned to progressive politics than to the religious populism of the royalists.

Stephen Collis's discussion of Howe's "anarcho-scholasticism" is of great use in discussing these questions of freedom and sovereignty. In what he calls "a little book on Howe's scholarly project," he draws on Derrida's *Archive Fever*, which posits two poles, one conservative and one revolutionary, to scholarly endeavor: "The anarcho-scholastic demands the impossible—demands, of history, both archive (entrance) and namelessness (escape)—seeks the place of power and the vacation of all seats of power. Howe everywhere gives voice to just this paradox."[43]

This holds in place contending impulses in Howe's work, and Collis helpfully provides an account of "radically open, decentralized (collage-based), and non-linear texts" that "erase (as far as possible) the line between poetry and prose, primary and secondary text—to upset all discursive hierarchies."[44] Although Collis's model is often persuasive as an account of Howe's critical writing, it does not do enough, perhaps, to question this fundamentally dyadic paradigm and expose the ways in which it might *not* usefully be read across such discrete phenomena as the antinomianism of the 1630s, textual editing, and the poetics of Transcendentalism.

The "gap in ideology" that is exploited by Sidney's shepherdess serves as a partial recontextualization, through gender, of the contending ideologies of *Eikonoklastes* and *Eikon Basilike*. Although the network of associations that leads to speculation on broader issues of guilt, authority, sacrifice, and authorship is complex, the core opposition of the poem is not sufficiently troubled by the feminine third term. This, in turn, has a tendency to reaffirm the association of feminine writing with tropes of absence, indirection, and fragmentedness: a willed inarticulacy that is enabling as a notion of poetic speech but inhibiting when it becomes the reserved domain of the feminine.[45] Once again, the parallel ambitions of Howe's poetry—to be at a "miraculous reach" from the world and conventional language use (*MED*, 13), and at the same time to be involved in the rhetoric of politics—create immense tensions. In its efforts to reserve for itself a specifically poetic form of expression, the poem displays impatience with the political prose of *Eikonoklastes* and a concomitant attachment to the pathos of Charles's execution. This thread in the work short circuits the poem's ethical ambitions and risks tipping into the kind of fascination with sanctified authority that provoked Milton's scornful dismantling of the Christological maneuvers that hold the readers of the "King's Book" in thrall to "a Masking Scene...set there to catch fools and silly gazers."[46]

Each of the foregoing objections has merit and, taken together, they might serve as a useful caution against reading the poems as Howe sometimes appears to be asking us to read them. Yet the question of intelligibility is central here, and to dismiss *Eikon* on these counts would, in the end, be to treat it as if its primary value were as an encryption of topoi drawn from the literary and critical theories of its moment. Howe surrounds her poetry of the 1980s and early 1990s with such critical discourses (and seems thus to answer to the readings thus engendered), but the dense, refractory poetic language of *Eikon* resists such translation at least as much as it invites it.

The Nonconformist's Memorial

The Nonconformist's Memorial takes its title from an 18th-century book cataloguing the silencing of nonconformist ministers following the Act of Uniformity in 1662.[47] Howe's poem, however, attempts a different kind of memorialization. In her 1995 *Linebreak* interview Howe describes it as "a meditation on the marginalization of women in religious history."[48] The historical figure around whom Howe organizes her poem is Mary Magdalene, the first witness of the resurrection. Magdalene becomes a representative of the woman poet; as so often in Howe's work of this period, the vocabulary of religious experience is used to frame questions of poetic speech. As elsewhere, it is hard to determine which of the two should be accorded interpretative priority. *The Nonconformist's Memorial*, however, is Howe's most direct attempt to think the aesthetic and the religious alongside one another.

Given the historical reach of Howe's work and the range of material from which she draws her allusions, religion is inevitable subject matter—it is privileged in her work because of its predominance in the history of her, and our, culture. Moreover, the language of the sacred is the most culturally elaborated means of speaking around the limits of figuration. *The Nonconformist's Memorial* situates itself on the boundary between saying and non-saying, drawing out affinities between poetic speech and mystical experience. Howe adopts an explicitly Christian frame of reference without subscribing to Christianity itself.

A remark in a letter to Norman O. Brown indicates the direction of her thinking on this point:

> Like you I have a Christological stamp on my imagination. I keep hoping that someday I will get there and will be able to BELIEVE. I cannot get past that resurrection. I can't believe it. And if you can't believe it you are out. I *can* believe in some fearful judging God. That I can believe, which is too bad. But not that we will all rise again and will be saved. So while I glory in the language of John or Genesis or The Song of Solomon (KJV) I can't see and know the risen Christ and say Master and trust. Language goes pretty far—but....Are words enough? They almost almost are—I hope I will reach the point where they are—maybe that will be peace— just to know words are enough.[49]

The Nonconformist's Memorial might be read as an exploration of the American nonconformist imagination. For Howe, poetic language's affiliations with silence and the ecstatic lever it into religious space. If Wallace Stevens sought to replace the supreme being with the Supreme Fiction, Howe seems to think that you cannot have one without the other. Yet this belief can only find expression in negatives. "Absence is what has not been said or spoken, the place to where our imagination keeps returning," she writes in a letter to Taggart. "So poets admire and desire this absence."[50] Again and again, her poems return to this absence: a gap where belief is directed, a void in the place of paternity, a silence that brings speech to a stuttering halt.

In a 1994 conversation with the poet Robert Creeley, published in the *Village Voice* magazine, Susan Howe remarks that "poetry is, I hate to say it, something holy."[51] Howe is talking about the marketing of a poetics course that she and Creeley taught at the State University of New York, Buffalo. (The university prospectus of the time marketed the course by listing a number of high-profile journals to which former Buffalo poetics students had contributed poems.) In her dialogue with Creeley, Howe laments this emphasis on worldly renown, preferring the apparent indifference to the reading public shown, in different ways, by Emily Dickinson and George Herbert. Her lack of regard for the values of mainstream American poetry publishing is unsurprising, but her use of the term "holy," marked as it is with the ambivalence and embarrassment of "I hate to say it," immediately separates her from most of her peers. In a 1989 interview, she says more, with less embarrassment, on the relation between poetry and the religious: "Carpentry, teaching, mothering, farming, writing, is never an end in itself but is in the service of something out of the world—God, or the Word, a supreme Fiction. This central mystery, this huge Imagination of one form is both a lyric thing and a great 'secresie,' on an unbeaten way; the only unbeaten way left. A poet tries to sound every part."[52] Is Howe's writing, then, best understood in Peter Quartermain's terms, as "essentially religious, devoted to a lively apprehension of the sacramental nature of our experience of the world, and of the sacramental nature of the world"?[53] It is more plausible, I would argue, to suggest that in such statements Howe is repeating the ultimately desacralizing movement of her subject in her book *My Emily Dickinson*, who, she says: "takes Sovereignty away from God and bestows it on the Woods" (*MED*, 80). Yet, again and again, religious experience seems to offer the best available vocabulary for the "unbeaten way" she wishes to track across centuries of human culture.

The highly distinctive voice Howe had developed by this stage in her writing folds absence into every level of the poetic process. The divinity that is invoked in her poetry may best be described as the divinity of "the obscure negative way" (*NCM*, 33). Whatever the nature of the mystery at which Howe is gesturing, the poetry is written around a silence that finds a kind of voice in what Nicholls has called the "noncognitive" aspects of her poems—the visual aspect and, above all, the sound of words.[54] A set of material factors in the writing, notably repetition and especially rhyme, create a phonic expectation of fullness, but the irregularity of the patterns means that the ear is never sure where this fullness will fall. The diction of the poetry, moreover, creates an atmosphere of allusiveness that is itself never fulfilled. The reader is more likely to perceive polyphony as a textual effect when lines from Hopkins, say, or Aristotle appear in the poem, than to be able to identity the precise source of the allusion.[55]

Built on a network of effects indicating absence, *The Nonconformist's Memorial* circles around questions of embodiment and intangibility; bearing witness, particularly poetic witness; the metaphorical freight of terms such as "light" and "dark"; and the ramifications of the posited encounter between an inaccessible Logos and a fallen language. Although there is an evident investment in such a transcendent Logos, almost as a historical legacy, the workings of the poetry itself meet this skeptically, as if trying to extricate themselves from a metaphysical alignment which they acknowledge as inevitable. At the same time, there is a more earthbound preoccupation with the historical marginalization of women by institutionalized religion.[56]

There are, as in most of Howe's works of the 1980s and 1990s, three parts to the poem. These are numbered. A prefatory section, outside the main three, begins with the poem's seed text: the passage from the Gospel of John (John 20:xv–xviii) that cites Mary Magdalene's witnessing of the risen Christ. This passage, which narrates the "*noli me tangere*" or "Touch me not" incident—a popular subject for painters—is cited at the beginning of Howe's poem and is at the heart of its preoccupations.

The first section embraces the theologico-literary motifs that the poem treats: history, incarnation, transubstantiation, and darkness. It is formally mixed and includes text that runs upside-down, perpendicular to the main lines, and diagonally. The brief second section begins with an epigraph from the Book of Revelation, 19:17—"And I saw an angel standing in the sun"—and contains two poems that use upside-down text. Each of these first two parts of the poem series combines strongly biblical language with more opaque passages such as "Arreption to imagery/ of drift meadow edge/ of the woods here" (*NCM*, 17). The final section is the most thematically unified, with several recurring strands—wandering, love, confession, redaction, and negativity. This third part is headed "Immediate Acts," which indicates a specifically Protestant experience of direct and private communion with God. There is a "she" in this final part of the poem that may be Mary Magdalene and a vestigial narrative that may speculate on her life after the Resurrection. There are more or less oblique references throughout the poem series to the encounter between Mary Magdalene and the risen Jesus in the garden. There are several indications that the central "love impelled figure"—a version of Mary Magdalene or Anne Hutchinson or Emily Dickinson, perhaps—is caught up in a moment of religious and aesthetic rapture that involves great privation. There is, as in Dickinson's Master Letters, a note of masochism in such lines as "Lay at night on thorns" (*NCM*, 25) and "It is the Word to whom she turns/ True submission and subjection" (*NCM*, 30). However, as with Dickinson, there is also a powerful note of spiritual rebellion: "Parallel to the mind/ a reprobate mind clings/ close/ inner outlaw impenitent" (*NCM*, 24).

If *Articulation of Sound Forms in Time* and *Thorow* are concerned with relating language to the limit points of civilization and the role of the wilderness in the American literary imagination (see my chapter 4), *The Nonconformist's Memorial* transposes this concern with boundaries and wandering to the field of religious discourse.[57] The figure of Magdalene allows Howe to make a point both about the past and about the role of the poet.

Writing to Lyn Hejinian in 1989, three years before the publication of the poem, Howe remarked,

> This moment when [Mary Magdalene] sees and knows and says Master and is pushed back—maybe it's in that space that some women work—I think this can apply to HD. The Master Letters Dickinson wrote are the most mysteriously powerful and central pieces of her work to me—they were found *in her poems*, not among letters that were to be burned—and yet all the critics want to find a specific Master and by this they are closing her in the very prison she is breaking out of. Now Mary at that tomb acts from pure disinterested love—and that space between the Master and the world that cannot ever be crossed may be...a space so powerful that it is another power—a space of silence, mystery, *unacknowledgement*.[58]

A similarly enthused letter to Norman O. Brown, written in the same month, says more about this "space":

> I think in that moment of turning, of hearing, and turning, and seeing—there is a space that is the space of Art for some women—in that gap—in the space between. That's where I think Dickinson's Master Letters touch HD's *Trilogy* and *Tribute to Freud*.... Dickinson first wrestles with the Angel Jacob but in the Master Letters she turns to see and say Master. To dare to enter that terrible Touch Me Not. That's what I'm trying to figure out now.[59]

Howe is writing of a disempowerment that is oddly and paradoxically enabling. At issue is the generative absence discussed above. In *My Emily Dickinson*, she writes of the Puritans' "obedience to a stern and Sovereign Absence" (*MED*, 39). That book's intense focus on the word "Sovereign" later yields the perception "Janus-faced, *Sovereign*, signifying liberty and submission, is infinitely beguiling" (*MED*, 84).[60] It also reverses the traditional gendering of the poetic Muse: "After a good day's writing with her Master's inspiration, the poet, alone, in her clearing of Becoming, keeps on experimenting, deciphering" (*MED*, 105).

The Nonconformist's Memorial appears to hover in beguiled fascination around a fusion of freedom and obedience. Mary Magdalene's encounter with Christ in John's Gospel is another of the metaphysical tableaux—like Ophelia's death or the metamorphosis of Daphne (discussed in the following chapter)—that haunt Howe's work. This time, it is the notion of feminine witness that organizes her perceptions, and the poet-witness is in the presence of a kind of authority. Dickinson, both proto-Nietzschean metaphysical rebel and publication-shy recluse, seems an important precedent.[61] Here, rather than the dynamism of "light letters exploding" in *Thorow* or the "rushing light" of the last page of *Melville's Marginalia* (*MM*, 150), Howe discusses poetic language in terms of "silence, mystery, *unacknowledgement*."

I understand that, in describing the "Master" of Dickinson and Mary Magdalene as separated by a space that "cannot ever be crossed," Howe is thinking of poetry as akin to the practice of negative theology, arising in the presence of a divinity whose very inaccessibility is generative. Whereas positive theology reflects on the nature of God, negative theology is, in Kevin Hart's words, "a discourse which reflects on positive theology by denying that its language and concepts are adequate to God."[62] This inadequacy is the aporetic motor of poetic speech. Divine or paternal authority is invariably absent in Howe's work. If the absence of Howe's father during the Second World War or the ghosts of Swift or Hamlet's father are examples of this, in *The Nonconformist's Memorial* and *Eikon Basilike* this apprehension of absence takes on a more theological character.

Mary Magdalene's experience speaks, for Howe, of both this encounter with divinity and the troubled history of the feminine in religious representation. In her *Linebreak* interview, Howe links Magdalene to her research on captivity narratives and antinomianism, describing Magdalene as "the first, original biblical nonconformist...in a Puritan, protestant sense."[63] Mary Magdalene's place in the Christian narrative was downplayed and serves, for Howe, as a prototype for the editing, by men, of early American captivity narratives or the banishment of Anne Hutchinson from the nascent Bay Area Colony in the 1630s:

> When you look at the history of religious sects—for example, the Quakers, splinter groups that are very radical—very often women are involved at the beginning who are then written out of the story. As it's popularized and institutionalized then the men take over... By the Book of Acts Mary Magdalene is nameless—the fact that she might have been a strong partner, a disciple and fellow teacher of Christ at the beginning.... The only place that's acknowledged is the one brief mention in John.[64]

In *The Nonconformist's Memorial*, Howe directs her attention to a woman who is at once central and peripheral to the inaugural moment of Christianity. In all four gospels, Mary Magdalene is the first to witness the resurrection. In John's gospel, Christ urges her to tell the disciples that he has risen, and she is, therefore, the first apostle. In Matthew, however, Christ appears to the disciples before the women have reached them, and in Luke and Mark she is disbelieved. Susan Haskins points out that, under Judaic law, women were not trusted as witnesses.⁶⁵

Back usefully discusses the idea of testimony, via Shoshana Felman, as a speech act.⁶⁶ However, she psychologizes the utterly irretrievable figure of Mary Magdalene as a "nonconforming spirit" who may have even have had Howe-like reasons for her "refusal... to apply an explanatory narrative structure to the 'empty-tomb' phenomenon."⁶⁷ This may be too explicit. The notion of feminine witness is vital, it is true, in this and other of Howe's poems, to the elaboration of a poetry that can in some way acknowledge the "anonymous, slighted" voices of the dead ("Leaves," 14). However, this imperiled witness does not find positive expression, even in the folds of Howe's text.

Howe's assimilation of Mary Magdalene to Emily Dickinson in her letters to Hejinian and Brown appears to indicate a kind of expressive ecstasy in the presence of a Master figure—the tangible/ intangible borderline invoked by daring "to enter that terrible Touch Me Not."⁶⁸ This, in turn, suggests that authority, witness, absence, and poetic speech are entangled in troubling, historically embedded ways on which our own emancipatory narratives have only slight purchase. For Howe, the negativity that her poetry courts appears of somewhat greater import than any restitutive project designed to recover marginalized speech—what Megan Williams has called a "poetics of recuperation."⁶⁹ Howe's "meditation on the marginalization of women in religious history" (Linebreak interview) continually bumps up against the intransigent absence of its object. This, in my view, makes Howe's project not less but more radically unsettling, since its unassimilability is the most persuasive token of its claims to critique the existent. As she remarks of her prose style in *The Birth-mark*, "By choosing to install certain narratives somewhere between history, mystic speech, and poetry, I have enclosed them in an organization, although I know there are places no classificatory procedure can reach, where connections between words and things we thought existed break off" (*Birth-mark*, 45). These are the places of her poems too—their "space of silence, mystery, *unacknowledgement*."⁷⁰ Magdalene's slighted experience remains ungraspable.

* * *

When, in an interview with Lynn Keller, Howe discusses the lines "The nets were not torn// The Gospel did not grasp" (*Nonconformist's Memorial*, 7) she remarks,

> By 'nets' I mean to associate Jesus as fisherman; somehow the net gets torn, the idea gets broken—the Gospel when it becomes Gospel, when it

is written, grasps (this is all vaguely sexual but then think about all the meanings of the word "conception"). Mary, the disciple, the first one who witnesses the resurrection, the one whose story we go by, gets dropped away almost at once.[71]

The points at which the net gets torn and the text presents itself as insufficient are central to *The Nonconformist's Memorial*'s concern with suppressed speech. Two different kinds of silence are at issue. At one level, Howe's talk of slipping through the net appears to describe the historical failure of the Christian church to recognize women—a certain category of narrative, defined by gender, is suppressed. Yet the net analogy also suggests a failure of reference—a problem of representing something that is resistant to capture. This inexpressibility is a defining characteristic of negative theology, a recurring motif in Howe's poetry.[72]

In *The Nonconformist's Memorial*, Howe uses the figure of darkness in an attempt to gesture toward unrepresentability. The presiding spirit of negative theology, Pseudo-Dionysus, is cautious on this point. In his *Mystical Theology*, he writes: "It [i.e. divinity] falls neither within the predicate of nonbeing nor of being. Existing beings do not know it as it actually is and it does not know them as they are. There is no speaking of it, nor name nor knowledge of it. Darkness and light, error and truth—it is none of these. It is beyond assertion and denial."[73] In Howe's poem, the distinct ideas of darkness, absence, and nay-saying are encompassed in her synoptic survey of the language of negation.

This is most evident in the cluster of references to darkness or negation toward the end of the third section of the poem sequence: "Steal to a place in the dark" (*NCM*, 23); "Undertype Shadow Sacrifice" and "the clear negative way" (ibid., 26); "Spirit snapping after air/ dragged down to visible" (27); "The abiding and transitory/ were negative and no echo" and "darkness rushing and the true" (28); "As night to understanding/ or truth to fiction" (29); "if in silence hidden by darkness/ there must be a Ghost" (30); "Isled on all removes/ When night came on" (32); and "Dense in parameter space/ the obscure negative way" (33). At these points, the poem appears to gesture toward the potential eloquence, in poetic terms, of such dark spaces. Such moments in the text have their origins, perhaps, in the issues broached in Howe's early essay "The End of Art" (1974), which discusses black and white in the work of Ad Reinhardt, Robert Lax, and Ian Hamilton Finlay. In her interview with Keller Howe cites the work of Reinhardt as an early influence.[74] Her essay takes its title from the last line of Reinhardt's essay "Art as Art," which is written in a style that recalls negative theology. As an epigraph, Howe cites Nicholas of Cusa, from a note in Reinhardt's daybook:

"How needful it is to enter into the darkness and to admit the coincidence of opposites, to seek the truth where impossibility meets us" ("The End of Art," 80). Writing of Hamilton Finlay, with whom she had an important correspondence, Howe quotes Pseudo-Dionysius on the "Darkness beyond Intelligible" (ibid., 82).[75] Kaplan Harris suggests in his discussion of this essay that it marked Howe's turn to poetry: "the end of art prepares the ground for an experience of language."[76] By the time *The Nonconformist's Memorial* was published almost twenty years later, Howe had transformed darkness into a central motif in her own work, operating across numerous discourses in an inarticulable yet intractably linguistic space of insufficiency and impossibility.

The light/ dark opposition is, of course, among the most conventional available to literature. The prologue to the Fourth Gospel equates light with Logos and divinity and human salvation with the illumination of darkness. Christ, in the prologue, is envisioned as the passing of the divine into the earthly order—the incarnation of the Logos. The oppositions in John 1 are stark: on one hand are Spirit, Light, and Logos, and on the other matter, darkness, and the fallen language of humanity. Christ's appearance on earth is a transaction between earthly and divine, and John the Baptist's act of witnessing at the outset of Christ's ministry anticipates that of Mary Magdalene at the end of the Gospel of John.

The movement of negative theology, with its rejection of the vocabulary of divine presence, has been compared to that of deconstruction, with its emphasis on the unfigurable category of *différance*, or the trace. The late 1980s and early 1990s—the period of the gestation of *The Nonconformist's Memorial*—saw several treatments of the question, and Jacques Derrida himself devoted an article to the subject in 1989.[77] This essay was an extended differentiation of deconstruction and negative theology, developing distinctions made in a succinct passage in his book *Margins of Philosophy*:

> The detours, locutions and syntax in which I will often have to take recourse will resemble those of negative theology, occasionally even to the point of being indistinguishable from negative theology. Already we have had to delineate *that différance is not*, does not exist, is not a present-being (*on*) in any form; and we will be led to delineate also everything *that* it *is not*, that is, *everything*; and consequently that it has neither existence nor essence. It derives from no category of being, whether present or absent. And yet those aspects of *différance* which are thereby delineated are not theological, not even in the order of the most negative of negative theologies, which are always concerned with disengaging a superessentiality beyond the finite categories of essence and existence, that is of

presence, and always hastening to recall that God is refused the predicate of existence, only in order to acknowledge his superior, inconceivable, and ineffable mode of being. Such a development is not in question here, and this will be confirmed progressively. *Différance* is not only irreducible to any ontological or theological—ontotheological—reappropriation, but as the very opening of the space in which ontotheology—philosophy—produces its system and history, it includes ontotheology, inscribing it and exceeding it without return.[78]

Derrida acknowledges the resemblance between his thought and negative theology but asserts that negative theology preserves a doctrine of "superessentiality," a reinstallation of the Godhead over and above the very assertions of absence that would deny to God any mode of conceivable existence. *Différance*, however, remains immune to such a hypostatization of absence. As a principle of radical difference, it is nothing and nowhere, irreducible even to the hypothetical presence implied by the notion of absence.

Although it does not offer itself as a corollary of deconstructive thought, the resistant quality of Howe's work is indebted to a notion of absence that approaches the blankness of a God under erasure. The turn in Howe's poetry toward inexpression and absence, enacting the difficulty of negotiating "the only unbeaten way left," demonstrates the paradoxes of poetic utterance in a way that can be said to get its hands dirty with the labor of negation. The work performs a double bind that sees it caught up in the nets of metaphysical terminology. As it invokes "the obscure negative way" (*NCM*, 33), it must, in seeking to speak of that obscurity, eventually transgress its own commitment to negation.

The mode of communication that Howe implies is hesitant, broken, and fissured; it addresses a category of religious experience that bypasses not only "text" but utterance itself. Howe's work, because of its investment in an extrinsic grace of this kind, might be said to be vulnerable to the terms of Derrida's critique of the "superessentiality" preserved by negative theology.[79] In other words, Howe frequently invokes a metaphysical vocabulary of negative transcendence. Her language tends to imagine any divinity or ground of authority as absent, yet the very terms it uses to express this ineffability serve to endorse the possibility of a transcendent guarantor of meaning. Her writing is underpinned by the idea of an authorizing absence that is analogous to the residual attachment to the category of presence that Derrida discerns and critiques in negative theology.

In *The Nonconformist's Memorial*, these ideas are central: the issues of speech and presence are brought to the fore as, in Christ's resurrection,

Howe explicitly addresses issues of incarnate divinity—the point, prepared by the opening of John's gospel, at which human language meets divine Logos. A poem from early in the poem sequence is preoccupied with the figure of Christ as a speaking subject:

> In the Evangelist's mind
> it is I absolutely I
> Word before name
> Resurrection and life are one
> it is I
> without any real subject
> all that I say is I
> A predicate nominative
> not subject the I is
> the bread the light the door
> the way the shepherd the vine (*NCM*, 10)

The poem appears to contain elements of a critical text or texts Howe might have encountered when researching the Fourth Gospel—lines 1, 3, 4, 6, and 8 appear to derive from a scholarly commentary on the prologue. Interpolated are assertions of "I," and the poem concludes with a compressed reference to Jesus's various "I am" statements in John—with the "I am" removed.[80]

Howe's two voices allow a poetic consideration of presence—both of the author and of immediate physicality. First, the poem speculates—"In the Evangelist's mind"—on the intentions of the author of the Fourth Gospel. The line is interrupted by "It is I absolutely I"—a voice that strives to assert its presence through an address to another. The phrase "It is I" occurs in all four Gospels when Christ walks on water, and it is used in Luke (24:39) when Jesus meets the disciples after the resurrection. It is thus uttered at moments when miracles—signs of Jesus's divinity—threaten to make him unrecognizable as a human.

The line also echoes a literary "It is I." In her interview with Foster, Howe refers to a passage from Melville's journal that describes a woman beside a new grave, crying "Why don't you speak to me? My God—It is I." Howe comments,

> The woman is wailing, "My God, it is I," but Melville is saying, "My God, it is I." He is the woman. There is everything in that to me. She's calling to the dead. Who has been buried? Is it her husband, a parent, a child? Melville doesn't know her. He doesn't name her. There is no nam-

ing and no answer. She is herself, and he sees himself in her. I think that detail holds everything. (*Birth-mark*, 179)[81]

Back aligns this comment with Howe's grief at her husband David von Schlegell's approaching death. However, the remarks also combine what Howe calls the "Christological pull" of late Melville with a feminine identification on Melville's part. Placed in the context of *The Nonconformist's Memorial*, "It is I," read through Melville, functions as an act of precarious transgendered identification, rather than an assertion of selfhood. The "I" of *The Nonconformist's Memorial* is an empty vessel whose absoluteness masks an absence.

The page-poem continues as a set of utterances that gather round the elusive evangelist and a nameless presence that asserts its own being but nothing else. It is, thus, a telescoping of the prologue's distinction between an inaccessible Logos and its earthly incarnation in Christ. The relation between finite worldly utterance and the unboundedness of Logos is conveyed in the succession of "I am" analogies that continually revise what it is "I am."[82]

"Word before name" again suggests Logos, an absolutely anterior Word beyond human naming. "Resurrection and life are one" appears to develop the thought of the first line, suggesting a commentary on the theology of the prologue to John. This is followed by "without any real subject": the subject pronoun I of "It is I" is presented as an empty index of subjectivity and the formulation summarized with "A predicate nominative."[83] Interposed between the two, "All that I say is I" stresses the personal pronoun with even greater urgency; it is as if grammar and the speaking subject are at loggerheads.

"Not subject the I is" is itself ungrammatical and, typical of Howe's fissiparous short lines, it lends itself to various constructions. It might refer to the "predicate nominative," it might look forward to the absent I of the "I am" analogies, it may be a contorted restatement of "It is I," or it may simply underline the earlier "without any real subject." The repetitions of "I"—six in nine lines—lend an anxious quality to an assertion that falls short of predication, or becoming the subject of a statement. Indeed, the subject, I, itself becomes a predicate in the phrase "It is I." To follow these nervously presented "I"s with the series of identifications—bread, light, shepherd, and so on—that Jesus invokes suggests a restless movement of metaphorical substitution that is propelled by the insufficiency of each term on the list.

In these lines, we can identify a version of Howe's metaphysical anxiety about origins: the sovereign "I" is an index of presence that is repeatedly invoked but found to conceal an absence. The "I" in Howe's poem dramatizes a troubled negotiation with both language and the very question of origin. Although the writing never, of course, attains this originary point—here we might adduce Howe's "God, or the Word, a supreme Fiction"—neither does it relinquish its desire for an origin. In Derrida's terms, even if "God is refused the predicate of existence," negative theology will, at a further remove, acknowledge his presence. Howe's borrowing of Stevens's "supreme Fiction" is a "superessentiality" that can be identified with the sustaining guarantee that underpins negative theology. Yet it has a more radical orientation, akin to the destabilizing "name of God," at once "*unthinkable* and *authorizing*," of de Certeau's account of mystic speech. Mary Magdalene's encounter with the risen Christ might appear to be a materialization of that guarantee, but it, too, is beset with uncertainty: "Touch me not," says Christ, "for I am not yet ascended to my father."

Howe's metaphysical ambitions at such moments are accompanied by a parallel commitment to the material presentation of text—its physical appearance as a book and the materiality of sound. Similarly, *The Nonconformist's Memorial*'s meditation on incarnation is accompanied by an earthbound reflection on the marginalization of women in religious history. The word-becoming-flesh motif is appropriate because the poem seeks to explore the full communicative potential of that materialized utterance. What Howe is attempting might be described as a metaphysical maneuver of capture that seeks to articulate what Howe has elsewhere called, speaking of Benjamin, the "entrance of the messianic into the material object."[84]

CHAPTER 3

Susan Howe's Renaissance

Two key texts, written concurrently, helped to cement Howe's reputation in the early 1980s. These were *Pythagorean Silence* (1982) and *Defenestration of Prague* (1983), originally published separately but later collected alongside *The Liberties* in *The Europe of Trusts* (1990) in the Sun and Moon Classics series (subsequently republished by New Directions). Although Howe was by this point corresponding with both Lyn Hejinian and Charles Bernstein, and in this sense loosely involved with language writing, it is immediately evident how different her work was from texts of the same period such as Hejinian's *My Life* (1980), Ron Silliman's *Tjanting* (1981) or the collaborative publication *Legend* (1980) coauthored by Bruce Andrews, Charles Bernstein, Ray DiPalma, Steve McCaffery and Ron Silliman. Indeed, her correspondence shows that Howe was skeptical of, if not hostile to, much language writing from the outset.[1]

In a 1985 letter to Silliman that underlines some of these differences, Howe remarks that she is a lyric writer, that she believes in what she calls the power of "Mystery in poetry," and that she is deeply committed to the past. She continues, choosing a conspicuously canonical example: "Unlike you I think Shakespeare IS a GREAT writer. Yes—I will use that terrible word GREAT. I know all the problems of that word too—because it has particularly shut women out—but I think too that the enigma of Power—that includes the idea—great—is as puzzling as the structure of the atom."[2] This "puzzling" "enigma of Power" bears a relationship in Howe's writing to the texts of the past, the role of the woman writer, and the kind of contract with the reader that is implied by the poetry. *Pythagorean Silence* and *Defenestration of Prague* both draw substantially on motifs from the literature of the Renaissance. I will be concerned with Howe's adaptation, via Ovid, of the notion of metamorphosis and of her use, when I come to discuss *Defenestration*, of the aesthetics of the masque and of Renaissance pastoral.

Whereas many of Howe's peers in the American avant garde were, broadly, adapting a post-Williams paradigm that reflected a skepticism about English literary tradition, Howe frequently engages with major canonical texts from the past: Shakespeare, Spenser, Milton, the Bible. A good deal has been made of Howe's revisionist approach to literary history and her involvement with marginalized figures, but relatively little has been said about her profound sympathy for texts that could hardly be less marginal. In discussions of the poems collected in Howe's key work *The Europe of Trusts*, it is the preface and *The Liberties*, rather than the two 'Renaissance' poems, that have drawn the most attention.[3]

Howe's anachronistic achievement in both *Pythagorean Silence* and *Defenestration of Prague* is to present late-twentieth-century anxieties about identity and authority through a Renaissance filter without doing violence to either set of perspectives. (By 'Renaissance', I mean a Renaissance understanding of classical notions—notably, ideas attributed to Ovid and Pythagoras.)

Another key preoccupation of Howe's work of this period is the idea of dissimulation, which is particularly important to *Defenestration*. Here, again, Howe works across distinct literary epochs. She adapts a motif, the suspicion of authenticity, that was widely current in postmodern aesthetics and was common to the assault by various of the language writers on a lyric selfhood "in which the specifics of experience dissolve into the pseudo-intimacy of an overarching 'authorial voice.'"[4] For many language writers, the ideological underpinnings of late-twentieth-century language use were addressed through a synchronic exposure of contemporary usages in which the literary was a highly suspicious (because it was hierarchical) category. In Howe's hands, however, this motif of inauthenticity is read diachronically for its historical resonances. Howe has a striking tendency to use a forcing method of poetic inquiry that reads across periods to discern parallels between very different kinds of artwork. Thus, the mask can be read back through Yeats to Jonson and Shakespeare. Jonathan Edwards and Wallace Stevens may be aligned through a pragmatist prism. Or, as Howe suggests in a 1981 letter to Hejinian, Marcel Duchamp's *Large Glass* may be brought into contact with the *Faerie Queene*.[5] Howe's interest in the back and forth between twentieth-century aesthetics and the past marks many of her works. It is as important to stress the contemporary nature of her preoccupations as to discuss her involvement in history. In works such as *Pythagorean Silence* and *Defenestration*, theoretical and historical projects are subsumed within the larger poetic project. The poems are so dense and broken that neither their historical backgrounds nor their contemporary ambitions are clearly discernible. Theory—a parallel practice at the very least for many language writers—remains an adjunct of the poetic text, rather than its expressive goal.

Pythagorean Silence

...Nature knows
No stedfast station, but, or ebbs, or flows:
Ever in motion; she destroys her old,
And casts new figures in another mold. (*Metamorphoses* [trans. Dryden] XV, 176–77)

Pythagorean Silence is a long, meditative serial poem strewn with allusions to pre-Socratic philosophy and Renaissance thought and literature. First published in 1982, it appears in Howe's 1990 collection *The Europe of Trusts* immediately after "Leaves." The poem comprises three sections: "Pearl Harbor," "Pythagorean Silence" and an untitled third section. "Pearl Harbor" reprises some of the material in "Leaves" in poetic form. This first section and the final one are relatively short and are formally mixed, whereas "Pythagorean Silence" runs to seventeen parts of similar length, all using the combination of single lines and couplets that Howe had used in *Secret History*, but not in *The Liberties*.

Drawing on Ovid and Shakespeare, the poem is particularly concerned with the notion of metamorphosis. Howe's interest in borders and boundaries becomes focused on the boundary between life and death. Developing some of the questions broached in "Leaves," the poem uses the symbol of the laurel tree in Ovid to explore the public role of poetry and offer itself as a particular kind of poetry of witness—one that seeks to communicate what falls outside the historical record through a language of severe ellipsis. Representation itself is an anxiety of the poem and, with whiteness and silence as persistent motifs, it often threatens to fade into the blankness of the empty page. *Hamlet* is the poem's chief Shakespearean resource, and Howe devotes particular attention to the death of Ophelia, which comes to represent a moment of embattled lyric potential. Howe probes a distinctly metaphysical vocabulary throughout the poem and, with Nietzsche's reading of the pre-Socratics in the background, begins to pick apart the battery of gendered dualisms that sustain the metaphorical separation of body and spirit in Western thought.

In another letter to Silliman, Howe notes that the tripartite structure of *Pythagorean Silence* corresponds to the three stages of creation in the Pythagorean tradition: "1) undifferentiated unity. 2) the separation out of two opposites to form the world order. 3) the reunion of opposites to generate life."[6] Howe links her poem to the event at Buffalo that is described in her prefaces to both *The Europe of Trusts* and *Frame Structures*, speculating that "maybe those polar bears and my father became Pythagoras."[7] She continues:

> That applies to P SILENCE. 1) the real. Buffalo Pearl Harbor being the day of the vanishing of my father. 2) Father now mythical father Pythagoras separation of us all endlessly chattering as if just the sound of voices explaining or of writing being written can ward off the terror of Silence or the idea of emptiness. 3) Out of both of these former (and in a Freudian sense I guess—out of both parents [opposites]) how do I as a woman pulling words and influences attempts at answers from a largely male tradition how do I marry these ideas and influences to make something new and something that is my own voice that will go on talking.[8]

Although Howe immediately inserts the caveat "that's only the shadow of a shadow in the piece," her gloss of *Pythagorean Silence* is both helpful and confusing. A letter to Norman O. Brown indicates the aesthetic resonances of the early Buffalo memory, remarking on "hearing of War in a place with a white jewel that is made under water in a shell, combined legend, violence and beauty so that they are forever together for me."[9] Putting her various thoughts together, we might say that *Pythagorean Silence* is a poem predicated on public and private catastrophe: Pearl Harbor and the disappearance of Howe's father for four years. Her father is partly identified with Pythagoras, and the poem as a whole grapples with the problem of the woman poet making something new for herself within a largely male tradition.[10] These themes are played out in an atmosphere dominated by whiteness: the snow of Buffalo; polar bears; the blank page and the "white jewel"—the pearl. Pythagoras is thought to have ordered his disciples to wear white and to have recommended that the dead be dressed in white.[11] Howe, moreover, sees Pythagoras himself dressed in white.[12]

Absence and silence are crucial to the conceptual terrain of the poem, which juxtaposes the preoccupation with mark-making in *Secret History* with the idea of a lyric poetry that is intimately concerned with death. However, the network of associations in the poem is large—the poem does not, in the end, make silence or death its ultimate goal. Rather, it positions itself on the borders of intelligibility—an index of the volatile transformations of meaning-making. Against a background of silence, or blankness, Howe's poem is, above all, a poem of metamorphoses, with roots in Ovid and Shakespeare. Such metamorphoses link Ovid's Daphne to Shakespeare's Ophelia as an image of a gendered lyric born in adversity.

Chief among the Pythagorean motifs of *Pythagorean Silence* is its exploration of a complex of ideas around metempsychosis, death, and metamorphosis.[13] In using Pythagoras as a point of departure, Howe touches on a set of associations that spans many centuries and that incorporates numerous reformulations. Indeed, it might be argued that the very elusiveness of the name under which the poem develops is another aspect of the weakening of authorial purchase that Howe's poetry, with its extensive use of collage, enacts. Notwithstanding the amorphousness of the mass of ideas associated with Pythagoras, Howe's poem can be said to be Pythagorean in three particular ways: because of its attribution, via Emerson, of a positive moral value to silence; its desire to engage with (and destabilize) the theory of opposites; and, above all, the manner in which it addresses the concept of the transmigration of souls. The key dividing line in this poem is that between Being and Non-being and, filtered through Renaissance readings of Ovidean metamorphosis, this transitional point becomes, for Howe, the point at which lyric poetry takes shape. Crossing this line is, moreover, a preoccupation that extends beyond this poem: at several points in her work—for example, the human-bird shifts in *The Liberties*, her treatment of Bartleby in *Melville's Marginalia*, or the interleaf in *The Midnight*—poetry is located in just such a transitional space.

The idea of a Pythagorean silence is an allusion to the injunction against idle chatter among the initiates of the Pythagorean cult.[14] It is also linked to Howe's desire to respond to American literary history: in section 15 of the central part of the poem, entitled "Pythagorean Silence," the line "Long Pythagorean lustrum" occurs (*PS*, 63). The phrase is drawn from one of Emerson's addresses, "Literary Ethics":

> Come now, let us go and be dumb. Let us sit with our hands on our mouths, a long, austere, Pythagorean lustrum. Let us live in corners, and do chores, and suffer, and weep, and drudge, with eyes and hearts that love the Lord. Silence, seclusion, austerity, may pierce deep into the grandeur and secret of our being, and so diving, bring up out of secular darkness, the sublimities of the moral constitution.[15]

Emerson, drawing on the high moral tone of American Puritanism, attributes an ethical weight to silence and asceticism. A certain austerity, he argues, allows access to otherwise hidden and privileged aspects of morality. Howe finds common cause with the legacy of the Calvinism of the American northeast, which has marked her writing from the outset.[16] Howe's poetics, however, are intimately concerned with negative theology and mystical speech, and her 'silence', although it shares Emerson's moral fervor, is unwilling to bring to light comprehensible objects retrieved from the "secular darkness" into which it dives.

Darkness is an aspect of the divine for Howe, and revelation in her work is a fleeting and inscrutable occurrence. Howe's work seeks to perform, through an encounter with the obscurity of language itself, the shadows at the fringes of philosophical language and the resistance of eschatological questions to rational enquiry.[17] Furthermore, the cultural meanings that accrete around the opposition of dark and light are an important part of the poem's work. It is at the moments when Howe's language finds itself confronted with the vacuum of the blank page or restlessly turning away from reference, that it pursues the "sublimities of the moral constitution." However, rather than seeking, with Emerson, to bring something hidden into the light, *Pythagorean Silence* questions the metaphorical underpinning of the term Enlightenment.

In an early interview, Howe comments on her interest in the theory of oppositions that has been assigned to the Pythagoreans. In this system the world was held to ten fundamental oppositions: limited/ unlimited, odd/ even, one/ many, right/ left, male/ female, rest/ motion, straight/ crooked, light/ darkness, good/ bad, square/ oblong. Howe remarks in this interview that she is interested in the equation of femininity with darkness, yet her "Promethean aspiration [is] to be a Pythagorean and a woman."[18] Howe is asserting that her work recognizes the generative power of such antinomies in our culture, while at the same time working to overturn them.

Howe's work in the poem—and elsewhere—is to follow an explicitly metaphysical trajectory even while subjecting it to a skeptical unpicking. In other words, her writing of this period has both an investment in examining the space to which Western culture assigns the feminine, darkness, spirit, and the unsayable and a desire to overturn the concrete instances of oppression that are sustained by such categories. Schultz's description of silence in Howe's work as both a "negative social fact for women and a positive religious state" can be modified to include an ambivalence about the gendered mysticism of that "religious state."[19]

In an April 1986 letter to Norman O. Brown, Howe outlines her interest in aspects of Renaissance thought, particularly as explored through Frances Yates's investigations of hermeticism. For Howe, though, the emphasis is on the significance of such thought in an American context:

> I am interested in how all these strands re-surface in America. It seems to be that reading and thinking about the seventeenth century helps in understanding our present dark and bloody history. There is a deep turn in some mysterious way that I can only grope at through poetry—from the 20th to the 17th century. This turn is heralded by certain 19th century writers. Melville particularly and Dickinson too. What fascinates me is metaphysical revolt hemmed in by political ambition.[20]

This last phrase captures the oscillation in Howe's work, as it probes the "enigma of power," between distinct registers of revolt.

My reading of *Pythagorean Silence* is organized around the dominant Pythagorean strand in the poem sequence: the transformative metaphysical motif of metempsychosis. The poem opens with an allusion to Ovid's Daphne, turned into a tree as she seeks to escape the amorous attentions of Apollo:

> we that were wood
> when that a wide wood was
> In a physical Universe playing with
> words
> Bark be my limbs my hair be leaf
> Bride be my bow my lyre my quiver
> (*PS*, 17)

The etymology of wood takes us to "possessed by a devil"; and, via Latin and Old Irish, "seer, poet"; or "going beyond all reasonable bounds."[21] "When that a wide wood was" rehearses the scene-setting stage directions at the beginning of Milton's *Comus*, which specify a "wild wood." However, the key to this sequence is Daphne's metamorphosis from human to plant form. Pursued by Apollo, her conversion into a tree is an imprisonment that opens on to the role of the poet, as Howe notes in a letter to Taggart:

> The image of turning into a tree I took from a lovely and utterly haunting small painting by Pollaiulo of Daphne turning into a laurel....
> Well here, of course bark (dog bark loud noise) is in the word bark of a tree. Transformation—and I think of Daphne becoming a laurel (the poet's tree) as a beautiful thing (unlike Dante and Shakespeare, who put people trapped in trees in Hell). So I am bride with my bark, married to the danger and turning and singing it, playing it. With the play on bow

(violent) and musical and on quiver—trees make arrows, arrows go in quivers, a string quivers when playing music and of course the rapture in quiver on and on.[22]

I read this transition in the context of later metamorphoses in the poem series, as a specifically Pythagorean transition, a metempsychosis, when a soul passes from one physical host to another. This might be read as an analogue of the process of poetic creation, a version of writing that amounts to a continual recasting of the texts of the past.

The conclusion to Ovid's *Metamorphoses* contains an account of the beliefs of Pythagoras that, in the Ovid of Arthur Golding's influential 1567 translation, retrospectively casts the long foregoing series of transformations in a Pythagorean light. For Golding, in his introductory epistle, "The oration of Pithagoras implyes/ A sum of all the former woorke."[23] The soul is described as follows in his version of Ovid:

> And even as supple wax with ease receyveth fygures straunge,
> And keepes not ay one shape, ne bydes assured ay from chaunge,
> And yit continueth always wax in substance: so I say
> The soule is ay the selfsame thing it was and yit astray
> It fleeteth into sundry shapes.[24]

Howe's version of the metamorphosis is a passing-into-stasis that retains spirit within a "physical Universe." Her account of Daphne's transformation cannot be disentangled from the theme of violence that pervades her 1980s poems: the classical role of the poet being to praise the exploits of the heroes of war. In "Bark be my limbs my hair be leaf" the speaker is apparently both Daphne and Howe. Yet there is a shift in the following line, "Bride be my bow my lyre my quiver." In Golding's translation, these are close to the words spoken by Apollo to Daphne, as he explains how she will adorn his hair, his "harpe," and his quiver—and those of all victors.[25] Dryden succinctly writes, "Be thou the prize of honour and renown;/ the deathless poem, and the poet, crown./ Thou shalt the *Roman* festivals adorn,/ And after poets, be by victors worn."[26] This formulation in turn recalls the title of the preface to *The Europe of Trusts*: "THERE ARE NOT LEAVES ENOUGH TO CROWN TO COVER TO CROWN TO COVER," which abstracts a line from Wallace Stevens's "United Dames of America." Behind that, perhaps, lies an allusion to the reflections on violence and poetry in Stevens's wartime essay "The Noble Rider and the Sound of Words."

In *Pythagorean Silence*, Howe's lines represent a complex, half-ironic appropriation of Ovid's account of Daphne's metamorphosis, which is at once "married to the danger and turning and singing it, playing it." The speaker takes for herself Apollo's emblematic bow, lyre, and quiver. Daphne, and not Apollo, becomes the figure of the poet. Howe's lines—"Bark be my limbs my hair be leaf/ Bride be my bow my lyre my quiver"—demonstrate her poetry's tendency simultaneously to inhabit and to question the discourses in which it is framed. Her relationship to power—or "danger"—is frequently colored by this affiliation with authority that "turns" to "play" it.

The questioning of the public role of the poet may contain an allusion not only to Stevens, but also to Robert Duncan's Vietnam-era book *Bending the Bow*. The introduction and the poem "Bending the Bow" both refer to the bow and the lyre of Apollo.[27] Moreover, in her use of Ovid, Howe is developing a tendency in the work of three Anglo-American modernist poets: Pound, Eliot, and HD.[28] Pound's *Personae*, for example, opens with "The Tree": "I stood still and was a tree amid the wood,/ Knowing the truth of things unseen before;/ Of Daphne and the laurel bow/ And that god-feasting couple old/ That grew elm-oak amid the wold."[29] The myth is also referred to in "A Girl"[30] and sections III and XII of "Hugh Selwyn Mauberley."[31] In "Notes on Elizabethan Classicists," Pound describes Golding's Ovid as "possibly the most beautiful book in our language."[32] Several of HD's early poems, such as "The Garden," touch on the motifs of the tree and of erotic pursuit, and consecutive poems in her early book *The God*—"Adonis," "Pygmalion," "Eurydice"—are based on book X of the *Metamorphoses*.[33] Pound (in Cantos IV, LXXVII, LXXVIII, and LXXXII) and Eliot (in *The Waste Land*) both make use of the Tereus and Philomela story, with its bleak conjunction of violation, metamorphosis, and song.[34] Howe, therefore, condenses an extraordinary range of classical, Renaissance, and modernist instances of these themes.

Howe's writing of this period approaches the theme of Ovidian metamorphosis through the lens of a late-twentieth-century interest in issues of gender, power, and poetic speech. She is commemorating a Pythagorean movement of spirit, but she is also asking what happens to women during times of war. In her reading of Ovid, both the feminine and the poetic, through the laurel tree, become an adornment—even an endorsement—of the martial ethos, the celebration of victors. Her poem asks at its outset how a contemporary American woman poet can speak a language that somehow resists this ethos. Howe's mutation of Ovid at the beginning of her poem is a reorientation of an earlier text—a central text for Western poetry—that she causes both to hymn and to query the role of the poet. Howe seeks in this passage, and in the poem that follows, to explore the entanglement of the lyric poet in the wreckage of war—what in the introduction to *Frame Structures* she calls the "sadism" of the Cold War and the "fiery impossibility" of Vietnam (*FS*, 28). Through poetry, she hopes to find a language that will neither be consigned to silence nor be co-opted by an incipiently bellicose discourse.

* * *

Howe's oblique and many-layered engagement with Pythagoreanism in her poem-sequence is organized around the separation of body and soul.[35] Her poem is particular interested in the borderline—death—at which, conventionally, spirit is free of its physical burden (even if, in the scheme of metempsychosis, momentarily). This is a violent, tensile space that becomes an analogue of the volatility of poetic language. Death is also a borderline that her poetry transgresses in its pursuit, through the motif of metempsychosis, of the ways in which the present can harbor the elusive voices of the past.

In *Pythagorean Silence*, the words "mimic presentation stained with mortality" (*PS*, 45) encapsulate the poem's various treatments of the link between death and representation. Spirit is always shadowed by the impermanence of the tangible, carnal world, which is present in "mortality." Howe is writing here of embodied consciousness. The line "mimic presentation stained with mortality" binds the multiple representations of mental processes to the mortal body and the material world. It is as if, in the world of the poem, death is the condition of the enabling transformative motifs of metamorphosis and metempsychosis.

Prominent among the cited material in *Pythagorean Silence* are passages drawn from Shakespeare, notably *Hamlet*.[36] Central to these are two references to Ophelia. Like Ovid's Daphne, she is a virgin who undergoes a poetic metamorphosis—Gertrude's account of her death applies the metaphor "mermaid-like." This metamorphosis, again, has repercussions for poetic language. The first occurrence runs as follows:

> Their words are weeds wrapped around my head
> Roses are withered—it grows rigidly dark
> Body and Soul (*PS*, 32)

The first of these lines adapts Gertrude's speech describing Ophelia's death (*Hamlet* 4.7, cited below) and brings about an identification of Ophelia with one of the poem's speakers. The weeds around her head develop the image of Daphne and the "my hair be leaf" of the poem's epigraph. The meeting of martial and lyric duties symbolized by Daphne's laurels becomes Ophelia's "coronet" of "weeds" and her "weedy trophies," silent in death. The two women follow similar routes as they pass out of humanity and into silence. The "weeds," echoing "words," represent a deathly counterpart to the laurels of the victors. However, out of that silence comes another poetry that acknowledges the irretrievable experience of history's victims.

Howe's poem is at once aligned with the dark, feminine aspect of the Pythagorean contraries and critical of the boundaries that safeguard dualisms of this kind. In this sense, the Pythagorean silence represents an attempt to speak from the place of Ophelia or Daphne, a place that is not "rigidly dark."

"Withered," in these lines, may allude to the violets (held to represent faithfulness) that withered, in Ophelia's words, when "my father died" (*Hamlet* 4.5.182). "Roses are withered" also initiates another set of associations (besides the children's rhyme): Laertes describes Ophelia as the "rose of May" (*Hamlet* 4.5.157) and Ophelia, in turn, offers him rosemary, "for remembrance" (*Hamlet* 4.5.173). *Ros marinus*, moreover, is the rose of the sea, so Ophelia's drowning can be interpreted, in the light of these associations, as a passing of the insubstantial phenomenon of memory into the primal element of water.[37] "Rosemary" brings together "rose" and "may/ Mary" and, as Philippa Berry notes, Ophelia's flowers add, though their May Day associations, a quality of pagan fecundity to her death.[38] Gertrude's description of Ophelia's death lies behind these associations:

> There on the pendent boughs her coronet weeds
> Clamb'ring to hang, an envious sliver broke;
> When down her weedy trophies and herself
> Fell in the weeping brook. Her clothes spread wide
> And, mermaid-like, awhile they bore her up,
> Which time she chanted snatches of old lauds,
> As one incapable of her own distress,
> Or like a creature native and indued
> Unto that element; but long it could not be
> Till that her garments, heavy with their drink,
> Pulled the poor wretch from her melodious lay
> To muddy death.[39]

For a brief moment, as she passes into death, Ophelia almost metamorphoses into a siren, or a creature "native" to the water.[40] This is a moment of transformative potential. Ophelia's loss of her "coronet" (for Berry a "metaphorical defloration")[41] and the clothes that are "spread wide" strengthen the force of the fertility associations and allow the motif of childbirth to run against that of the passage from life to death.

Ophelia sings old songs as she drowns and, in alluding to this speech, Howe may here be drawing an implicit parallel with her own selection from older texts. Moreover, as her lays are also "lauds" (and hence religious), there is a mingling of the Christian and the secular that corresponds to the Mary/ May combination suggested by "weeds." Ophelia's "fantastic garlands" offer a momentary recovery of Daphne's laurels: the poet enters a revised civic role. In the figure of Ophelia, then, Howe imagines the glancing effect of words emerging from silence. She is identifying with a death-bound mermaid caught at the point of metamorphosis who offers a brief opportunity to recover the lyric potential of poetry—a potential that is defined by its processual and transitional nature.

The metaphysical ambition of Howe's allusion, moreover, is heavily underlined in her text with the words "Body and Soul." Later in the poem, the line "I lay down and conceived" (*PS*, 44) resonates with the associations of fertility around Ophelia's death, but Howe is also suggesting that the "lay" that precedes "muddy death" is a resurrection before the fact: a metamorphosis in which spirit emerges in song. In Ophelia's death, Howe focuses on this transitional moment of metamorphosis itself, the bridge between living and inert matter. In both Ophelia and Daphne, she associates this bridging point between Being and Non-being with the potential for poetic speech. When Howe, in her preface to *The Europe of Trusts*, asserts her wish to "tenderly lift from the dark side of history, voices that are anonymous, slighted—inarticulate," she is organizing a lyric poetry of history around this transaction between the dead and the living ("Leaves," 14).

Among the many other allusions to *Hamlet* in the poem, a passage on page 42 is especially pertinent to the present argument:[42]

> ...   Lost
> to grief   How lust
> (these were the ghost's words) crawls
> between heaven and earth
>
> Dust is birth
> of earth we make loam   substance
>
> and strange shadows
> But I am reaching the end   Sky
> melts away into sand
>
> sand into Sound (*PS*, 42–43)

The key phrase here is "crawls// between heaven and earth," which derives from Hamlet's words to Ophelia: "What do such fellows as I do crawling between earth and heaven? We are arrant knaves all, believe none of us.

Go thy ways to a nunnery. Where's your father?" (*Hamlet* 3.1.128). The "arrant knaves" do the crawling for Hamlet, but Howe conflates these with "lust," drawing on the ghost's "won to his shameful lust" (*Hamlet* 1.5.45). Again, Howe is focusing on the passage between life and afterlife and linking poetry's annexation of religious experience to the productive moment in death. The poem continues—"... Sky/ melts away into sand// sand into Sound"—by linking the sounding of poetry to "Dust is birth," an adaptation of Hamlet's "Alexander died, Alexander was buried, Alexander returneth to dust, and dust is earth, of earth we make loam" (*Hamlet* 5.1.201–3).

The words "substance// and strange shadows" come from Sonnet 53's "What is your substance, whereof are you made/ That billions of strange shadows on you tend?" Here, the allusion is a clipped citation that plays the material against the shadow world. It is as if Howe is setting the materiality that Hamlet stresses with his "dust is earth" against the insubstantial ghost that plays on his mind. Howe echoes Hamlet's words with her Sky-sand metamorphosis and further suggests—"But I am reaching the end"—that the sounding of poetic language, echoing obscurely with the shadows of past injustice, is found in her condensation of death and rebirth. If there were no paternal ghost, after all, there would be no *Hamlet*.

Howe, then, twists her Shakespearean material to suit her interest in with poetic voice and metamorphosis. Her re-editing of *Hamlet*—"lust" now crawls, not "knaves"; "earth" becomes "birth"; the sonnet's question on substance is abruptly elided—bring the poem to its fundamental concerns of desire and death, matter and the immaterial. *Pythagorean Silence* returns insistently in this way to fragmentary "texts torn out of context" (*PS*, 67) that hover around these themes. It is a process of distillation that demonstrates Howe's methods in refined form: the texts are removed from position and reoriented to take part in another, ostensibly narrower, meditation. The words in this case communicate with each other as a reverie on death. However, these citations trail their contexts behind them, and wider reference to the source texts cannot be discounted—the elliptical treatment of Ophelia's death, for example, forms part of a rich parallel with Daphne's metamorphosis.

At the end of the final section of *Pythagorean Silence*, fifty pages later, Ophelia makes a second appearance in death: "weeds shiver and my clothes spread wide" are the last words of the poem (*PS*, 84). Again, the identification is direct, with Gertrude's "her clothes" becoming "my clothes." The weeds that she wished to hang on the "pendent boughs" are placed alongside "shiver," a pun on the "envious sliver" that broke beneath her weight. With "shiver," the cold weather that is the poem's background climate is finally linked to the coldness of the grave, a point at which the words/ weeds (*PS*, 32) break apart. In her letter to Taggart, Howe asserts that Daphne can divert herself from the ambitions that Apollo has for her, and here, too, she finds a redemptive moment in Ophelia's death.

The broken mode of utterance that "shiver" implies shatters the narcissistic suspension offered by Shakespeare's "glassy stream" and echoes the earlier line "pantheon of history shivered into/ ruin" (*PS* 61–62). Narcissus's perception of a singular self is destroyed as he metamorphoses into a flower, whereas Ophelia's flower-strewn lay both beckons the fantastic, imaged in the mermaid, and shivers her siren song into the historically layered polyphony of Howe's poetry.

Defenestration of Prague

The shivering of representation discussed above can be approached in a different way through the question of perspective in Howe's poetry. *Defenestration of Prague* roots itself in an exploration of ideas of representation in the Renaissance imagination, seeking to consider questions of power and literary form alongside one another. Although Shakespearean material is present in the poem, *Defenestration of Prague* is less concerned with tragedy than *Pythagorean Silence*. Instead, comedy, masque, and pastoral are its modes. It has an interest in lightness and surfaces that is unusual in Howe's writing of this period. Howe focuses in particular on Spenser and, less visibly, the work of Ben Jonson and Inigo Jones in the masque tradition.

In an interview, Howe acknowledges Spenser to be the seed for *Defenestration of Prague*: "Edmund Spenser led me by a very long and crooked route to the actual defenestration in Prague."[43] Howe is referring to an incident in 1618, when Bohemian Protestants tossed two Catholic councilors and their secretary out of a window, thus precipitating the Thirty Years' War. (Most of the nations of Europe, both Protestant and Catholic, became embroiled in the conflict.) There are, as far as I can discover, no direct references in the poem to the defenestration.[44] However, at the fringes of Howe's text is a questioning of the role of the poet similar to that explored through Daphne and Ophelia in *Pythagorean Silence*.

Howe's engagement with her sources raises questions about the implication for Spenser's poetry of his involvement in the 'plantation' of Ireland; fragments from Spenser's tract *A View of the Present State of Ireland* find their way into *Defenestration of Prague*.[45] Behind the text lurks a preoccupation with the doubled identity of the landowning class that was to become known as the Anglo-Irish and that would preside over the period of the Protestant

Ascendancy. As we have seen, Howe's own dual affinities, developed by the pull between her Anglo-Irish mother and American father, are one source of the combustible antinomies in her writing. In *Defenestration of Prague*, such ideas of doubling and identity are obliquely addressed at a level that is far removed from the personal. One of *The Faerie Queene*'s female characters, Florimell, for example, is taken up in Howe's poem, which refers both to Florimell and her double (a witch creates a counterfeit Florimell). Moreover, play with masks, masques, and deceptive appearances occurs throughout *Defenestration of Prague*.[46]

In her treatment of *The Faerie Queene*, instead of subjecting Spenser's poem to a reading that would simply brandish evidence of a latent barbarism, Howe finds, instead, a kind of freedom in its ability to construct an imaginary pastoral world. In an interview she has said, "In Spenser's allegory, symbolic things become real and reality melts into sound outsensing distance. This poem of the Mind is a pastoral *free* place. In Book II, Canto VIII, the author, *who is also an invader*, asks: 'And is there care in heauen? And is there love?' "[47] Although the mutual implication of culture and colonialism is a key theme for Howe,[48] her reading of *The Faerie Queene* appears more responsive to the role of artifice in Elizabethan and Jacobean culture. The blurring of the line between real and ideal orders is a central preoccupation of *Defenestration of Prague*. Questions of authority and of moral probity coded as English are everywhere in Spenser, but the degree to which the rhetoric of colonial adventure denudes Spenser's poem of its poetic integrity remains a subsidiary concern for Howe. Instead, *Defenestration of Prague* revolves around figures of insubstantiality and elusiveness and probes territory in which an event and its representation threaten to become indistinguishable.

The most prominent representative of the evasive "mystery" of Howe's conception of poetry is Florimell, whose chastity is continually threatened in Spenser's poem. There are several parallels to be drawn between the presence of Florimell in *Defenestration of Prague* and the treatment of Daphne and Ophelia in *Pythagorean Silence*. All of the women are pursued by amorous males. As with the two virginal women of *Pythagorean Silence*, Florimell's chastity is central to her literary identity. Like Ophelia and Daphne (daughter of the river god Peneus), Florimell is associated with water: she is held in an undersea dungeon by Proteus and linked by Spenser to "Venus of the fomy sea."[49] Florimell's flight is, moreover, at one point directly compared in Spenser's poem to that of Ovid's Daphne.[50]

Reading outward from these associations, the unattainable object of Petrarch's affections, Laura, was often compared to Daphne. Howe is exploring a conventional mode of figuring the feminine in order to ask what happens when a woman becomes the speaker and not the addressee of lyric poetry. If past "poet-invaders" such as Spenser and Raleigh mapped "virgin" land how might Howe's "poetry unsettled by history" both preserve and question that tradition?[51] The poem probes the connections that fascinate Howe in Spenser and Raleigh—the traffic, that is, between what Howe in interview describes as "allegory, iconoclasm, colonization, punning and the idea of the feminine."[52] Through Raleigh, Howe finds in her investigation of literary history a point of connection to the colonial experience in America—a theme she would explore more thoroughly in *Articulation* and *Thorow*. As a poet immersed in the American tradition, she is to an extent implicated in the colonial adventure—an irony that contributes to the obliquity of the poetry.

In the poem, Florimell represents an "idea of the feminine." Howe appears to find a resistance to translation in the character that is analogous to her poem's pursuit of meaning—a pursuit that is both playful and troubled. On each of the three occasions that the elusive Florimell appears in Howe's poem, it is in the context of the difficulties of mimesis: "Florimell flees away into the forest// Hide her there/ an illusion (fiction)" (*Defenestration*, 107); "Florimell embarks blindly/ (being lost)// to interpret the world" (Ibid., 109–10); and "Florimell and her false double/ True and false beauty" (Ibid., 135).

In these lines, Spenser's character is lost both to herself and to her pursuers. At one level, Howe is dramatizing the figure of femininity in lyric poetry, with its Petrarchan narrative of pursuit and endlessly deferred possession. At another, she is communicating a broader difficulty about separating world and representation. Can Florimell and her "false double" be distinguished? Through the allegorical figure, Howe allows the poem to dissolve into a play of fictive worlds. The aspiration to distinguish between "True and false beauty" gives way as "Words and meaning meet in// feigning" (*Defenestration*, 107). Howe's poem understands falsehood to be a condition of mimesis. Its response is to revel in the dreamlike forest scenes it establishes. Despite the lightness of the text's meditations on appearances, there is an accompanying anxiety about the points at which poetry and the world appear to be at odds, when the assertion of colonial power, in other words, meets its literary expression. These include the dissonance between Spenser's appreciation of the natural beauty of Ireland and the stylized pastoral of his poem, and that between Lord Grey—the despotic Lord Deputy of Ireland, under whom Spenser served—and Artegal, the *Faerie Queene*'s representative of justice. Although the accent is on fantasy, beneath the play of fictive worlds, the text knows itself to repress a violent real.

The stage for Howe's investigations—as in much of *Pythagorean Silence*—is the forest. Although numerous literary antecedents of the woods of Howe's "sylvan/ imagery" (*Defenestration*, 89) in *Defenestration of Prague* might be adduced, Howe mainly draws on *The Faerie Queene*, *A Midsummer Night's Dream*, and, again, the "wild wood" of Milton's *Comus*.[53]

As a girl Howe took part in stagings organized by her mother of *Comus* and of *A Midsummer Night's Dream*, both of which, she has said, left a powerful linguistic imprint.[54] In *Comus* she was a wood-nymph, or hamadryad, aged four—hamadryads, incidentally, are supposed to live and die with the trees they inhabit. In *Defenestration of Prague*—as with Daphne's flight into the woods in *Pythagorean Silence*—the obscurities of the forest prepare a consideration of the functions of lyric:

> Benevolent woods and glades
> hamadryads
>
> plots and old-plays
>
> A fictive realm
> Words and meaning meet in
>
> feigning
>
> without a text and running from
> true-seeming
>
> Florimell flees away into the forest
>
> Hide her there
> an illusion (fiction)
>
> Beauty of the world
>
> becoming part of the forest (*Defenestration*, 107)

The forest is a place where a drama of representation is staged. The work of mimesis—here at once "feigning" but evading "true-seeming"—is made complicated by the ceaseless flight of Florimell into the forest.[55] The forest becomes a space for the continual creation and unmaking of fictions. Yet verisimilitude—"true-seeming"—is not the goal. The fictive Florimell, hidden in the forest, is as much a fake as her false double. The original object of representation is simply not accessible. Mimesis, in this sequence, is a process of staging—or coming into being—that is never fully achieved. Instead, like the radically curtailed portions of language in Howe's poetry, it is a venture that is aware of its own artifice and that can only communicate through the gradual, processual accumulation of small utterances. When Florimell becomes "part of the forest," it is as if she is almost lost to representation. She is accessible only to a form of expression that could rival the insubstantial shadowplay of the forest—for which we might understand Howe's own writing.

* * *

Defenestration of Prague engages in another important way with this play of fictive worlds. In this case, a complex of ideas concerning words and pictorial representation is approached, albeit in a very oblique manner, through the Jacobean masque. In a 1983 letter Howe wrote, somewhat elliptically, to Charles Bernstein on this theme: "Defenestration *of Prague* is very much involved with Masque tradition—and perspective of such— Inigo Jones vs. Ben Jonson—artificer/architext vs. writer. The eyepoint centered on Royalty etc. The political implications."[56] *Defenestration of Prague* is ambivalent about the courtly masque: enthralled by its capacity to stage the fabulous (which becomes an analogy for a hallucinatory understanding of the act of reading) but troubled by the spectacle's endorsement of the ideology of Divine Right. The many voices of Howe's poem are a means of substituting a multiperspectival model of viewpoint for the single monarchical sight-line encouraged, as we will see, by the masque.

The front and back covers of the original edition of *Defenestration of Prague* are devoted to a sketch by Inigo Jones entitled "Cloud Containing Divine Poesy," part of his design for *Temple of Love: The Queene's Shrovetide Masque*, which was performed on 10 February, 1635.[57] In the masque, the visual spectacle, the words and the music were of roughly equal importance.[58] As in Spenser's *Faerie Queene*, the characters of masques were typically allegorical personifications—Virtue, Pleasure, and so on. Moreover, in the Jonsonian form, the masques incorporated grotesque or comic antimasques, designed to contrast the behavior of the lower orders with that of the aristocrats whose virtues were hymned in the texts. The masques, then, were victory celebrations in which nobility and order invariably triumphed over baseness and wildness.[59]

Inigo Jones discovered perspective sets in Italy, and he used the innovation for the extraordinarily lavish spectacles that he staged for James's court.[60] These made use of complicated machinery, scenery, and lighting effects.[61] However, to the Renaissance eye, the idea of conveying spatial depth through flat pieces of board and converging lines was new. The effect of perspective, moreover, would be most apparent to those in the best seats, and most of all to the king, who would be placed in the seat that offered the best view of the new sets. Howe's reference to "eyepoint" in her letter to Bernstein suggests that she follows Renaissance scholar Stephen Orgel's argument that representation in the art of the masque is designed to reflect back to those in power a world in which their dominance is entire and, indeed, part of the order of things. Orgel writes,

> Jones's stage subtly changed the character of both plays and masques by transforming *audiences* into *spectators*, fixing the viewer and directing the theatrical experience toward the single point in the hall from which the perspective achieved its fullest effect, the royal throne.... Through the use of perspective, the monarch, always the ethical centre of court productions, became in a physical and emblematic way the centre as well.... It is no accident that perspective stages flourished at court and only at court, and that their appearance there coincided with the reappearance in England of the Divine Right of Kings as a serious political philosophy.[62]

If *The Faerie Queene* is a highly aestheticized celebration of order, virtue and Elizabethan Protestantism, the Jonsonian masque seeks to effect an analogous eulogy to the prevailing social hierarchy with its material staging of the miraculous. Howe's poem sets out, on one hand, to unpack the organization of space that constructs the official viewpoint and, on the other, to exploit the mystificatory maneuvers that endow the king with divine authority. At the level of the artwork, Howe posits a convergence between the iconoclastic "wild interiority" of language and the sense of wonder that pervades the Jonson-Jones aesthetic.[63] As with her later work *Eikon Basilike*, it is not possible to read her poem as straightforward iconoclasm; it is too much in sympathy with the masque's investment in awe. Rather, the poem seeks to investigate the hallucinatory aspect of literary experience and to decouple this from its authoritarian trappings in the texts that she explores.

Defenestration of Prague, with its affirmation of lightness and revelry, is in partial accord with the mood of the masque. However, Howe's poem does not echo the plotting or style of Jonson's masques. Rather, it mimics the atmosphere of stylized and confected performance and often returns to a vocabulary of ephemerality. In Jonson's masque *Oberon*, for example, there is a fairy palace with transparent walls. The combination of insubstantiality, extraordinary staging, and the mirroring of earthly authority is revealed in the following stage direction: "*There the whole palace opened, and the nation of Fays were discovered, some with instruments, some bearing lights, others singing; and within, afar off in perspective, the knights masquers sitting in their several seiges.*"[64] This spectacle is followed by a song:

> Melt earth to sea, sea flow to air,
>   And air fly into fire,
> Whilst we in tunes to Arthur's chair
>   Bear Oberon's desire;
> Than which there can be nothing higher,
> Save JAMES, to whom it flies:
> But he the wonder is of tongues, of ears, of eyes.[65]

Jonson, in cahoots with Jones (who staged this masque), is presenting the audience with a spectacle of wonder that reflects back to the court its own glamour. However, this is presented in the language of the immaterial and the melting of elements into one another. In Howe's poem, there is a tendency to take up this emphasis on insubstantiality and to use it as a weapon against the singleness of kingly perspective. Howe assents to the ephemerality of the spectacle but puts it into the service of a kind of imaginative disobedience.

This engagement with the airiness of masque—and the perilous pleasures of its narcissism—can be seen at many points in *Defenestration of Prague*. Howe writes, for example, lines such as the following: "figural shadowing of invisible" (*Defenestration*, 103); "Fantasticality/ nimble phantasma capering on a page// with antic gesture" (*Defenestration*, 110); "Worlds pass mirror-worlds in shelter" (*Defenestration*, 118); and "Revolution repetition Doubling// Self around self/ mimicking and lengthening// Layer after layer/ mirror characters pursue each other" (*Defenestration*, 127).

The hallucinatory masque space that Howe sketches in *Defenestration of Prague* is an environment in which the traffic between ideal and real is sufficient to blur the distinction between the two. The attention given to the question of presence finds an analogue in the vestigial nature of the actors. This nexus of ideas around insubstantiality and unstable identity in the poem is most evident in the lines "evanishing of the actors into// one another" (*Defenestration*, 108) and "Players melt into one another" (*Defenestration*, 136). The lines echo the aftermath of the masque scene in Shakespeare's *The Tempest*:

> Our revels are now ended. These our actors,
> As I foretold you, were all spirits, and
> Are melted into air, into thin air[66]

This quality of being on the point of dissolution is pervasive in *Defenestration of Prague*. The fairy-like actors and "sylvan" setting of the poem are a means of invoking a version of Renaissance pastoral: the forest as a magical space in which the rules of court and city are suspended.[67] Standing as a figure for contemporary poetry, this environment makes of the page a site of refuge from more transparent language use, a place in which meanings appear and disappear in much the same manner as the "evanishing actors" of the masque. At numerous points, the poem uses language that resists any interpretation other than a staging of this ephemerality. Howe appropriates the masque's capacity for realizing the fantastic but allows a highly associative dream logic to dismantle the sovereignty of perspective that would be the prerogative of the king—or his proxies, the author and reader.

Although Inigo Jones's importation of perspective is seen as a device through which depth of field was put into the service of a self-confirming quasi-religious ritual of sovereignty, Howe's shifts in the poem reaffirm the subsequent democratization of perspective in theatrical representation. When Howe writes, for example, such opaque lines as "Fable over the mountain// abash negation/ gnashing pattern of alliteration" (*Defenestration*, 122), she renounces, with forceful lyrical diction, any singleness of viewpoint—neither writer nor reader can lay any definitive interpretative claim to such sequences.

* * *

The representational mobility of *Defenestration* is discernible in another aspect of the staging of pastoral tradition on which Howe draws in her depictions of the forest: that of revelry, the "nimble phantasma capering on a page// with antic gesture" (*Defenestration*, 110). The forest, through this lens, is a "Hide-and seek border region" (*Defenestration*, 111). It is an inversion of the "drear wood" of *Comus*, in which The Lady appears, lost and hoping she does not attend the bacchanal presided over by Circe's son: "I should be loth/ To meet the rudeness and swilled insolence/ Of such late wassailers; yet O where else/ Shall I inform my unacquainted feet/ In the blind mazes of this tangled wood?"[68] In Howe's case, the wassailers, like the rambunctious strawboys of Irish tradition, are welcomed into the poem.

Defenestration draws on the "moonlight revels" of *A Midsummer Night's Dream* (2.1.141), with their aura of temporal suspension, masquerade, and stylized amorous misrecognition. The first section of *Defenestration*, "Tuning the Sky," for example, refers to Shakespeare's "Mechanicals" (*Defenestration*, 96) and is followed by the words "casement(*open* of great moone," an adaptation of lines from *A Midsummer Night's Dream* (3.1.53–54). The "tatterdemailion [correctly, tatterdemalion, meaning ragamuffin] revel" or "wassail" of Howe's text (*Defenestration*, 103) would mean a scruffy or tattered celebration—the opposite of the courtly masque. There are several allusions to popular oral forms: the long "Speeches at the Barriers" section opens with the lines "Say that a ballad/ wrapped in a ballad" (*Defenestration*, 99), and there are references to "oldest chronicle" (*Defenestration*, 131), "fable" (e.g., *Defenestration*, 133), and "nursery tale" (*Defenestration*, 125). Howe is sometimes thinking of an open-air event—"Revels under open sky" (*Defenestration*, 129)—and sometimes of a shamanic disclosure—"Wild man of pageant and poem/ wild man in a dream" (*Defenestration*, 135). The latter recalls Spenser's injunction against the "wilde" Irish "bardes," who celebrate "lycentious" and "most bolde and lawlesse" behavior. "Mock reign of a mock king" (*Defenestration*, 136) brings a carnivalesque pathos to the temporary inversion of the existing order. It is clear, too, that the modes of popular celebration invoked by Howe are linked to something that occurs within the linguistic order, a "Stanzaic glade" (*Defenestration*, 131) in which "Nimble and subtle/ words jig and double catch" (*Defenestration*, 127).

Moreover, the idea of mimesis in these moments, rehearsing again the "evanishing of the actors into// one another," recurs with a collapsing of the 'true' and 'false' selves of performance. The "Players melt into one another," and "Layer after layer/ Mirror characters pursue each other" (*Defenestration*, 127). These characters may be the characters in a fiction or the typographical characters that exist on the surface of Howe's pages. Howe pursues this mirroring further, with "Worlds pass mirror-worlds in shelter" (*Defenestration*, 118). Spenser's moralizing aesthetic falls apart in the "Hide-and-seek border region" (*Defenestration*, 111) of the forest. Howe works with reversal and inversions, urging oppositions to "melt into one another." Player and person, dream and reality collide in a "chemical wedding" of "Self and Anti-self" (*Defenestration*, 142)—an allusion to Yeats's opposition of Self to the liberatory imaginative mask of Anti-Self.[69]

The theme of popular celebration, a poetical anti-masque to the theme of masquing, is evident at points in the poem such as "Fairs held on hilltops/ (mummer and strawboy)" (*Defenestration*, 145) and "Straw dress/ straw mask" (*Defenestration*, 142). The word "mumming" has its origins in the French, *momer* (to mask oneself), but mumming was an English form, thought to have been adapted by the Irish with the arrival of the colonizers of the seventeenth century.[70] Strawboys were straw-masked revelers, usually uninvited, who participated in wakes or wedding celebrations—it was considered bad luck to turn them away. *Defenestration*'s third and final section, "Bride's Day," brings an Irish dimension to this treatment of popular revelry. Its title refers to the Irish festival of Imbolc or Candlemass, a celebration of the arrival of spring.[71]

It would be a mistake, however, to suggest that, in opposing aristocratic forms to popular ones, Howe is simply investing the latter with greater transgressive potential. Jonson and Jones, for all their differences, argues Orgel, had a similar attachment to producing a state of wonder. The masque was a kind of staging or realization of fantasy, its fabulous metamorphoses conjoining real and ideal. So, in Orgel's words, "the realistic and the marvelous—that which produced wonder, the end of drama—were neither antithetical nor, on the whole, even distinguishable. What was marvelous about the spectacular machinery was precisely the realism of its illusions."[72] Howe's evocation of a hallucinatory forest seems an attempt to stage the fabulous through the formal means available to the late-twentieth-century poet. A poetry of fragments, it represents the discontinuities of the linguistic realization of fantasy. Although the multiple viewpoints of Howe's poetics suggest a critique of the ways in which the masque served to authenticate divinely ordained kingship through the exercise of monarchical perspective, the desire to produce a state of irrational transport is susceptible to the lure of that very mystification of authority, as in *Eikon*.

Wonder at the miraculous artifice of the courtly masque is combined, then, with an insurgent populism that incorporates the aesthetic maneuvers of the Irish peasantry under colonial rule. The masks that mummers and strawboys wear are another version of the mobile identity that Howe accords her "evanishing actors." There is repeated "flight from true-seeming" in the poem, as figures such as the strawboys echo the elusiveness of Florimell. Whereas performers and spectators melted into one another during the courtly revels that concluded the Jacobean masque, these aristocratic figures in Howe's poem are jostled by the unruly entrance of the strawboys and the tatterdemalion revelers. Sovereignty, a mystifying form of authority, is pitted against an unruly popular iconoclasm, but neither term of the conflict is cancelled in the encounter.

The political oppositions of Howe's work, in other words, can never be understood as a straightforward endorsement of alterity. Howe's interest in the mechanics of exclusion, whether ritualized through scapegoating or as bloody as the extermination of native American tribes, runs alongside a concomitant fascination with the figure of the center that guarantees or authorizes representation, whether it is the (absent) king or the elusive "center around which Poetry gravitates."[73] The fairyland of Shakespearean pastoral comedy is the scene of these tense conceptual crosscurrents in *Defenestration*, with the forest imagined as a space of self-renewing ficticeness that is available to both hieratic and demotic forms.

In *Defenestration of Prague*'s setting of "benevolent" pastoral (Defenestration, 107), poetic language is given an evanescent, sportive quality that is quite different from the more threatening American forests of *Thorow* or *Articulation*. Yet all of this 1980s writing shows a complicated awareness of the formal and ethical problems facing a woman poet writing in the American context. Howe is a New England poet, with all the baggage that entails, and she often returns to the themes of social authority and colonization.

What is valuable about Howe's poetry of this period is her ability to sustain just such a complicated relation to authority. The gendered identifications of *Pythagorean Silence* are similarly hard to pin down as Howe attempts to rethink the figures of Daphne and Ophelia. From their metamorphoses, Howe seeks to express a predicament that embraces both marginalized feminine and marginalized poetic speech. Howe's act of resistance, however, risks folding in on itself and becoming a valorization of a silenced-ness that remains, in the end, silenced.

Her answer to the dilemmas in these related poems could find no other expression than through the disjunctions of her poetry. It is a struggle between muteness, on the one hand, and authority, on the other, which is generative in the extreme. Her use of motifs from the sixteenth and seventeenth centuries is similarly double-edged: it binds her to the literary mainstream in a way that makes her different from her peers among the language writers. It is true, certainly, that she reinflects such works in her own poems. However, her *détournement* of these texts does not amount to a wish to reject some sort of overbearing and hegemonic canon. Rather, it is a far more ambivalent engagement that insists on close rereading of Shakespeare, Spenser, Milton, and the Bible—texts that are no longer forcefully inscribed in cultural memory. Howe's poems of this period splinter these works as they seek to find a means of approaching the "enigma of Power."

CHAPTER 4

The Poetics of American Space

Howe begins her long poetic engagement with American history in *Chanting at the Crystal Sea* (1975). Throughout this early sequence, there are passages that read as though they have been abstracted from the narratives of early settlers. There are many apparent references to the precarious situation of the early arrivals, their experience of 'wilderness', and the mixture of piety and violence in their lives: "Monday, massacre, burning, and pillage/ On Tuesday, gifts, and visits among friends" (*Chanting*, 70). The poem concludes with a striking invocation of the paternal:

> I see my father approaching
> from the narrow corner of some lost empire
> where the name of some great king still survives.
> He has explored other lost sites of great cities
> but that vital condition—
> the glorious success of his grand enterprise
> still eludes him. (*Chanting*, 72)

The lines probe the confused legacy of imperialism, finding only uncertainty and amnesia, rather than the clear mapping of territory: "some lost empire...some great king...other lost sites of great cities." The father is spellbound by the past, but now he finds it increasingly unintelligible. "Greatness" and glory are no longer to be found. The twentieth century, the poem suggests, has shown the bankruptcy of such rhetoric. The poem ends elusively, the certainties of the father's archaeological project dissolving into vagueness and conjecture. The failings of conquest become an important concern for Howe in her subsequent writing, and the sheer difficulty of recovering voices from those "lost sites" exerts greater pressure on the syntax of later poems. The two major serial poems of *Singularities*—*Articulation of Sound Forms in Time* and *Thorow*—show Howe wrestling into being a form of poetic speech that is adequate to a constellation of issues involving the archive, the transplantation of the Western tradition to another territory, femininity, and power.

Articulation of Sound Forms in Time and *Thorow* are Howe's most discussed works. For many observers, their representation, through a language of rupture, of the underside of American colonial history has rendered them exemplary among Howe's poems. One notable feature of much of the criticism has been to find in the poetry's intractable wordscapes a kind of freeing gesture. For Ma, for example, the poetry breaks "free from grammar as 'repressive mechanism'"; for Back, language finds its "liberation"; for Perloff, the writing effects a Cagean "demilitarization of syntax"; for Reinfeld it breaks through "narrative and referential frames"; for Frost, it "explores ways to obliterate linguistic and social constraints"; and, for Schultz, it "desystematize[s] history."[1] There is, as I note in my discussion of *Articulation of Sound Forms in Time*, much in the text to justify such an opposition of the (bad) systemic and the (good) asystemic. There is also, as Ma observes of Howe's interview with Edward Foster, authority from Howe for such a reading. "I think a lot of my work is about breaking free," says Howe. "Starting free and being captured and breaking free again and being captured again" (Foster interview, 166). However, I believe that Howe's own accounts of her writing, particularly in interviews, can sometimes hinder, as well as help, her readers. In particular, as I will argue in my account of *Thorow*, I believe the writing to be greatly colored by forms of constraint. If the return of the repressed is a guiding model for our understanding of the writing—and everything in Howe's historical poetics points toward this—then it is important to recognize that the unconscious is precisely *not* a space of freedom. Rather, it is a space in which we do not exert the control we would wish to exert; indeed, we are susceptible to control by an agency that feels other to ourselves. Another way of reading the linguistic deformations of the *Singularities* poems would be to see them as attenuated stagings of certain historical and cultural determinants. These guide and even enslave a form of poetic speech that has sought to lay itself open to the twin fields of text and landscape.

In a recent piece of self-commentary that may be more helpful than the remark cited above, Howe writes of her earlier work,

> During the 1980s I wanted to transplant words onto paper with soil sticking to their roots—to go to meet a narrative's fate by immediate

access to its concrete totality of singular interjections, crucified spellings, abbreviations, irrational apprehensions, collective identities, palavers, kicks, cordials, comforts. I wanted jerky and tedious details to oratorically bloom and bear fruit as if they had been set at liberty or ransomed by angels. (*Personal Narrative*, 16)

In this cluster of thoughts, there is a desire for the assimilation of poem and place and a desire (perhaps frustrated) for truncated and often unexceptional fragments of language to be rescued and transformed through the medium of poetic speech. Again, liberty is at issue, albeit conditioned by a wary "as if." It is significant that the various linguistic materials that Howe seeks to gather are delivered through "immediate access," which suggests some kind of suprarational communion through poetry with the historical, textual, cultural, and geographical layers of meaning that the writing invokes.[2] This way of thinking about the work has, I believe, proved both liberating and confining for Howe. Its liberatory moment is best understood through her engagement with American antinomianism, and, as she goes on to say in *Personal Narrative*, with her assimilation of the "absolute freedom and wildness" that Thoreau found in Nature to the "freedom and wildness" she found in libraries (ibid.).[3] However, the tangled mesh of material brought to light by her vigorous and brilliantly associative researches leads to many contradictions, as Howe would undoubtedly acknowledge. It is my belief that the poetry "oratorically" blooms in ways that have nothing to do with the angels or, indeed, with a liberty that is not thoroughly circumscribed by pressures that are both internal and external to subjective experience and that, collectively speaking, belong to both past and present.

The poems of *Singularities* reflect the research that Howe was doing in the 1980s on early American history—work that found a prose outlet in the audacious criticism of *My Emily Dickinson* and *Birth-mark*. It is clear from the latter that Howe became very interested in dissent from the Puritan establishment in seventeenth-century New England—itself, of course, a social group that belonged to a dissenting tradition. Antinomianism is at the heart of this dissent from transplanted Dissenters.[4] However, I will argue that this designation of revolt has sometimes led to incomplete accounts of both her poetry's power and its relation to the phenomenon of power. In her introduction to *Birth-mark*, Howe describes the antinomian conflict of the 1630s that gripped colonial New England at its very inception as "the primordial struggle of North American literary expression" (*Birth-mark*, 4). This dispute among the Puritan settlers offers Howe not only a point of purchase on her literary antecedents, but also a way of grounding her own poetics. In her polemical reading of the controversy's influence, issues of authority and poetic inspiration collide with the policing of literary works by academic and publishing institutions in the twentieth century. She writes,

> The issue of editorial control is directly related to the attempted erasure of antinomianism in our culture. Lawlessness seen as negligence is at first feminized and then restricted or banished.... For me, the manuscripts of Emily Dickinson of the early American female preacher and prophet Anne Hutchinson, and the comparison of her opinions to monstrous births, is not unrelated to the editorial apprehension and domestication of Emily Dickinson. The antinomian controversy in New England (1636–38) didn't leave Massachusetts with its banished originator. The antinomian controversy continues in the form, often called formlessness of Emily Dickinson's letters and poems during and after her crisis years of 1858–60. It continues with this nineteenth-century antinomian poet's gesture of infinite patience in preferring not to publish. Her demurral was a covenant of grace. The antinomian controversy continues in the first recording and revision of her manuscripts according to a covenant of works. (*Birth-mark*, 1)

The covenant of grace, in the language of the Puritans, was God's compact with the Elect. The covenant of works, declared redundant by Calvin, corresponded to the importance of earthly deeds in gaining salvation. The antinomian current in American literature, for Howe, follows a line that runs from the banishment of Anne Hutchinson from the Bay Area colony through Emily Dickinson to the marginalization of the poetic avant garde in the late twentieth century: "I see a contemporary American practice that isn't what necessarily gets into the canon and has trouble getting published. It is an echo of an undervoice that was speaking from the beginning and is peculiarly American. This voice keeps speaking *against* the grain" ("Encloser," 192).[5]

Howe, choosing to work to one side of academic criticism, made her critical writing, which is indebted to Olson's *Call Me Ishmael* and Williams's *In the American Grain*, an extension into prose of her highly associative manner of thinking. This mode enables her to negotiate a structural analogy between antinomianism and radical poetics. In a remarkable—and questionable—feat of conflation, she sets up an opposition between grace, spiritual immediacy, poetic inspiration, and a "contemporary American practice" of writing, on the one hand, and an array of legislating religious, political, and literary forces on the other. Howe at some times, as in the citations above, appears to valorize the asystemic; at others to strive for balance between law and grace (and their various analogues); and at still others to complicate this opposition with a third term, often gendered as feminine. Her use of dichotomies is itself rooted in the exigencies of place. "Contradiction is the book of this place," she writes in *My Emily Dickinson* (45). Although they are undoubtedly resonant and fertile texts, her critical essays run the risk of unsustainable and ahistorical comparisons—suggesting, for example, a continuity between what Charles Bernstein has called "official verse culture" and the authorities of the Bay Area colony—that fail to illuminate either side of her stacked dualisms.

Nonetheless, in Howe's reading of American religious and literary history, it is possible to find grounds for the arguments around the inarticulate that proliferate in her work. Anne Hutchinson, the woman at the center of the antinomian controversy, was accused of propounding the view that the Puritan ministers of the Bay Area colony preached a covenant of works, not of grace.[6] She was said to be alleging, in other words, that they placed greater emphasis on deeds in the world than on the believer's knowledge that he or she was among the Elect, predestined for salvation. Her opponents feared that her views could lead to a disregard for moral law that might shatter the social cohesion of the fragile colony. In her defense, during her public examination in 1637, Hutchinson cited a passage from 2 Corinthians: "Who also hath made us able ministers of the new testament; not of the letter, but of the spirit: for the letter killeth, but the spirit giveth life."[7] Hutchinson seeks to contrast literal interpretation with the directness of intuitive understanding. The turning point of the examination concerns this directness, when Hutchinson admits that God spoke to her in what she calls "an immediate revelation," with the words: "I am the same God that delivered Daniel out of the lion's den, I will deliver thee."[8] This spiritual encounter leaves Hutchinson skeptical of the worldly authority of her examiners: "But now having seen him which is invisible," she says, "I fear not what man can do unto me."[9]

In her *Linebreak* interview, Howe speaks of an "immediate infusion," which is "what Anne Hutchinson is about, being instantly infused with grace so there would be no text—there would be no need for law because this direct experience would come that had no use for print."[10] Similarly, alongside an early reference to Hutchinson in *My Emily Dickinson*, Howe writes, "Grace caused a civil war in the Calvinist soul. Grace often visited the elect, with visionary intensity born in ecstasy and trance" (*MED*, 47). Howe's account of Hutchinson describes a desire for an unmediated experience of divine grace. Mystical speech, at such moments in her thought, is accorded a charged communicative pre-eminence over the fallen form of text.

The antinomian dispute, as Patricia Caldwell has argued, also involved language itself.[11] During the trial that led to her excommunication from the church and banishment from the colony, Hutchinson made a distinction between word and referent, saying, "I confess I have denied the Word Graces but not the thing itself."[12] The first governor of the colony, John Winthrop, says of her "immediate revelation": "Ey it is the most desperate enthusiasm in the world, for nothing but a word comes to her mind and then an application is made which is nothing to the purpose, and this is her revelations when it is impossible but that the word and spirit should speak the same thing."[13] For Winthrop, Hutchinson's enthusiasm, far from the passing of the divine into human language or the first glimmerings of an incipiently American form of speech, is a whimsical and socially irresponsible challenge to the communal bond of language.

Howe's writing seeks an understanding of the ways in which the linguistic indirection that she associates with antinomianism might be regulated by the discourses that seek to deny it. In so doing, it attempts a historicization of the category of the outside in American culture and proposes a literary resistance to the marginalization of this antinomian element. Having unsettled the would-be theocracy of the settlers, Hutchinson is described by Winthrop as the "American Jesabel." Hutchinson's banishment from the colony is followed a year later, in what is claimed as a vindication by her persecutors, by her death in a massacre carried out by Native Americans. In *Birth-mark*, Howe traces a line between the suppression of antinomianism and the "repudiation of alterity, anonymity, darkness" in contemporary America (89).

Howe's business, however, is with the underside of history, not with explicit commentary on the present—the repressed, in her work, returns mutely, arriving as a linguistic effect. At issue, as a consequence, is the coexistence of distinct kinds of silence: that of historical actors rendered inarticulate in various ways and that of a metaphysical notion of absence. Part of the combustible energy of Howe's poetry, problematic as it is, lies in its ability to map and overmap such incommensurable models of otherness. The risk that such a poetry of homologies runs is to appear to conflate these different versions of the outside.

In Hutchinson's "immediate revelation," Howe finds a prototype for the experience of poetic language. In Hutchinson's banishment, the poet detects a scapegoating impulse responsible for contemporary ills that range from social marginalization to the shaping power of cultural conservatism in the process of canon formation. Configurations of language and power have a long half-life in Howe's reading of American history. There is, however, a danger in ethically oriented readings of Howe that view the poetry chiefly in terms of the way it tracks phobic responses to social 'otherness' (e.g., femininity, the racial other, and so on). This account is certainly justified by passages in some of Howe's critical texts, but it leaves the poetry marooned in a banal counter-hegemonic project in which numerous 'others' are conflated and, worse, held to share in an implied coalition against what Back terms "normative language functions."[14] Such interpretations risk muffling the force of Howe's writing by being too quick to name the negativity that informs it; the poetry is not primarily carrying out a work of redress. Readings such as Back's accentuate the problems caused by neglecting the complex polyphony and the many ambivalences of Howe's poetry and, following oppositions that the writing sometimes encourages, reduce the poetry to a conflict between the systemic (always repressive) and the asystemic (inevitably liberatory). Power and authority are endowed, in this view, with a monolithic rigidity that is of little help, as a conceptual tool, to those in pursuit of radical alternatives.

Howe found the voice that appears in the *Singularities* poems long before she embarked on serious research on captivity narratives and Anne Hutchinson. Although it is not hard to find elements of quasi-Puritanical, typology-driven dogmatism in the politics of the American Right,[15] it may not be especially helpful to apply an "antinomian" counter to these forces in the poetic practices of the late-twentieth-century avant garde. Such a designation, indeed, appears mainly to be a means of providing a historical grounding for topics characteristic of the American academy of the 1980s and 1990s: interrogations of national and cultural identity; exploration of the marginalization of the other (eventually, of course, "othering"); feminism; the new historicist re-examination of the operation of past ideologies; and poststructuralist attention to the discursive sleights of hand through which texts repress their metaphysical underpinnings.

Reading Howe's work through an antinomian lens does, however, help provide a literary and historical context for her poetry's fascination with a form of American literary language that privileges hesitancy and indirection. As Howe's research on antinomianism did not fundamentally alter the character of her poetry, the presence of antinomianism in her work can be better understood as the result of an anxiety about origins that causes her to fashion a particular literary genealogy around her own preoccupations. Like many other writers before her, she implicitly writes herself into her own strong reading of literary history.

Articulation of Sound Forms in Time

Articulation of Sound Forms in Time is one of Howe's most powerful texts, a searching realization of her historical poetics. The poem sequence was first published by the small press Awede in 1987 and then reprinted by Wesleyan as part of the *Singularities* collection in 1990. It was the first American-themed book she had published since 1978's *Secret History of the Dividing Line*.[16] *Articulation of Sound Forms in Time* and *Thorow* are her most sustained poetic attempts at addressing the colonization of America and its ramifications for American literary identity.

The initial setting of *Articulation of Sound Forms in Time* is a 1676 battle between settlers and Native Americans near the colonial settlement of Deerfield in the Connecticut River Valley.[17] The poem contains three sections: "The Falls Fight," comprising a short prose text and a letter from the late eighteenth century; "Hope Atherton's Wanderings," a sequence of 16 short page-poems; and "Taking the Forest," a series of 25 short page-poems.[18] The poems of "Hope Atherton's Wanderings" are more varied in form than those of "Taking the Forest," which use the single lines and couplets that Howe had favored in *Pythagorean Silence*, *Defenestration of Prague*, and *Secret History of the Dividing Line*. Both the prose text and the second section are grounded in the experience of a minister named Hope Atherton, who in 1676 was involved in a skirmish known as the Falls Fight (later called the Turner's Falls Massacre) during King Philip's War, a conflict that involved settlers and Native Americans.[19]

During the hostilities, a party of English soldiers massacred an Indian encampment of about 300 people, most of whom, Howe notes, were women and children. In their bloody retreat, a small group of Englishmen, including Hope Atherton, became separated from their compatriots. When, after several days spent hiding in the woods, the settlers surrendered to the Indians, they were put to death, with the exception of Atherton. The letter from 1781 that Howe appends to her narrative of these events suggests that Atherton was spared because the Indians thought that he—hatless and dressed in a black coat—was a god among the English. The letter also notes that Atherton's story was not believed by some among his congregation, who considered him to be "beside himself" (*Articulation*, 5).[20]

Articulation moves outward from this prose section through "Hope Atherton's Wanderings," which can in several places be linked to the historical material excavated in the first section, to the expansive poetry of "Taking the Forest," which ranges across many discursive fields. In *Articulation*, Howe's commitment to intelligibility often appears so slender as to threaten any idea of the story within history. *Articulation* meditates on the legacy of the doctrine of predestination and its consequences for the contemporary poet. The poems are subject to a perplexing temporality that crushes past and present together. The relation between history and prophecy, in particular, and the kind of authority that underpins each of these discursive modes is of great interest to a poet seeking to rethink narratives of the settlement of New England. Schultz, a perceptive reader of Howe, has made an important extended discussion of the question of authority in this poem. It will become clear, however, that I do not concur with Schultz's optimistic contention, "By performing and taking apart the central ideologies that separate Puritan theology from the native American context in which they found themselves, Howe aims to get back to a point where the story can begin again, where it can be more inclusive."[21] This "point where the story can begin again" remains elusive for Howe, as does any representation of the "native American context."

Howe's poem resonates with the dictum "Prophecie is History antedated and Historie is Postdated Prophecie," cited in the first section of the poem (*Articulation*, 4). (Howe attributes this to the Massachusetts Bay Colony minister John Cotton; Sacvan Bercovitch notes that the formulation was used "repeatedly" by early New England ministers.)[22] *Articulation* is informed by the New England acceptance of the Calvinist idea of predestination, which gave the seventeenth-century settlers' own experience both literal and figurative meaning: their own history was the chronicle of a specific earthly community and, at the same time, the unfolding of the narrative of God's chosen people.[23] Bercovitch writes,

> The newness of New England becomes both literal and eschatological, and (in what was surely the most far-reaching of these rhetorical effects) the American *wilderness* takes on the double significance of secular and sacred place. If for the individual believer it remained part of the wilderness of the world, for God's "peculiar people" it was a territory endowed with special symbolic import, like the wilderness through which the Israelites passed to the promised land.[24]

This combination of secular and sacred, literal and eschatological, is everywhere evident in Howe's poem, which claims the fusing of these realms for a poetic language that works against, rather than with, the teleological imperatives of the Puritan typological marriage of Bible and history. For Howe, the interpenetration of secular and sacred represents an anti-narrative impulse that is ultimately antinomian—a suggestion I will explore below. The fusion of literal and eschatological registers in Puritan writing finds an analogue in the doubleness of Howe's texts, in which an expanded but obscure associative range is substituted for religious symbolism.

In using a citation that assimilates history to prophecy in her preface, Howe indicates that she believes the idea of predestination still has purchase on the American political imagination. It is this fantasy of pre-eminence, of being "God's 'peculiar people,'" that she wishes to undo. Howe's treatment of America's Reagan-era present is, therefore, a treatment of what that present represses. Her gloss of a line from *Articulation* in a 1987 letter to Taggart makes her ambitions clear: "Well I meant by 'migratory path to massacre'— the migration that lead us on as an Errand into the Wilderness in which we *massacred* Indians—that was our corrupted Errand. Of course I mean future too and present as I do always in all these 'meditations.'"[25]

Howe's tracking of a "Migratory path to massacre" (*Articulation*, 22) can be understood as both a summary of the Puritan errand and a longer, quasi-typological view of American history. In the same May 1987 letter to Taggart, Howe also comments on the lines: "Cries open to the words inside them/ Cries hurled through woods" (ibid.). She remarks, "The woods were a region of terror and the only answer was to hurl brutal cries of war through them—to cut down the wood—even to burn and defoliate the forest in Vietnam."[26] This reduction of language to fragmentary particles that nonetheless retain the potential to knit together the distant past—Atherton's adventure—and a twentieth-century war (Vietnam) is characteristic of Howe's historical poetics.

* * *

Howe writes from within a twentieth-century tradition of the "poem containing history"; the scale of her historical ambition places her in the Pound/ Olson line of poets. Her long poems, like theirs, are transhistorical and polyphonic, and they place great emphasis on the role of the fragment in larger cultural narratives. However, this is a current in poetics that she writes both with and against.[27] Howe's evident admiration for the formal and theoretical range of verse epics such as the *Cantos* and the *Maximus* poems is combined with a critique of the will to power that sustains them. Other genealogies—Dickinson and Stein, HD and Duncan, or Eliot and Stevens—might therefore also be plausibly argued.

Atherton's excursion, is, as we have seen, described by Howe as "an emblem foreshadowing a Poet's abolished limitations in our demythologized fantasy of Manifest Destiny." Once again, an apparently forthright assertion opens onto ambiguity. Manifest Destiny was the nineteenth-century doctrine that justified the continuing expansion of America into Mexican and Native American territory. This project of conquest by a nation attempting to free itself of the anti-egalitarian weight of European history was based, in its formulation by John L O'Sullivan in 1839, on the "sacred and true and noble idea of equality."[28] Howe's remarks on Vietnam in her correspondence with Taggart suggest that the idea of Manifest Destiny has continuing currency in the late twentieth century. Against this, she offers the figure of the poet, whose "limitations" have been "abolished." What Howe means by these "limitations"—literary history? formal restraints? institutional disregard?—is left unclear. The "emblem" is thus permitted to stray across several fields as a principle of radical uncertainty. Poetry, in this view, is a corrosive, negative force. Its operations can begin the task of unpicking an explicitly or implicitly colonial language that sustains damaging constructions of alterity and their practical consequences in political and cultural life. However, a less instrumentalized version of poetic speech, in which the negative bears a quasi-theological weight, remains equally plausible.

Time plays a curious role in these last few lines of Howe's introduction to the poem: "Putative author, premodern condition, presently present, what future clamors for release?" she writes of Atherton (*Articulation*, 4). His name "draws its predetermined poem in" (*Articulation*, 4). Howe is exploring the idea of destiny—central, of course, to Puritan theology. The word has two meanings in Howe's preface: first, a political "fantasy" fuelling American imperialism and, second, predestination. The latter version of destiny retrospectively inscribes a poem—Howe's poem—in the emblematic figure of Atherton. Howe's rhetorical feat is to reach into the past to meddle with destiny and unsettle the teleology of predestination. She is flattening time, but she does so from the point of view of the future. Atherton, a "presently present" footnote of history, is made available to the contemporary artist, whose poem becomes a self-fulfilling prediction.

The past is apprehended through language, not only in what Nicholls identifies as an "antimetaphorical" and "cryptic" non-figural use of words,[29] but also in the powerfully figural sense—discernible, for example, in Howe's discussion of "bark," "bow", and "quiver" in her November 1981 letter to Taggart on *Pythagorean Silence* or the extended examination of the word "sovereign" in *My Emily Dickinson*. Howe's method is often, much like Bercovitch's characterization of Puritan sensibility, to pursue literal and allegorical tracks simultaneously. Words in her poems can sometimes present themselves with cryptic obduracy, almost actively repelling interpretation, but, at other times, there are abundant metaphorizing energies at play.

In the concluding lines to page 36, for example—"Scythe mower surrender hereafter// Dear Cold cast violet coronal// World weary flesh by Flesh bygone/ Bridegroom"—a stanza is concluded with figural zest. "Mower" suggests, with "Scythe" and "hereafter," a reference to death and judgment. Howe is perhaps echoing the language of Cotton Mather's *Agricola* as it reflects on Psalm 37's "They shall soon be cut down as the grass": "Uncertain the time when the mower will come, the offspring of the earth is not always of one age and of one bulk when the mower applies the scythe unto it."[30] "Violet coronal" sounds like a literary citation, but it is drawn from the language of astronomy—the word coronal can mean garland or crown, so the line functions as another metaphor for sovereignty.[31] "World weary flesh by Flesh bygone" again suggests death, suffering, and succeeding generations. The combination of "flesh" and "Flesh" invokes the biblical "flesh of my flesh."[32] "World weary" has connotations of apocalypse, and the word "bridegroom," echoing "bygone" and standing in enigmatic isolation at the end of the poem, recalls the Puritan minister Thomas Shepard's sermons on the parable of the wise and foolish virgins.[33] The stanza thus develops an intricate figural web of reflections on death and resurrection.

In "Taking the Forest," Howe repeatedly reminds the reader of the resistance to efforts of interpretation of the scattered material that she assembles. She writes, for example, "Predecessor and definition/ incoherent inaccessible muddled inaudible" (*Articulation*, 21). The enigmatic lines leave the reader grasping at what might be communicated. In the end, the passage, which almost reads like a hostile review, advertises its own incoherence and inaccessibility as a means of the enacting the difficulty of the poet's task. Later in the poem, there is a similar sense of eavesdropping on a conversation that cannot quite be heard: "muffled discourse from distance/ mummy thread undertow slough// Eve of origin Embla the eve" (*Articulation*, 32). This time, there is a different emphasis, as a hidden "undertow" of coherence is attributed to a maternal inheritance (Embla is a Norse version of Eve).[34] Extreme prominence is given to hesitancy and uncertainty in her poems. The material unearthed by her scholarship—despite the apparent directness of her critical prose at times—is equivocal, and its messages are "muffled" to the point of inaudibility.

It is in the work of Charles Olson, another poet with a passion for the archive, and one of the 'fathers' in the background of *Eikon*, that Howe's historical poetics finds its clearest precedent.[35] Kathleen Fraser has argued persuasively that, for writers such as Howe, "Olson's idea of high energy 'projection' engaged an alchemy of colliding sounds and visual constructions, valuing *ir*regularity, counterpoint, adjacency, ambiguity...the movement of poetic language as investigative tool."[36] When Howe began to make the transition from visual art to poetry in the late 1960s, Olson's writing was a crucial enabling influence. This is surprising for several reasons. Olson's epic concerns would appear to be at a considerable remove from Howe's preoccupation with silence, space, and the marginal. His overtly phallic mythopoesis seems at odds with the importance to Howe's work of a provisionality that is coded as feminine.[37] Olson desires to restore physicality and breath to poetic utterance, whereas Howe places decisive weight on the physicality of the text itself—the look and feel of the poem on the page. Nonetheless, in an interview Howe has said, "Much of my inspiration as a poet comes from Modernist writers. At first Charles Olson (a late Modernist or first postmodernist) gave me a certain permission. The early edition of *Maximus IV, V, VI* was crucial."[38]

Howe was particularly interested at the time in the typographical experiments of *Maximus* poems, which seemed to afford a point of connection to her use of texts in her visual art: "At his best, Olson lets words and groups of words, even letter arrangements and spelling accidentals shoot suggestions at each other, as if each page were a canvas and the motion of the words—reality across the surface" ("Where Should the Commander Be," 6).[39] Both Howe and the Olson of *Maximus* are concerned with events occurring during the settlement, in the seventeenth century, of what would become New England. Each suggests that a damaging template was established for American culture through the violent ambition of the Puritan leadership of the Bay Area Colony. Surrounded by a wider argument couched in mythical terms, Olson's *Maximus* is a "demythologizing" counter-history that draws on a vast range of historical sources in its attempt to diagnose the ills of Olson's America.[40] Howe's work is similarly counter-historical in its revisionism and, in relating Hope Atherton to the figure of the contemporary poet, it attempts to imagine the creative act as a collapsing of past and present that recalls an Olsonian notion of poetry's capture of simultaneity.

Melville, in Olson's view, made possible a reconceptualization of time in which the artist could roam freely and moral oppositions were suspended. Melville's time, however, "was not a line drawn straight ahead toward future, a logic of good and evil. Time returned on itself. It had density, as space had and events were objects accumulated within it, around which men could move as they moved in space. The acts of men as a group stood, put down in time as a pyramid was, to be re-examined, re-enacted."[41] Olson evinces a quasi-mystical faith in the ability of the poet to discern a discontinuous past in the present. When historical knowledge inheres in present reconfigurations of past events in the mind of the historian or poet, an understanding based on chronological sequence is replaced by a gathering-in of fragmentary matter.

Words, for Howe, are minutely inscribed with the "Malice" of history: "Malice is the history of Progress" ("Commander," 9). The poet can explode a word's condensed significance, releasing a chaotic freight of earlier meaning and intertextual reference.[42] "Etymologies and genealogies are precious allegories for poets swimming through libraries," writes Howe, adapting a famous Melville passage ("Commander," 11).[43] Howe, in linking Olson and Melville, is doing more than tracing a male genealogy and reading the feminine against the grain of their texts. She introduces herself, a woman poet, into a familiar pattern of influence and rivalry: "[Olson's] first book shows that we see everything and nothing in laws. Artists bow to no order. In a duel of emulation one figure eternally confronts another. Sympathy/Antipathy. The conflict is projected into space. Emancipation of a Subject from body and destiny is a never- never play of resemblance and rivalry" ("Commander," 6). Howe is, by strong implication, writing herself into this "play of resemblance and rivalry." Gender, however, alters the terms of her emulation; her writing must interrogate the problematic gendering of this her own stuttering voice. It is typical of Howe's paradoxical mode of thought to find herself caught between a rejection of her antecedents and an assimilation of their methods. She sees the poet as simultaneously a law-abolisher and lawmaker: "Olson-Ishmael-Maximus subjugated while yielding to subjugation, and captured while freeing, the protean splendor of Herman Melville's restless, hieroglyphical nature" ("Commander," 4).

Similarly, in her reading of Dickinson, the language of rupture and regeneration is used, "the past, that sovereign source, must break poetic structure open for future absorption of words and definition. Velocity, mechanics, heat, thermodynamics, light, chaos of formulae, electromagnetic induction must be called back into the Sublime, found and forgotten" (*MED*, 116). Howe's "infinite miscalculation of history," is a suggestion that temporal being is built on quicksand, rather than solid ground (*Articulation*, 17). The historical insight afforded the poet—much like Melville's idea of truth, "forced to fly like a white doe in the woodlands"—is transitory at best.[44] Language is a "word Forest" (*Thorow*, 49) and any quest for origins a deluded search for a "Corruptible first figure" (*Articulation*, 17). The poet's "precious allegories" are not archetypal but provisional—volatile constellations of meaning that momentarily arise in poetic language's negotiations with past and present. The couplet "Predominance pitched across history/ Collision or collusion with history" (*Articulation*, 33) suggests that there is a violence to her poetry's encounter with the past—it must either collude with existing narratives or, in search of something outside the record, collide with them, producing the shattering effect found everywhere in *Articulation*, from the visual poems of pages 14–15 to the broken sense that pervades "Taking the Forest." Yet the poetry's resistant qualities are combined, as Peter Middleton argues, with an attenuated purchase on the borderline phenomena that it hopes to render: "Howe's work shows that literary experiment is not necessarily 'destructivism,' but can also be an exploration of what is never clearly text nor clearly other, only a history of boundaries, captures, escapes, genocides and glimpses of something 'seen once.'"[45]

The historical poetics that emerges in Howe's mid-1980s work has an ambition similar to that of both Olson and Pound. It privileges the artist, or poet, with the capacity to effect a visionary synthesis of past and present, yet it vigorously resists the overbearing and legislating voices that drive the epics of Olson and Pound. Indeed, it resists the impulse to completeness or coherence that sustains the epic mode. Howe arrives at something like a negative version of Pound's "luminous detail," effecting conjunctions across diverse historical periods but adopting a faltering style of enunciation that enacts the resistance of that historical material to revisiting by contemporary investigation.

Pound's didacticism, literary authoritarianism, and aim of treating the thing directly are utterly distinct from Howe's exploration of the antiauthoritarian implications of hesitancy. Howe is similarly removed from Olson's heroic ambition and "phallic energies."[46] If Pound's "ego scriptor" continues to resonate in Olson, Howe's "unconscious scatter syntax" (*Articulation*, 36) shifts the writing process away from the organizing certainties of either. Her linguistic intransigence separates her from her antecedents in the formulation of a modernist poetics of history. Her notion of the fragment appears in her writing at the levels of the broken word—the "velc," "ythian" or "quagg" (*Articulation*, 10); citation; private reference; and interrupted syntax. Yet, in addition to this insistence on disjunction, Howe's commitment to "lines of association" offers her a means of asserting the importance of occulted histories through etymologies and word associations.[47]

The "short, quick probings at the very axis of reality" that Melville celebrates in Shakespeare are, for Howe, comparable to the voices she strains to discern issuing from the Hope Atherton episode in the Connecticut River Valley.[48] The lines "Snatched idea/ Recollection fallen away from ruin" (*Articulation*, 19) suggest the evanescence of the perceptions she is pursuing, as if the "ruin" of history were accessible only to "snatched" forms of "Recollection." The same page's "slipping from known to utmost bound" asserts once again the liminality of the experience to which the poem dedicates itself.

In the juxtaposition of material, whether apparently unconnected words or shreds of cited text, Howe's poetry pushes itself with cultivated uncertainty into territory that Olson had prepared. "I felt an immediate shock of recognition," Howe has said of her first encounter with Olson's poetry. "It was his voracious need to gather 'facts', to find something, a quotation, a place name, a date, some documentary evidence in regard to a place. To collate the collection quickly with something else without explaining the connection."[49] It is this simultaneous commitment to the decontextualizing energies of collage and the rootedness of historical particulars in place that most strongly situates Howe in the post-Olsonian line of historical poetics.

* * *

Coming after the treatment of Atherton in the first section of the poem and the related poetic treatment of landscape and New England history in the second section, "Taking the Forest" moves into wider intellectual and historical parameters. This third part of the poem bears no obvious—or indeed apparent—relation to the previous sections of *Articulation of Sound Forms in Time*. The sequence is not immediately grounded in the historical or linguistic fallout of colonial violence on the eastern coast of the United States. The clearest reference to American history is to westward expansion, not to New England:

> Luggage of the prairie
> Wagons pegged to earth
>
> Tyrannical avatars of consciousness
> emblazoned in tent-stitch (*Articulation*, 36)

It is through this last couplet that we can find a way into Howe's poem. The lines suggest a Western consciousness knitting itself into the fabric of American experience. The idea of a transplanted intellectual heritage that only partially takes to the new soil is probed in "Taking the Forest." Certain motifs, it is implied in the poem, are characteristic of the Western, or European, thought-habits that took root in America. Among these are artistic representation, the uses of historical knowledge, and patricidal monotheism. This concluding and longest section of the poem is, thus, continuous with aspects of her European-history-themed writings: the interest in representation in *Defenestration*, for example; the prominence of literary-historical material in *Pythagorean Silence*; and the theologically inflected treatment of regicide in *Eikon Basilike*.

None of the twenty-five poems in "Taking the Forest" is more than a page long.[50] The longest runs to twenty-eight lines and the shortest to eight lines. Individual poems are comprised of sequences of lines that often bear little apparent relation to one another. Within lines, although syntactical relations are often absent, associations of sound or sense bind words to one another. The line "hideout haystack hunter chamois" (*Articulation*, 26), for example, combines heavy alliteration with the language of the hunt— the implicit needle suggested by "haystack" renders the chamois as elusive as Melville's "white doe in the woodlands." Such thematic and aural continuities are discernible within and across individual poems, and across the sequence as a whole. However, the poem sequence is highly volatile, and any integrative impulse suggested by such connections is stretched to breaking point. Several lines—"unconscious scatter syntax," (*Articulation*, 36) for example, or "Fledgling humming on pathless" (*Articulation*, 35)—reinforce the tendency toward disintegration by directly stating it. In such cases, the energies of dispersal contained in such words as stumbling, wandering, and anarchy are plainly aligned with poetic language.

The vocabulary that Howe uses comes from many fields. Prominent among these are history, philosophy, and religion. Also widely represented are the themes of psychoanalysis, law and, language. There are many references to the ideas of doubling and dissimulation that also found frequent expression in *Defenestration of Prague*: "Splitting nature's shadow/ splitting the world" (*Articulation*, 18); "mimic tracery/ mimic swaddling" (28); and "All things double on one another" (ibid.), for example. Brief discussion of three prominent strands in *Articulation*—history, system, and authority—will, I hope, serve to describe its operations.

At several points in "Taking the Forest," history is depicted as an impenetrable and unknowable process. "Infinite miscalculation of history" (*Articulation*, 17), for example, suggests both the misreadings perpetrated by scholars and the endless catalogue of misjudgments that constitutes human activity. This is, therefore, a reading of history as catastrophe. The lines "Migratory path to massacre/ Sharpshooters in history's apple-dark" (22) suggest a colonial enterprise that is oriented around indiscriminate violence; once again, there is the implication that historians themselves are merely taking pot shots. Lines such as "antecedent terror stretched to a whisper" (17), "Cries open to the words inside them/ Cries hurled through the Woods" (23), "Destiny of calamitous silence" (25) and "muffled discourse from distance" (32) suggest that a confluence of trauma and historical distance renders messages from the past incomprehensible to the latterday investigator. Other lines imply that traumatic repressed material lurks, not quite articulated, at the fringes of speech: "Recollection moves across meaning" (33), "Visible surface of Discourse// Runes or allusion to runes" (36), "Memory mutinies contours cling" (23), and "pilings of thought under spoken" (30). The implications of such lines can, again, be applied to the endeavors of the historian—that violence and dispossession, the experience of the victims of the Falls massacre, for example—will remain at the fringes of narratives of American history. In all these cases, historical narratives are shown to fail for two reasons. First, they are insufficiently aware of the operations of power within the discursive frameworks that shape their own perspectives. Second, they are not adequate to the affective content of the disastrous events they purport to describe. Moreover, the psycho-political afterlife of the doctrine of Manifest Destiny, a ghostly typology inscribed in the American political unconscious, buckles in the presence of the dissociative energies that unmake any teleology.

Many poems reflect the philosophical freight of Enlightenment. In the context of the poem as a whole, this must be read as a concomitant of the European imprint left on the intellectual life of the Americas. There are references to Parmenides (*Articulation*, 17); phenomenology ("Consciousness grasps its subject/ stumbling phenomenology," [17]); Spinoza (28); and Hegel ("The Now that is Night/ Time comprehended in Thought" [28]). However, the philosophical strand in the poem is most evident in references to pattern and system: "Universal separation/—Distant coherent rational system" (17); "Logical determination of position" (18); "Step and system" (19); "Chaos cry carrion empirical proof proving" (21); "total systemic circular knowledge/ System impossible in time" (28); "Wedged sequences of system" (34); and "—emending annotating inventing/ World as rigorously related System" (35). In such instances, system is clearly given a pejorative, almost coercive weight.

There is in the poetry an apparent resistance to such systematizing impulses: "Kneel to intellect in our work/ Chaos cast cold intellect back" (*Articulation*, 34) is one statement of the opposition in question. The poem appears to identify itself with a logic of disintegration, an enactment of productively asystemic thought that is performed at the levels of both syntax and meaning. Narrative is replaced by stumbling, speech by stuttering, and linear progress by wandering. This mode—clearly a means of theorizing both poetic speech and the vagaries of the archive—is reflected in such word-bundles as "Omen of stumbling" (*Articulation*, 23); "Untraceable wandering/ the meaning of knowing" (25); "Left home to seek Lost// Pitchfork origin" (25); "Lost among equivocations" (32); "Anarchy into named theory/ Entangled obedience" (32); "Dear unconscious scatter syntax" (36).

Howe is not, of course, anachronistically assigning an Enlightenment-before-the-fact worldview to the earliest settlers. The poem clearly addresses both the colonial era and the subsequent hegemony of European intellectual culture in the United States. However, a prominent thematic chain in the poem confronts the categorizing, empirical impulse in Enlightenment thought with the variously uncoercible properties of language, nature, and the unconscious. Howe at times seems determined to supplement the Atherton narrative with the suggestion that European thought, with its implicitly colonial subjugation of the natural world through descriptive procedures, encountered something ungovernable in the Americas. In her works of the late 1980s and early 1990s, the hesitancy and stuttering of

Hutchinson, Dickinson, Billy Budd, Bartleby, and Howe herself are indications of an intellectual culture that is pressing against its own limits. Howe's poetry at such moments presents itself as a corrosive counter to American self-belief.

Yet these provisional namings of the asystemic other to rationality are not unequivocally endorsed. Rather, the poem, itself necessarily enacting a movement of "Entangled obedience," is as pessimistic about "Chaos" as about "Cold intellect" (*Articulation*, 34). "Taking the Forest" situates its own unfolding, of course, within the diverse intellectual histories to which it alludes. The liberatory energies of the writing are only produced and encountered through a reflexive self-questioning that cannot cut itself loose from the European past. The forest, in other words, has already been taken, once and for all. Howe's glancing encounter with this prototypical image of secular-sacred wilderness knows that such a vision of the free is itself open to tyrannical abuses. Liberation is ultimately discernible, and dimly at that, only as a kind of negative potential.

Allied to the opposition of system and scattering impulses in "Taking the Forest" are numerous references to an idea of power that is invested with religious weight. Howe appears to be alluding to a genealogy that has its origins in Freud's theories of social authority, in which the social bond is cemented by the guilt and remorse that follow the sacrifice of the tribal patriarch. The line "Conscience in ears too late" (*Articulation*, 25) links this theme to the importance of *Hamlet* in earlier Howe poetry—the representation, for example, of Swift in *The Liberties* as an emblem of a patriarchal divinity that coincides with the ghost of Hamlet's father. In a manner that anticipates the poems collected in the later *Eikon* and *The Nonconformist's Memorial*, this power-wielding divinity is depicted as an absent paternity that guarantees social authority.

The very first line of "Taking the Forest" embodies this key theme: "Corruptible first figure" (*Articulation*, 17). Other references to a law-making patriarchal divinity include "Patriarchal prophesy at heels of hope" (22); "Lawless center/ Scaffold places to sweep" (ibid.); "seclusion in symbol sovereign" (23); "great unknown captaincy" (ibid.); "tribunal of eternal revolution/ tribunal of rigorous evaluation// Captive crowned tyrant deposed/ Ego as captive thought" (25); and "Occult ferocity of origin" (30). What is suggested is the operation of social authority as a figural mechanism dependent, even in secular cultures, on the phantasmatic recreation of a divine origin that is absent as a condition of its divinity. This is read across several fields, but the English revolution and psychoanalysis are prominent. The stern lawmaker of the Puritans is held, by implication, to have left a deep mark on American political and literary culture.

In the context of *Articulation*'s opening section, religious authority is expressed by the rather comical figure cut by Hope Atherton. However, "Taking the Forest" shows this episode to be guided by a predominantly European intellectual culture. Atherton's position, crossing and recrossing the territorial boundary separating settler from indigenous people, implies that the American story both is and is not a European story. Howe's poetry, with its enormous investment in canonical English literature and its simultaneous preoccupation with American speech inhabits a space of non-fixity similar to that of Atherton's wanderings. He is, as her prefatory section suggests, an "emblem" of the contemporary American poet.

If the "Destiny of calamitous silence" (*Articulation*, 25) suggests that the voices of the past are condemned to mutism, the poem's surfaces nonetheless beckon the reader with the promise that they conceal layers of hidden knowledge—what are described as "Pilings of thought under spoken" (*Articulation*, 30). Howe's dissolution of Olsonian authority blows apart the possibility of a history energized by the force of the poet's ego; her poems-containing-history offer, instead, a polyphony that gravitates around manifestations of authority and a stuttering energy that suggests that the flow of retrieved words is forever on the point of running dry.

Thorow

Thorow both describes and enacts a thesis based on the mutual embeddedness of colonial power and language. It has its origins in the first months of 1987, when the poet was a writer in residence at the Lake George Arts Project in upper New York State. The poem interleaves material based on Howe's own encounter with the landscape around Lake George with literary and historical documents. The poet's two main textual resources are the writings of Henry David Thoreau and the papers of an eighteenth-century Irishman named Sir William Johnson.[51]

My aim in this chapter is, in a sense, to historicize Howe's poem—to ask questions of both the intellectual context that informs it and the nature of the poetic radicalism that it represents. Rereading *Thorow* in the light of Howe's 2005 CD recording of the text, I suggest that Freud and Thoreau offer us a way of rethinking the poem in which the link between the poetic and the political appears less easy to endorse than, for example, when considering Back's remark that two pages of *Thorow* "enact language's liberation, its release from the bonds of syntax, word units, and normative use of page space."[52] This position typifies certain assumptions about the politics of poetic form in the poetry and criticism of the 1980s and 1990s avant garde. In my discussion of *Thorow*, I wish to complicate my remarks above about the energies of dispersal located in Howe's texts. Her writing is certainly influenced by the critical discourses of pluralism and multiplicity, from subjectivity to social being, with which postmodern theory sought to counter anything smacking of a *grand récit*. However, I suggest that, severing the poems from some of the claims that both Howe and some of her critics make for them, the figures of sameness and repetition may provide more powerful means of articulating the poetry's aims.

Although Howe's poetry from the early 1990s onward is less involved than it had been previously in sifting the linguistic residues of historical violence, Howe has remained attached to *Thorow*, continuing to include it in her poetry readings. In 2005, it received a notable revamp when Howe issued a recording of the poem made in collaboration with the musician David Grubbs, a co-founder of the influential 1990s Chicago post-rock group Gastr Del Sol.[53] With interests ranging from rock and American folk to John Cage and the minimalist drone music of Tony Conrad, Grubbs is an example of a young musician whose avant-gardism combines hard-edged experimentalism with popular idioms.[54] He is as likely to work with a song-based rock trio as to produce electroacoustic music. It is the latter tendency that he adopts in his work on *Thorow*, which is built on drones created through the electronic processing of cello and saxophone improvisations.[55]

The recording of *Thorow*, issued alongside an abbreviated version of *The Nonconformist's Memorial*, is more than a document of a poetry reading and more than poetry accompanied by music. The piece in this form works as an integrated aural unit, Howe's words given additional force by Grubbs's slow-moving, drone-based sonic sculpture. Speaking of his collaboration with Howe, Grubbs has observed, "I'm stuck with a motto: no foreground, no background."[56] These drones are combined with finely timed editing of Howe's voice, sometimes to produce an aural analogue of the visual scatteredness of parts of the work on the page, sometimes to dust the main text with fragments from Howe's prose introduction. The demotion (demolition might be a better word, given the sound editing) of the introduction, which makes certain polemical claims about power and language, is the most significant textual shift introduced by the recording. As I will argue, it effectively returns the poem to itself. The musical element of the recording sits in equivalence with the spoken words, changing the reader-listener's encounter with the poem. The sound editing introduces skips and jitters that mimic the stuttering quality that pervades Howe's thinking on poetry.

The relative abstraction of the musical component of the work allows it to function as a textural foil to Howe's voice, running both with and against the grain of the text. The music does not have a melodic or harmonic argument that might pull the listener too strongly into some sort of musical narrative. An interpretation of the music of *Thorow* is conceivable. It might be suggested, for example, that the looming tones of *Thorow* amount to a materialization of the "Underthought" (*Thorow*, 53) that encrypts the traumatic past in Howe's writing. Yet that seems almost too literal a translation. In the end, the sound retains its intractability and untranslatability, entangling itself in the dense aural weave of the voiced poem.

* * *

Thorow follows the triadic form favored by Howe in most of her long poems, although, unlike in the contemporaneous *Articulation of Sound Forms in Time*, the introduction stands apart from the numbered sections of the poem proper. The first section of the poem incorporates much material drawn from Johnson's papers.[57] The second is more concerned with Howe's own experiences at Lake George, as the landscape speaks through her and enacts the introduction's "I heard poems inhabited by voices... The Adirondacks *occupied* me" (*Thorow*, 41).[58] In this section, Howe at various points reprises in miniature Thoreau's descriptions of nature—either as quotation or imitation. The brief third section is the most fragmentary and, on pages 56–57, contains one of Howe's most impressive poems of textual scattering.

A problem for twenty-first century readers, perhaps, lies in Howe's highly condensed introduction to the poem, one of her most polemical pieces of writing on colonial New England. The introduction's highly compact and polemical prose alludes to certain thinkers who were in the air as Howe wrote—Baudrillard, Deleuze, and Todorov (in his later historicist guise). As if in acknowledgement of a certain theoretical distance, the introduction is only present in the *Thiefth* recording as sliced and diced utterances that interfere with the unfolding of the poem proper. This, I would argue, amounts to a significant revision of the poem. The introduction to *Thorow* is more programmatic than those of her other long poems, offering a prefatory mini-poetics that orients the poem in relation to the history of the landscape that provides its ostensible setting.

One of the introduction's defining statements is the following:

> In the seventeenth century European adventurer-traders burst through the forest to discover this particular long clear body of fresh water. They brought our story to it. Pathfinding believers in God and grammar spelled the lake into *place*. They have renamed it several times since. In paternal colonial systems a positivist efficiency appropriates primal indeterminacy. (*Thorow*, 41)[59]

In describing the territory through which the colonists blazed their trails as undifferentiated wilderness, Howe revoices the views both of the early settlers who sailed in search of a "Virgin land" and of Thoreau's understanding of nature. European place names, she contends, force the wilderness into culture. Nature, it is implied, is inevitably viewed through a European lens because of the imprint left on the landscape by place names.

Naming, rather than offering the potential for anarchic punning that Howe elsewhere celebrates,[60] is in *Thorow* in the service of human agency and specifically linked to the exercise of colonial power: "Every name driven shall be as another rivet in the machine of a universe flux" (*Thorow*, 42).[61] Naming, then, is the point of entry of nature into culture. It is hard to escape the implication that the relative indeterminacy of Howe's text is therefore to be read as a partial recovery of wilderness—an atavistic return, in other words, to Thoreau's belief that poetry should strive for wildness.[62]

Back argues persuasively that the links between language and colonial power that Howe draws were influenced by Tzvetan Todorov's *The Conquest of America: the Question of the Other*.[63] Early in his book, Todorov describes Columbus's near obsession with naming features of the landscape and the islands he came upon: "Columbus knows perfectly well that these islands already have names, natural ones in a sense (but in another acceptation of the term); others' words interest him very little, however, and he seeks to rename places in terms of the rank they occupy in his discovery, to give them the *right* names; moreover, nomination is equivalent to taking possession."[64] Although Todorov's argument about colonial discovery and nomination changes considerably when he begins to discuss Cortes, his assertion about naming and possession—suggesting an identity between linguistic and actual violence—is certainly close to Howe's comments in her introduction. *Thorow*'s meditation on meaning and political power shares Todorov's perspective on the links between cartography and political domination. However, the equivalence of which Todorov speaks—and which is found in Howe's radically condensed polemic—deserves to be met with some suspicion. Language may be a form of power, even a realization of power, but nomination might more plausibly be described as a consequence, rather than the equivalent, of taking possession.

Howe's introduction raises further problems: the non-European, Native American presence is swept into a category of inarticulate otherness that assimilates it to the wilderness of the surrounding land. Language, through naming, is held to be part of the machinery of domination. It might be argued, in response, that any resistance to that domination is thereby denied coherent expression. The assimilation of the specific evils of patriarchy and colonialism to one another is troubling for various reasons, not least the sheer violence with which Howe brings together these distinct orders of oppression. The further extension of these categories into those of grammar and efficiency is questionable—Howe is erecting an edifice of overdetermined structural analogy that, in aligning grammar, patriarchy, and cartography, sheds little light on the operations of any of these terms.

In her introduction, Howe sets in opposition a force of conservative fixity, understood in terms of both language and politics, and a mobile, radical force of disruption. It might be argued that assigning the feminine—"she, the Strange" (*Thorow*, 41)—to the latter risks disenfranchisement by repeating the very equation of the feminine with inarticulacy that it seeks to attack. Despite the immense rhetorical energy of Howe's prose in such passages, its extreme elision of categories and an essentially dualistic vision tend to work against her endorsement of a thinking of "multiplicities" (*Thorow*, 42). Although the poem itself is a complex and resonant response to historical violence, the forced style of prose in Howe's preface, with its crushing together of categories and its declarative tenor, reflects elements of the programmatic language use that she seeks to dismantle.

In probing the colonial imagination, Howe often touches on the Puritan notion that the promised land would be the site of the redemption of God's chosen people.[65] Howe approaches this yearning for redemption as a desire for a return to Eden, specifically the "New Eden" or Arcadia of early accounts of America. When she writes "slipping back to primordial/ We go through the word Forest" (*Thorow*, 49) and "psychology of the lost/ First precarious Eden" (ibid., 52), it is as if the first settlers were experiencing the landscape in its pristine and nameless state.[66]

Such figures, read alongside Howe's polemical introduction, are highly questionable. They also sit uneasily with the poem's allusions to postmodern thinkers, for whom dreams of unsullied origins would be anathema. Yet, discussing *Thorow* in an interview, Howe herself has displayed ambivalence about this state of prelapsarian integrity:

> For some reason this beautiful body of water [i.e., Lake George] has attracted violence and greed ever since the Europeans first saw it. I thought I could feel it when it was pure, enchanted, *nameless*. There never was such a pure place. In all nature there is violence.... Uninterrupted nature usually is a dream enjoyed by the spoilers and looters—my ancestors. It's a first dream of wildness that most of us need in order to breathe; and yet to inhabit a wilderness is to destroy it.[67]

The remarks suggest that *Thorow* might be a wilier poem than either its introduction or some of Howe's admirers would allow. In this view, the poem is symptomatic as well as diagnostic. On one hand, Howe imagines the landscape as the Puritans did, as what she has called "a dialectical construction of the American land as a virgin garden preestablished for them by the Author and Finisher of creation" (*Birth-mark*, 49). On the other hand, Howe's poem attacks this "dialectical construction" from within, even as it appears to confirm it. *Thorow* is, moreover, like other of her texts, a historical investigation that is oriented toward the present. As she observes in "Incloser," "Dickinson, Melville, Thoreau and Hawthorne guided me back to what I once thought was the distant seventeenth century. Now I know that the arena in which Scripture battles raged among New Englanders with original fury is part of our current American system and events, history and structure" (*Birth-mark*, 47). The poem, in other words, could not help but embody some of the problems it wishes to expose.

Howe's writing, then, is both more knowing and pessimistic than the introduction might make it appear. Howe describes a compromised temporality—the feeling of being "outside of time" when writing *Thorow*—but her writing also knows that it can neither escape the context of its production nor think itself into a vanished past. As with *Articulation*, there is little in *Thorow* to offer hope of a new and (in Schultz's terms) "inclusive" American beginning.

* * *

Read in tension with the thought of Thoreau, Howe's *Thorow* is also an attempt to constitute an ambitious notion of poetry that would somehow evade the language of "domination," even as it bears its marks. This recourse to Transcendentalism generates problems similar to those discussed above, as it appears to depend on an opposition between a liberating, originary openness and the dead, controlling hand of human culture. Taking the polemical position that "naming delimits the open," Howe wants to assert the instability of nomination and reclaim some of this open territory by loosening the bond between word and place. Her point of departure in this is Thoreau's version of the wild, linking landscape, history, and poetry. If nature often appears in *Thorow* to be exactly the "neatly dialectical other to community" that Nicholls credits Howe with *avoiding* in her descriptions of wilderness, the reason lies in her close engagement with the work of Thoreau during her months at Lake George.[68] Yet, once again, Howe both enters the framework of Thoreau's thought and explores its internal contradictions. Her problematic pursuit of origins is a reawakening of Thoreau's version of the American wilderness, but one that is suffused with pessimism and ambivalence. As she observes in *My Emily Dickinson* (44), "In the desperate hunt for wilderness meat, an Elizabethan hunter-pilgrim desired and dreaded to become his own savage avatar."

Thoreau believed that the American wilderness encountered by Cabot, Raleigh, et al. could be found, even his own day, in the American interior.[69] For Thoreau, wilderness not only allows civilization to rethink itself, but is also emblematic of the possibilities of a literature no longer tied to the decadence of Europe. In "Walking" he writes:

> In Literature it is only the wild that attracts us....
> Where is the literature which gives expression to Nature? He would be a poet who could impress the winds and streams into his service, to speak for him; who nailed words to their primitive senses, as farmers drive down stakes in the spring which the frost has heaved; who derived words as often as he used them—transplanted them to his page with earth adhering to their roots; whose words were so true, and fresh and natural that they would appear to expand like the buds at the approach of spring.[70]

The very words to which Thoreau ascribes value are of a primitive quality, part of nature itself. A few pages further into "Walking," he assimilates this quality of natural language to the "savage":

> A familiar name cannot make a man less strange to me. It may be given to a savage who retains in secret his own wild title earned in the woods. We have a wild savage in us, and a savage name is perchance somewhere recorded as ours. I see that my neighbor, who bears the familiar epithet William, or Edwin, takes it off with his jacket. It does not adhere to him when asleep or in anger, or aroused by any passion or inspiration. I seem to hear pronounced by some of his kin at such a time, his original wild name in some jaw-breaking or else melodious tongue.[71]

Here, Thoreau bases his notion of language on a fantasy of uncorrupted wilderness: the only way for American culture to go forward is to go back in pursuit of "primitive senses." There is, in this view, a natural, originary language that lies beneath the secondary language of civilized humans. European culture obscures the chaotic flux of drives that it supersedes. Sleep, anger, passion, and inspiration permit the primitive name to return and obliterate the appearance of civilization.[72] "Primitive" names attach to things. The poet presses nature into her service, aiming to derive words from nature and nail "words to their primitive senses"; words must come from nature, and they should not be allowed to stray from their original senses.

The couplet "The literature of savagism/ under a spell of savagism" (*Thorow*, 49) could be read as an acknowledgement of Thoreau's theory of the "wild savage" within and its relation to the wildness in literature.[73] However, read in the context of Thoreau, it becomes clear that Howe's return to origins is only masquerading as such; it is better understood as an act of literary ventriloquism, read, like the "machine" of flux, from a contemporary perspective. Howe's refusal of the "scandal of materialism" (*Thorow*, 52) that her ancestors perpetrated is in sympathy with Thoreau's attitude toward commerce, but she appears to be both enthralled by and skeptical about the sort of immediate encounter with nature of which Thoreau writes. There is no recourse to the possibility of a prelapsarian language, yet poetry, in evading the instrumentalized language of commercial exploitation, contains the potential to voice the uncolonized areas of the psyche that Thoreau considers the domain of the savage.

Howe, following this tradition, transposes the sacralized nature she finds in Thoreau into the space of contemporary poetics. Her sustained interest—from her early installations to her work on Charles Sanders Peirce's symbolic logic or her late visual collages—in the relation between visual and verbal signification might be read as an extension of Thoreau's attempt to decipher the "hieroglyphic" of nature.[74]

Howe's lament that the "spirits have fled" from Lake George can be understood, through *Thorow*, as decrying the process of disenchantment that follows from the colonization of experience by the commercial imperatives of American capitalism ("There are two laundromats, the inevitable McDonald's, a Howard Johnson, assorted discount leather outlets, video arcades, a miniature golf course, two run-down amusement parks, a fake fort where a real one once stood, a Dairy-Mart, a Donut-land, and a four-star Ramada Inn built over an ancient Indian burial ground," *Thorow*, 41). Her attempt at the recovery of a 'wilder' speech is pursued through a wandering movement that is at once an asystemic resistance to colonial mapmaking, conducted in time and across the page, and a careful suspension of linguistic conventions. The errant Scout figure that Howe takes from Johnson's papers (*Thorow*, 43) treads a path that deviates from that of the "pathfinding believers in God and grammar." Instead, she suggests that her mission is to "Let myself drift in the rise and fall of light and snow, re-reading and re-tracing once-upon" (*Thorow*, 41).

Howe here uses another term from the postmodern lexicon, "drift." The word is crucial to *Thorow*, and the notion reappears at the end of section 2 in the lines "Dark here in the driftings/ in the spaces of drifting" (*Thorow*, 55). It is around this idea of drifting that some of the poem's core concerns coalesce. The term probably entered the poem via Lyotard's introduction to his *Driftworks*, another of the books Howe was reading at the time *Thorow* was composed.[75] Howe's poem imagines an encounter between her wandering version of Thoreau and postmodern theory. Howe does not begin to smooth over the obvious incompatibilities. Rather, what interests her are the affinities between Thoreau's proposal of wandering as a radical cultural practice and Lyotard's praise of the *dérive*.

Lyotard, in his introduction, proposes the principle of drifting as a position that resists the authoritarian implications of knowledge and (Marxian) critique: "Don't you see that criticizing is still knowing, knowing better? That the critical relation still falls within the sphere of knowledge, or 'realization' and thus of the assumption of power? Critique must be drifted out of. Better still: *Drifting is in itself the end of all critique*."[76]

In a move characteristic of postmodern aesthetics, Howe adopts asystemic methods to counter a late-twentieth-century capitalism that appeared all-encompassing and impervious to critique. Her strategy is to generate a mobile language that would seep through the cracks in the "European grid" and offer a literary formalization of an anti-authoritarian "politics of marginality."[77] Her aim is to write in language that is inimical to the operations of power, with its tendency, in Lyotard's scheme, toward a univocal monopoly of knowledge. As before, however, the use of metaphors of mobility and stasis to cement a notional assimilation of poetic form to the sphere of the political seems an act of questionable rhetorical value.

Howe does not cite Lyotard in her introduction, but she does quote two other French theorists of the postmodern, Deleuze and Guattari, on the proper name. Her citation concludes: "The proper name is the instantaneous apprehension of a multiplicity. The proper name is the subject of a pure infinitive comprehended as such in a field of intensity" (*Thorow*, 42).[78] Howe here finds a reconsideration of naming that rethinks Thoreau's savage, primal name as a principle of multiplicity. The Romantic pursuit of origins is superseded by an entirely different conceptual framework, one that would replace Thoreau's implicit topography of surface (civilization) and depth (the wild) with a collapsing of perspectives and a valorization of a more thoroughgoing intellectual nomadism. The two notions of naming, Thoreauvian and Deleuzian, share a quality of uncoercible motility that allows Howe to force them together. Thoreau's inner savage, with its implicit chaotic, atemporal space of drives, finds some echo in the language Deleuze and Guattari employ: "instantaneous apprehension," "a pure infinitive comprehended as such in a field of intensity."

Yet incompatibilities between the two vocabularies remain, and neither offers a compelling means of gaining a purchase on colonial violence or its ancillary linguistic imperatives. It is with Thoreau's glance within, at a symptomatology of trauma, rather than through the language of multiplicity, that a more satisfactory narrative of the relation of colonial cartography and prosody than Howe permits herself in her elliptical introduction can begin. I would also argue that *Thiefth*'s reappraisal of the poem's aural qualities buttresses *Thorow*'s attempts to engage an intransigent verbal territory that encompasses historical, linguistic, and psychological disturbance.

* * *

It is possible to discern in *Thorow* a representation of historical trauma that is embedded in Howe's use of repetition. There is no liberation of language or anything else envisaged in *Thorow*; rather, there is a close attention to a linguistic condition that is riddled with the indecipherable marks of past violence.

Thoreau, in "Walking," deploys the metaphor of the compass to play the cultured East against the "wildness" of the American West: "My needle is slow to settle" he writes, "but it always settles between west and south south-west.... Eastward I go only by force; but westward I go free."[79] Howe absorbs the metaphor but discards the trope of westward movement, preferring to wander: "Unconscious demarkations range// I pick my compass to pieces// Dark here in the driftings/ in the spaces of drifting" (*Thorow*, 55).[80] In *Thorow*, the drifting is not only spatial, but also temporal, as the textual space incorporates both present and past. In her introduction, Howe announces that her work of drifting is a kind of return or rediscovery: "Let myself drift in the rise and fall of light and snow, *re*-reading and *re*-tracing once-upon" (*Thorow*, 41, my emphases). The words "once-upon" stress the folktale fictiveness of the fantasy of origins.

This fantasy, evident at numerous places in the work, is shadowed by an emphasis on its unattainability. At the same time as the poem appears to invoke an unmediated encounter with wilderness—whether understood as the landscape or linguistic indeterminacy—Howe acknowledges the impossibility of achieving any such nearness. Although the work draws on both Puritan and Thoreauvian ideas of wilderness, the notion of "slipping back to primordial" is approached as a figure that is built into the American literary imagination.[81]

The obligation is felt not only as the private quest of the author but as a renunciation of agency: Howe seeks to depict the process of writing the poem as one of hearing "poems inhabited by voices." "The Adirondacks," she writes, "occupied me" (*Thorow*, 41). This opens the idea of possession to two interpretations: territorial occupation of natural landscape, and the possession of the internal landscapes by unconscious forces that appear external to subjective agency. It is with this doubled impulse that Howe's poem gains its communicative resonance. The summary incursions of landscape and voices into the writer's consciousness establish a mode of literary representation that collapses inside and outside, and temporality folds into the "present in the past now" (*Thorow*, 43).

The "return of the repressed" is one of the broad conceptual foundations of Howe's poetry—the voices of the dead return as an affective disturbance in the texts of the present. However, Howe's manner of working might also be compared to another of Freud's theories that has entered the cultural mainstream: the compulsion to repeat. The theory arose as a means of accounting for the tendency of analysands to repeat disguised versions of earlier trauma and, in *Beyond the Pleasure Principle*, is described thus: "The manifestations of a compulsion to repeat exhibit to a high degree an instinctual (*Triebhaft*) character and, when they act in opposition to the pleasure principle, give the impression of some 'daemonic' force at work."[82] Howe's poetry is similarly prey to an irresistible urge to return to the scene of the originating trauma.[83] As in Freud's hypothesis, her poetic speech demonstrates an abdication of agency on the part of the speaker. The imposition of the "European grid on the Forest" (*Thorow*, 45)—land-grabs, cartography, and European languages—generates a countervailing impulse that, akin to Thoreau's wildness, forces itself into the language of Howe's poem as a principle of disturbance. What Howe characterizes as "understory" (*Thorow*, 50) and "underthought" (*Thorow*, 53) asserts itself as the marker of cultural damage.

Freud allows that the compulsion to repeat does not only occur within the transference.[84] In one passage in *Beyond the Pleasure Principle*, he even proposes it as a rational way of understanding humanity's sense of the "compulsion of destiny."[85] My point is that Howe is enacting—again and again—a return to barely articulable but traumatic repressed material.[86] This material arrives in her poetry with the force of outsideness—it unsettles syntactical coherence and demonstrates the "daemonic" qualities of which Freud writes.

Howe, following Thoreau, has spoken of a wildness that is both inside and outside: "You open your mind and textual space to many voices, to an interplay and contradiction and complexity of voices."[87] For Howe, this wildness is distanced from its characteristics of primal intensity, even as her language repeats this essentially Romantic movement. For her, there is no naive encounter with nature. Rather than offering an encounter with an inner "savage," the language of the unconscious is a "transindividual" phenomenon—a place where the voices of others are encountered and where *echt* originary utterance is inconceivable.[88]

Early in *Thorow*, there is a metaphor for defenses destroyed by an incursion from outside: "Fence blown down in a winter storm// darkened by outstripped possession" (*Thorow*, 44). Howe might equally well be describing nature sweeping away the incursions of civilization or the subjection of the conscious mind to Freud's "'daemonic' force." For Thoreau, the fence is the emblem of possession. In "Walking," he yearns for a "people who would begin by burning the fences and let the forest stand!"[89] Indeed, he goes on, in hyperbolic mode, to describe a land surveyor as the "Prince of Darkness."[90] Freud and Thoreau, then, are at odds. In Thoreau's view, it is the civilizing forces—analogous to Freud's acculturated ego—that are the representatives of evil. By contrast, the natural world—an analogue of Freud's threatening "aboriginal population in the mind"—is benign and close to heaven.[91]

The "daemon"—let us say a principle of externality compelling speech—lives on both sides of the fence in *Thorow*, and it is implicated in the voicing of both paradise and apocalypse. The poem embarks on an attempt, which it knows must fail, to reimagine an Edenic wilderness and encounters instead a landscape marked by territorial strife. In her essay "Incloser," Howe writes of the difficulties the settlers encountered on arriving in a supposed paradise:

> Schismatic children of Adam thought they were leaving the "wilderness of the world" to find a haven free of institutional structures they had united *against*. They were unprepared for the variability of directional change the wilderness they reached represented. Even John Winthrop complained of "our wildernes troubles our first plantings." (*Birth-mark*, 48)

In attempting to re-encounter the wilderness, Howe is continually confronted with the recollection of events such as the "Armageddon at Fort William Henry" of 1757 (*Thorow*, 51).[92] When the voices of the past return—like the symptom—it is in a different guise: the elliptical, warped language of Howe's poem. In the poem's first section, much of this change derives from a sifting of the language in William Johnson's papers. The first three lines in the poem, for example, "Go on the Scout, they say/ They will go near Swegachey// I have snow shoes and Indian shoes" are taken from a letter to Johnson by his deputy, George Croghan (*Thorow*, 43).[93] On pages 46–47, the words "At Fort Stanwix the Charrokey/ paice," "Agreseror," and "that time the Shannas & Dallaways" also come from a Croghan letter.[94] The poem, then, reinserts these decontextualized fragments of language as a means of gesturing at the inscrutable pressure that the past—in this case an eighteenth-century tussle over land—exerts on the present.

The revisiting of trauma and *re*-tracing—encountering for a second time—is central to both the poem's temporality and its critique of Thoreauvian immediacy, and the idea of repetition is built into *Thorow* at the level of the individual line. On page 45, for example, there are the lines, "Must see and not see/ Must not see nothing/ Burrow and so burrow/ Measuring mastering," "So empty and so empty," and "Dear Seem dear cast out." On page 51, the following lines occur: "Besieged and besieged// in a chain of Cause/ The eternal First Cause" and "Author the real author." By repeating words such as burrow, empty, dear, besieged, and author within the space of these short lines, Howe's poem seems to depend on a frustrated urge to find the sameness in return.

Thorow briefly unites textual fragments of America in the pre-colonial and colonial eras (differing visions of wilderness), the eighteenth century (Johnson and the French and Indian War), the nineteenth century (Thoreau), and the present. Howe knows that her work cannot recover a virgin landscape or some notional space of pure poetic utterance. Neither can the battered speech of her poems perform any restitutive function. It can only testify to a banal present, compromised in its relation to the past, at which she gestures in her account of tacky souvenirs for sale in the Lake George gift shops. Although the introduction appears to be sustained by a fantasy of wilderness, in the body of the poem Howe acknowledges the mediated nature of these encounters with the landscape. Despite the immense pull of the Thoreauvian account of the wilderness, her poem knows that this is itself thoroughly cultural. Crucially, the poem recognizes that it is itself part of that European trajectory—"I am/ Part of their encroachment," and "My ancestors/ tore off the first leaves" (*Thorow*, 47, 52). What is less clear is whether it is itself susceptible to a reification of the opposition between nature and culture.

Repetition, as the repeated low-register drones of *Thiefth* suggest, is at the core of the poem's thought world, and the "primal indeterminacy" of the introduction is revealed within the poem to be a chimera, albeit one that has had an enduring life in American literature.[95] In addition to inhabiting the landscape, Howe is inhabiting the metaphorical environment that the landscape has generated. The poem attempts, in a necessarily glancing and indirect manner, an immanent critique of that encounter as it has been staged and restaged at various points in American history.

Thorow contemplates the place to which Enlightenment thought assigns "elemental irrationality" and explores the impossibility of a direct encounter with wilderness. Howe's poem seeks to reflect the allure of what might be termed the negative aspects of Reason without succumbing to the irrationality that the landscape represents. *Thorow* is suffused with Thoreauvian perspectives on wilderness and language, but it explores them from the inside; it diagnoses a way of speaking that knowingly remains a prisoner of a certain rhetoric but subjects it to such deformations that its ideological underpinnings begin to come apart.

Something went very wrong in American history, it suggests, and poetry is the means by which that failure can be voiced. The double bind of the poem is that, in conceding "grammar" to colonial linguistic identity, it leaves itself with the task of articulating the inarticulable. So *Thorow* situates itself on the borders of coherence, striving pessimistically for an experience of enchantment that it knows to be inaccessible. The poetic form of *Thorow* is a kind of acknowledgement that linguistic estrangement is always a negotiation with particles of syntax and meaning, not a liberation.

With the release of *Thiefth*, *Thorow*'s inarticulacy was given a pertinence that its own introduction was beginning to obscure. The CD's deft handling of nonverbal material propels the listener toward the kinds of obdurately unrecoverable historical material that Howe has placed at the centre of her poetic project. Even the title emphasizes the poem's urge to unspell. The use of music, the suggestion of multiple voices in the editing, and the imagination and vigor of the realization of the typographical dissarrangements of the poem's third section all give the poem an aural cogency that strengthens its claims to voice coherence within incoherence. Rather than being constrained by the dichotomies that shape Howe's polemic on grammar and God, the poem's greatest resourcefulness lies in its exploitation of the ironies of treading the boundary between an Anglophone literary culture and the natural other that the culture designates as external to it.

CHAPTER 5

Enthusiasm, Telepathy, and Immediacy

In the late 1960s and early 1970s, Howe was a visual artist, working with installations that combined text and photographs.[1] *Hinge Picture*, her first book of poetry, was published in 1974 by Maureen Owen's Telephone Books. It has as its epigraph a quotation from Marcel Duchamp, an artist she continues to cite in interviews:[2] "Perhaps makes a HINGE PICTURE. (folding yardstick, book....) develop in space the PRINCIPLE OF THE HINGE in the displacements 1st in the plane 2nd in space"[3] (*HP*, 32). The notion of the hinge is an early example of the taste for figures of duality that is discernible in many Howe texts. Borders, margins and dividing lines are, as we have seen, crucial to Howe's writing. The visual aspect of the work— the look of the words on the page—is clearly important, but spatial relations are important in other ways too. Howe's text suspends narrative in favor of webs of thematic concern. History and language are imagined spatially, with associations being made that may depend on a word's proximity to others on the signifying chain or to distant historical or literary echoes.

Hinge Picture was, as Howe tells Keller in an interview, initially intended to be an installation, with words to be placed on the walls. It was at the poet Ted Greenwald's suggestion that she decided to put the texts into a book.[4] In my opinion, Kaplan Harris is right to suggest that, in citing copiously from Gibbon's *Decline and Fall of the Roman Empire*, Howe is using material that is "basically disconnected" from her American and Irish "inheritance."[5] However, there are telling parallels between the installation-based collage from which *Hinge Picture* grew and the later work. Significantly, *Hinge Picture* uses textual collage to create a dialogue with the past and, importantly, with a particular author's writing. Also, *Hinge Picture* is closely concerned with the detail of arranging words on the page. As Howe says in a recent interview, "*Hinge Picture* is formal in the sense that I obsessively used a justified margin. In those typewriter days I went to great trouble to get this effect. Then I thought it was a visual imperative, but now it seems sound-based."[6] In my view, these two features of the writing are examples of an enthusiastic orientation that would find firmer historical and literary grounding in Howe's 1980s writing.

The use of justified margins in *Hinge Picture* sometimes leads to box-like arrangements of text. *Hinge Picture* contains several word-grids, along with irregularly shaped poems and more conventionally lineated writing. In her early work—as Kathleen Fraser, Rachel Blau DuPlessis, Gerard Bruns, and Brian Reed have all argued—Howe is interested in grid patterns. Fraser points out that these provide a bridge between the grids of Robert Duncan and the painter Agnes Martin's use of the space of the canvas (perhaps, as Reed suggests, acknowledging Rosalind Krauss's theorization of the grid as "a way of circumventing the age-old, ever-vexatious split between spirit and matter").[7] The artificially compressed space of the grid might also, as Bruns has suggested, point to the concrete poet Eugen Gomringer, whose essay "From Line to Constellation" Howe cites in her early article "The End of Art": "Restriction in the very best sense—concentration and simplification—is the very essence of poetry" (81).

Howe's word squares (to use the term favored by DuPlessis and Reed) impose a visual order on the words, breaking them unnaturally and adding artificially extended spaces between the words. What Howe achieves in this early writing anticipates her work on Dickinson, where she repeatedly asserts that the visual and material features of the manuscript are integral to the poetry. In her Dickinson essay "Flames and Generosities," for example, Howe writes, "In the precinct of Poetry, a word, the space around a word, each letter, every mark, silence or sound volatilizes an inner law of form—moves on a rigorous line" (*Birth-mark*, 145).

Although the text predates Howe's encounter with antinomianism, *Hinge Picture* evokes an "ecstatic frenzy" (*HP*, 39) that is suffused with images of light: the "god of light" (45), "fiery meteor" (45), "dazzled" (46). This suggests a transfiguring, quasi-religious experience of poetic language. Although *Hinge Picture* is a more uneven accomplishment than the later work, its themes anticipate the close of *Melville's Marginalia*, in which the poem's reflections on print and immediacy are bathed in Shelleyan rushing light. Howe uses citation in *Hinge Picture* to counter late-twentieth-century language usage with a history that absorbs into itself the predictive archetypes of mythical utterance. Citation summons a force of externality that, paradoxically, reinforces the poem's qualities of immediacy, sending it down obscure, collage-driven pathways that abstract the poem from the speaking subject and place it at the center of a humming network of decontextualized meanings.

In her essay on *Melville's Marginalia*, Megan Williams points the reader toward Howe's discussion in *Birth-Mark* of F. O. Matthiesen and his response to Whitman's "immediacy." For Williams, this is an index of the "'immediacy' and antinomian enthusiasm of [Howe's] own personal meetings with past authors."[8] Such a conjunction of enthusiasm and immediacy is evident not only in *Melville's Marginalia* and the *Singularities* poems, but also in other places in Howe's writing—"Emily Dickinson's writing is a premeditated immersion in immediacy," she writes baldy in *Birth-mark*, for example (139).

The materiality of the book is clearly of great importance to Howe, both as a poet and as a critic arguing for a reappraisal of the status of Emily Dickinson's manuscripts, as it is for scholars such as Jerome McGann and Johanna Drucker.[9] Less obvious is the suggestion (only made explicit in 2000's *The Midnight*) that materiality and collage are intimately related. It becomes clear in *The Midnight*—in a way that informs our reading of earlier work—that Howe's writing is predicated on paths of association that are driven by two kinds of communicative impulse: the nonverbal features of reading, actuated by the material encounter with the book, and the interchange between authors that occurs when one writer uses words or motifs derived, consciously or not, from another.

In attempting to describe these twin impulses, it may be helpful to suggest that different kinds of object are at play. The psychoanalytic notion of the object (in object relations theory) makes no distinction between the mental representatives of physical objects, experiences, abstractions, and people. This notion can help us conceive of an affective dimension to the activity of reading in which the thingness of books and the meetings between authors exemplified by collage and marginalia are not necessarily different in kind.

It is important to bear in mind that, for Howe, immediacy is always found alongside mediation. The encounter with books as objects is clearly mediated, and there are various kinds of conceptual mediation in the work: the endless deferral embodied in Howe's labyrinthine archival quests, the ever-receding figures of authorial authority, and the restless postponement of any kind of meaning-bearing compact with the reader in the line-by-line unfolding of the poetry. Immediacy and mediation, then, go hand in hand in this work, each located in the material-immaterial object. Affective intensity is encountered through the words of others, not through unmediated access to the author. A charged neo-Romanticism can be located, for example, in such physical phenomena as the dusty paraphernalia of textual scholarship. As Brian Reed helpfully suggests, "at every point in Howe's work transcendental impulses coexist with their antitheses."[10]

Nonetheless, in recent years, Howe has attracted criticism for her attitude toward the material. In particular, the neo-pragmatist critic Walter Benn Michaels opened his book *The Shape of the Signifier* (2004) with a discussion of *Birth-mark*, which he considers to exemplify a dangerous and politically irresponsible strand of postmodern thought on the "materiality of the signifier."[11] His arguments on Howe are strongly colored by the critique of literalism in art developed by Michael Fried in his essay "Art and Objecthood."[12]

In an interview, Howe has identified her intellectual background with Judd and Smithson, two of the artists that Fried seeks to criticize.[13] One way of understanding the matrix of thought engaged by Howe's writing is, therefore, through debates on the fate of modernism within the New York art world of the 1960s. On one side were those, like Donald Judd, Robert Morris, and Robert Smithson, who sought to sever the line demarcating the aesthetic object from the world; on the other were those, such as Clement Greenberg and Michael Fried, who saw in this tendency a fatal compromising of the autonomy of the artwork and the demise of the formal stringency that had characterized the modernist tradition.

Michaels criticizes Howe's argument in *Birth-mark* that editors of an autobiographical notebook kept by the Puritan minister Thomas Shepard had paid insufficient attention to the material written upside down in the back of the notebook.[14] Michaels argues that if the book becomes a "'material object' it ceases to become something that could be edited and thus ceases to be a text at all."[15] Textuality, then, depends for Michaels on reproducibility. His argument does not acknowledge the presence in Howe's texts, both critical and poetic, of a commitment to undecidability. Her argument about Dickinson's manuscripts, for example, does not make the case that facsimile is the *only* means through which the works can be read.[16] In discussing Peirce, she is struck by the ways in which his manuscripts *resemble and anticipate* twentieth-century artworks. Her arguments pose difficult questions about the nature of textuality and of the aesthetic. Howe believes that there is no way of establishing a radical separation between a text and its material manifestation. The text cannot with any honesty be divorced from its visual, aural, or tactile corollaries. The point about Howe's position is not to argue for pure abstraction, visuality, or materiality, but to present it as what she calls in *The Midnight* a "zone of contention." Michaels's attempt to extrapolate from the audacious performance of uncertainty in the *Birth-mark* a "thoroughgoing materialism" asks entirely the wrong questions of Howe's text.

This chapter addresses the matrix of ideas generated by these meetings between material and immaterial, mediated and immediate. *Melville's Marginalia* is centrally concerned with both the relations between authors and books as objects. Printing is presented in this poem as a falling-off from the kinetic activity of thought, a legislative fettering of the energies of the spirit. Yet print, the medium of this communication, is also handled with a rigorously applied inventiveness. The space of the page is treated in such a way that the page frequently assumes the force of a visual artwork. Much of *Pierce-Arrow* concerns the invidious status of manuscripts and the abilities of these artifacts to convey by visual means dimensions of writerly activity that are lost to the printed page. In what follows, I examine Howe's use of manuscript facsimiles in *Pierce-Arrow*'s unlikely alignment of Swinburne and Peirce.

Melville's Marginalia

The final poem in *The Nonconformist's Memorial* collection, *Melville's Marginalia*, addresses the relation between author and past in ways that invoke the play of determination in the psychoanalytic notion of *Nachträglichkeit*—the relationship, in other words, between the memory of past trauma and the present self. It is a long and complex work in which Howe is found, as in many of her poems, deep in the archive.[17] On this occasion, she is pursuing Herman Melville. However, she does so indirectly, through the figure of the Irish writer James Clarence Mangan (1803–49). Melville owned an edition of Mangan's poetry, and the American writer's annotations to this book are reproduced in Howe's chief source text, Wilson Walker Cowen's edition of Melville's marginalia. As she writes in a 1992 letter to Norman O. Brown, "marginal markings in the books of other writers *is* identity made up of identifications."[18] Marginalia demonstrates the self-fashioning that is wrought through the voices of others. The links between the texts that she covers effect a marriage between Irish and American literary traditions. Beneath the voluminous paperwork generated by her research—Melville's marginal annotations, Mangan's bizarre faked translations, the visual dynamism of Shelley's manuscripts—is a powerful reflection on the unconscious processes activated in the reading process. However, although *Melville's Marginalia* pursues numerous obscure lines of literary connection—it is a poem of unofficial genealogies—it is not simply a hymn to wayward scholarship. Indeed, it is one of Howe's most enthusiastic poems, with a less equivocal endorsement of spirit than is apparent in either *Thorow* or *Eikon*.

Approaching seventy pages in length, *Melville's Marginalia* was, on publication, Howe's longest poem series. The first section, after a brief preface, is a combination of prose, often quite straightforward and in the form of quotations, and highly fragmented verse texts. There is a sketch of Mangan's life; an account of Cowen's remarkable edition of marginalia; a description of Howe's pursuit of her intuition that Mangan was the "progenitor" of Melville's Bartleby; and several excerpts, typographically rearranged, from passages that Melville marked in his editions of Arnold.[19] The second half of the poem series mainly contains stanzas of fourteen or fifteen lines of even length, eschewing the series of single lines and couplets that Howe had favored in much of her earlier work. There are four main elements to this second part of *Melville's Marginalia*: a preliminary and a concluding section in which Howe's words predominate, and two middle sequences that draw heavily on texts by Shelley and Mangan. Toward the end, the poem adopts a progressively Promethean language of light and rebellion.

Melville's Marginalia investigates both the relations between writers and Howe's own relationship to Irish and American literary identity. Mangan is approached through Howe's construction of Melville's response to the Irish writer's life and writing. Mangan shunned the English literary establishment, and he remains a relatively obscure figure in English literature. In Ireland, however, he became a totemic author, greatly admired by Yeats:[20] Mangan (along with Davis and Ferguson) was one of three writers associated with the mid-nineteenth-century Young Ireland movement about whom Yeats wrote short essays. In these pieces, Yeats presented himself as the inheritor of a particular tradition of English-language Irish writing. Yeats makes the nature of his self-fashioning explicit in his poem "To Ireland in the Coming Times": "Know that I would accounted be/ True brother of a company/ That sang, to sweeten Ireland's wrong,/ Ballad and story, rann and song;... Nor may I less be counted one/ With Davis, Mangan, Ferguson." Yet, in his writing on Mangan, as in Howe's, the question of cultural nationalism is only obliquely addressed—Yeats speaks more directly of the peculiarity of Mangan the "magician."[21] He writes of the "electric flashes" of Mangan's style and observes, "He never startles us by saying beautiful things we have long felt. He does not say look at yourself in this mirror; but, rather, 'Look at me—I am so strange, so exotic, so different.'"[22]

This quality of strangeness pervades Howe's poem and the way it articulates literary relationships. A number of such relationships are suggested in the poem: intensely personal ones such as that of Melville to Hawthorne or of Shelley to Byron, and literary ones such as that of Melville or Joyce to Mangan.[23] However, a more unusual association dominates *Melville's Marginalia*: at the centre of the poem's first section is the speculative contention that Mangan, once a clerk, was the prototype of Melville's Bartleby.

Howe makes this assertion when describing her examination of Melville's edition of Mangan's poems: "I saw the penciled trace of Herman Melville's passage through John Mitchel's introduction and *knew by shock of poetry telepathy* the real James Clarence Mangan is the progenitor of the fictional Bartleby" (*MM*, 106; my italics).

Developing her point about identity and identification, then, we can see that a form of communication between authors is at issue, a direct encounter that resembles Howe's account of antinomian grace. The idea of "poetry telepathy" in *Melville's Marginalia* is a variant of an ambivalent preoccupation with immediacy that is to be found in many places in Howe's work. Howe uses the term as a way of discussing how one writer's words can be said to inhabit another.[24] The word progenitor might suggest a genealogy of direct influence, but Howe's poem is closer to endorsing a combination of conscious and unconscious determination, with a strong emphasis on the latter. Far from a Bloomian agonism of generations conducted in the shadow of Oedipus, Howe's work suggests a more casual dissemination of words. I will stress the enigmatic nature of such relations, which may depend less on any literary influence than on Howe's distinctive form of strong reading for the connections to be retrospectively assigned by the latterday reader.

Howe cites a letter from Melville to Hawthorne in the first section of her text: "Ah! It's a long stage, and no inn in sight, and night coming, and the body cold. But with you for a passenger, I am content and can be happy" (*MM*, 91). The notion of incorporation or assimilation suggested by the word "passenger" is important to the working of Howe's poem as an index of the strangeness that citation can bring to a text. Elsewhere, Melville's letters to Hawthorne evoke an embattled community of explorers in virgin territory:

> This most persuasive season has not for weeks recalled me from certain crotchety and over doleful chimaeras, the like of which men like you and me and some others, forming a chain of God's posts round the world, must be content to encounter now and then, and fight them the best way we can. But come they will,—for, in the boundless, trackless, but still glorious wild wilderness through which these outposts run, the Indians do sorely abound, as well as the insignificant but still stinging mosquitoes.[25]

Melville's "chain of God's posts" indicates a quasi-spiritual kinship among authors, who, in turn, are part of a cultural vanguard comprising "men like you and me and some others." Howe's "shock of poetry telepathy" is, like the title of her book *My Emily Dickinson*, a means of inserting herself as both reader and writer into this dialogue between authors. Perhaps, like Melville, she believes that "genius, all over the world, stands hand in hand, and one shock of recognition runs the whole circle round."[26] Yet her pursuit of the marginal, the excluded feminine, and the silenced voices of the past in her work indicates a more critical relation to Melville's global power grid of geniuses. Rather than inducting herself into a questionable confraternity, Howe celebrates the strangeness of the act of reading: the uncontainable and unpredictable short-circuits that are risked in one writer-reader's attempted assimilation of another's linguistic signature.

* * *

"Free association" is central to Howe's assertions in *Melville's Marginalia* about the affinities between poetry and telepathy. "Poetry is thought transference," she writes, and then, immediately, "Free association isn't free" (*MM*, 105).[27] With this formula, Howe follows Freud, who, in the *Interpretation of Dreams*, writes of two theorems that are fundamental to his clinical technique: "that when conscious purposive ideas are abandoned, concealed purposive ideas assume control of the current of ideas and that superficial associations are only substitutes by displacement for suppressed deeper ones."[28] This notion of a purposiveness operating at a level that exceeds readerly perception is central to the poetics of *Melville's Marginalia*. When Howe writes of "poetry telepathy," she might mean *poetic* telepathy, but she seems to be suggesting an equivalence between the terms, especially as the phrase follows "Poetry is thought transference." Neither poetry nor free association can escape the hidden operations of purposiveness. It is up to writer and reader to discern the movement of these currents of association. If there is an inaugural trauma behind the textual symptom, it would lie, for Howe, in the relation between literary texts and historical instances of violence and dispossession.

Howe approaches Melville indirectly, by means of his readings of other authors. In her preface she writes, "I thought one way to write about a loved author would be to follow what trails he followed through words of others" (*MM*, 92). In the first part of the poem, she adds, "If there are things Melville went looking for in books so too there were things I looked for in Melville's looking" (*MM*, 105). Howe's opening chronology lists such diverse events as an address given by Shelley on Fishamble Street, Dublin (possibly witnessed by an eight-year-old Mangan, who lived on the street); Mangan's death in 1849; and the appearance in the United States four years later of another scrivener, Bartleby. Then, in her preface, Howe cites an extract from Melville's journal that describes a visit to the grave of Shelley (*MM*, 89).

Howe is motivated, perhaps, by Cowen's speculation, in his own preface, that Shelley's relationship with Byron put Melville in mind of his own with Hawthorne.[29] From these details, Howe constructs links between the writers. Shelley functions as a kind of thread connecting Mangan to Melville. He is associated with both the young Mangan and the older Melville, and his death is linked to the abject deaths of Mangan and Bartleby. It is not merely Hawthorne that Melville carries as a "passenger"—he is carrying other authors as foreign objects, too, and Howe's poem attempts to give voice to some of these relationships. Howe does this in a way that writes herself into this writerly-readerly network of authorial interconnection.

The link between Mangan and Shelley is also made by Joyce in an earlier version of the paper on Mangan that is cited by Howe.[30] In another part of Joyce's lecture (a point that is unclear in Howe's extract), Joyce criticizes Mangan for what he perceives as his enslavement to nationalistic *ressentiment*: "Love of sorrow, desperation, high-sounding threats, these are the great traditions of James Clarence Mangan's race; and, in that miserable, reedy and feeble figure, a hysteric nationalism receives its final justification."[31] The phrase "love of sorrow" in the Joyce essay is one of several that echo the language of Mitchel's introduction to his 1859 edition of Mangan's poems—in this case that Mangan "seemed to revel in the expression of passionate sorrow."[32] Howe cites Mitchel's formulation (*MM*, 131), and it is important to the poem's network of literary conjunctions that she, Joyce, and Melville are working from the same selected edition of Mangan.[33]

With Melville's personal library at the center, Howe is exploring the links between Irish cultural nationalism and poetics. Yet Howe approaches this tangentially. In his 1907 paper, Joyce observes that "the poet who hurls his anger against tyrants would establish upon the future an intimate and far more cruel tyranny."[34] Howe's poem, however, finds in the very effeminacy of the "miserable, reedy and feeble figure" a stranger vocation, as his "passionate sorrow" is transposed to Bartleby's skeptical quietism. *Melville's Marginalia* uproots Mangan from his minor place in literary studies and inserts him into an alien tradition. Howe's attachment to such correspondences, with their flouting of temporal and national demarcations, plays predominantly on half-buried textual affinities, and ranges in its speculations far beyond the sphere of conscious influence.

Describing an analogous combination of recovery and elaboration in the psychoanalytic setting, Christopher Bollas compares the task of recollection to the creative work of historians in re-envisioning the past. He continues,

> [The] movement of the real upon the self has the effect of giving the self the feel of its own many deaths; but in a psychoanalysis this past,

transformed into a history, gives the real a place that is open to the continuously transformative workings of the imaginary and symbolic, the very movement that Freud termed *Nachträglichkeit*, translated into English as "deferred action" or into French as *après coup*.[35]

Bollas writes from the perspective of the present assimilation of the past. His account of the creative work of reconstruction in the analytical setting is comparable to Howe's work on Melville's marginalia, following "what trails [Melville] followed through words of others (*MM*, 92)." A good deal of the poem is devoted to present transformations of the past—her text is a reconsideration of those that cluster in the margins of Melville's library, a speculative construction of the aftershocks of deferral. Yet it is certainly not the case that Howe arrives, even momentarily, at a satisfactory narrative that would explicate the links between Mangan, Melville, Hawthorne, Shelley, Byron, and Joyce. What she is performing, in her free association, places her in the word-filled space between the analyst's chair and the couch; she offers evidence of a series of connections, but she is both unwilling and unapologetically incapable of imposing an interpretative narrative. This is partly, perhaps, because of her conviction that the traumatic 'real' that is the object of her literary investigations is in some final sense irrecoverable—the poet can only track its affective impact on the texts she examines and produces.

There is another way of looking at *Nachträglichkeit*, a view that reverses the priority of past and present and that is reflected in James Strachey's English translation of the word as "deferred action" in the Standard Edition of Freud. From this angle, the movement of the action of past trauma on the present is forward, rather than backward. In this version of *Nachträglichkeit*, the emphasis is on the inassimilable event—such as the infant's experience of desire, which reappears subsequently to provoke the interpretations of the sexualized adult. The initial experience, therefore, is, in the words of French psychoanalytic thinker Jean Laplanche, a kind of "time-bomb."[36] Here, we are reminded of the seventeenth-century formula "history is Postdated Prophesie" that Howe cites in her introduction to her work *Articulation of Sound Forms in Time* (*Articulation*, 4). The past is considered from the perspective of its action on the present, rather than as the subject of later elaboration.

Thus, at the same time as we read *Melville's Marginalia* as a creative reconstruction of the reciprocal connections between earlier authors, we can interpret Howe's response to these authors in the light of their action on her; she makes herself receptive to the action of submerged textual strands within Irish and American literature. Her position is poised between the alert passivity of the medium and the organizing activity of the editor.

It preserves the doubleness of *Nachträglichkeit*, containing both its forward-facing and retrospective orientations—what might be described, in the vocabulary of Laplanche, as its "deterministic" and "hermeneutic" moments.[37]

However, although Laplanche's translation of *Nachträglichkeit*—as "afterwardsness"—is intended to incorporate both these elements, he still finds the concept insufficient as a means of theorizing the relation between the present and a founding trauma. This is because of the constitutive part played by the desire of the adult—an affective force that would be incomprehensible to the infant—in the traumatic event. In other words, formulations of *Nachträglichkeit* tend to concentrate on the psychoanalytic subject to the exclusion of the other, who was present at the initiating moment of the trauma. Laplanche's Copernican revolution is to reinsert the enigmatic and unintelligible messages of the other's desire into Freudian metapsychology. He writes,

> It is impossible... to put forward a purely hermeneutic position on this—that is to say, that everyone interprets their past according to their present—because the past already has something deposited in it that demands to be deciphered, which is the message of the other person.... right at the start, there is something that goes in the direction of the past to the future, from the other to the individual in question, that is in the direction from the adult to the baby, which I call the implantation of the enigmatic message.[38]

To transpose this to the field of poetics is clearly to do a certain violence to Laplanche's concept of the "enigmatic message," and I would certainly not contend that the resistant qualities in Howe's writing are in any simple sense an untranslated communication of this enigma. However, in the context of the present discussion of temporality and literary genealogies, the concept can have a nuanced explicatory force. Howe's writing is capable of representing trauma in both progressive (deterministic) and retrogressive (hermeneutic) fashions. The textual marks of past violence and dispossession in her work present themselves in her reorganizations of historical texts, which become a symptom of the disturbance that exerts pressure on the present. At the same time, for all its difficulty, her work *is* a reorganization of material, and it does contain the kind of creative restructuring of the past that Bollas describes. If Howe has described her work as "a catastrophe of bifurcation," we might complicate this duality by insisting on the foreignness and heterogeneity of the texts she attempts to assimilate.[39] Indeed, one might even say that her work is a failure of incorporation. Caught in the cleft stick of *Nachträglichkeit*, the object remains unassimilated, and its enigmatic strangeness is not neutralized through full accommodation within Howe's poem.

Texts by Joyce, Mangan, Shelley, Arnold, and Melville are present in *Melville's Marginalia*, but they are often decontextualized and, unless the reader follows Howe into the archive, often also invisible. Howe's method of free associating around phrases from Cowen's compendium of marginalia also builds an element of resistance into her text. The method, combining the words of others with Howe's 'free' association, increases the hallucinatory potential of reading by installing a question mark over the relation between utterance and source.

The lines "According to/ Vallency every Irishman is/ an Arab" (*MM*, 135), an unreferenced citation from one of Mangan's "Literae Orientales" essays, are a case in point.[40] Mangan is critical of the idea that linguistic scholars could seek a founding extrinsic authenticity for the Irish language in Oriental origins.[41] In one of these essays, not cited in *Melville's Marginalia*, he disdains the "old Orientalists,"[42] preferring to annex a vagrant freedom for the imagination:

> The mind, to be sure, properly to speak is without a home on the earth. Ancestral glories, genealogical charts, and the like imprescriptible indescriptibles are favorite subjects with the composite being Man, who also goes now and then to the length of dying in idea for his fatherland—but for Mind—it is restless, rebellious—a vagrant whose barren tracts are by no means confined to the space between Dan and Beersheba. It lives rather out of the world.[43]

In citing Mangan's "every Irishman is an Arab," Howe perhaps wants her text to accommodate the Orientalism alluded to in the title of Joyce's "Araby" and also present in the writings of Byron and Shelley.[44] Yet the phrase is, it transpires, the opposite of Mangan's actual position, which is to confront an ideology of origins and authenticity with the veil, the cloak, imaginative fakery, and the nomadism of Cain.[45]

One aspect of the afterwardsness of Howe's text, then, lies in its preservation of the remnants of a once-faddish Orientalist exoticism. Yet this element is so decontextualized that it almost fails to communicate anything other than its own strangeness—"every Irishman is an Arab." The link between the initial context of the phrase—a debate within Irish cultural nationalism—and its reappearance in *Melville's Marginalia* is almost severed. The foreign material is never fully assimilated. The presence of extraneous texts in such abundance ensures that the disturbance in Howe's text is not in the full possession of the author. This foreign material is subsumed to the exigencies of her own voice through its identifiable formal signature, but that voice can never hope to contain the conflicting energies of the complexes of thought on which it touches. The fragments that she cites contain traces of other desires and imperatives—something akin to Laplanche's enigmatic messages—that are entirely alien to her text and whose associative potential continually exceeds it.

* * *

In addition to the investigation of textual otherness or externality in the poem, *Melville's Marginalia* directs its attention to the hinge between existence and death. This element of the poem can be read as a continuation of the treatment of Ovidian metamorphosis and Ophelia's death in *Pythagorean Silence* (1982) and of incarnation in *The Nonconformist's Memorial* (1992). It has broader affinities with the recurrent figure of the dividing line in Howe's work, from *Hinge Picture* (1974) or the territorial demarcations of her later American poems to the importance of the semi-transparent interleaf to *The Midnight*. I will explore this set of ideas alongside Giorgio Agamben's discussion of Bartleby in his 1993 essay "Bartleby, or On Contingency" not only because of its powerful theorization of Bartleby's inertia, but also because of the essay's links to Howe's conception of an immediacy that precedes the putting of pen to paper.[46] Howe's reading of Bartleby, whose suspended pen is the embodiment of a potentiality that evades the deadly fixity of print, draws on her antinomian understanding of grace in literature. In *Birth-mark*, she describes Bartleby's "I would prefer not to" as "an antinomian gesture" (12). In the same book, she writes of Dickinson's "gesture of infinite patience in preferring not to publish" (1). In her *Linebreak* interview with Charles Bernstein, she also remarks that, in contrast to the "instant infusion" of grace, "The moment a word's put on a page, there's a kind of death."[47]

Agamben finds in Bartleby a figure who might be linked to the Skeptics, especially as summarized by the writing of Diogenes Laertius on Pyrrho of Elis in his *Lives of Eminent Philosophers*, a book that Melville owned and which was published in the year that he wrote *Bartleby, the Scrivener*. For the Skeptics, writes Agamben, "what shows itself on the threshold between Being and non-Being, between sensible and intelligible, between word and thing" is the space of "potentiality," a point that is neither positive nor negative, but simply the "luminous spiral of the possible."[48] Agamben describes a position of generative stasis that derives its productive potential from the ability to at once be and not be. Bartleby's suspended state of being, contends Agamben, is Melville's approximation of this skeptical avoidance of affirmation or denial:

> As a scribe who has stopped writing, Bartleby is the extreme figure of the Nothing from which all creation derives; and at the same time, he constitutes the most implacable vindication of this Nothing as pure, absolute potentiality. The scrivener has become the writing tablet; he is now nothing other than his white sheet. It is not surprising, therefore, that he dwells so obstinately in the abyss of potentiality and does not seem to have the slightest intention of leaving it.[49]

In Howe's poem, behind the jostling textual fragments, is a linking of Bartleby's intransigence to Mangan. Howe mentions certain aspects of Mangan that might have drawn Melville to him, notably the "Irish poet's occupation as scrivener, the 'feminine softness of his voice,' the political rebellion in his writing, and his death by starvation in the city of Dublin" (*MM*, 107). Beneath this, beyond the fascination with the details of Mangan's life, is a reimagining of the Irish writer as a chaotic precursor of the figure to whom Melville brought such austerity and rigor. Howe finds that Mangan's "restless, rebellious," "vagabond" mind, his appetite for intoxication, and his dandyishness—the various ways, in short, in which he rejected his straitened circumstances—are refined in Bartleby into a pure ethic of refusal.

Although it might appear strange to suggest that a poem of nearly seventy pages can share a poetics with the verbally parsimonious Bartleby, especially in Agamben's metaphysically pregnant reading, it is continuous with other of Howe's writings. The stutter that Howe links to Melville, via Charles Olson, is a form of hesitancy that reaches its apogee in the scrivener. "It's the stutter in American literature that interests me," says Howe of Olson's reading of *Billy Budd* (Foster interview, 181).[50] Hesitation is integral, too, to Howe's characterization of Emily Dickinson:

> HESITATE from the Latin, meaning to stick. Stammer. To hold back in doubt, have difficulty speaking. "*He* may pause but *he* must not hesitate"—Ruskin. Hesitation circled back and surrounded everyone in that confident age of aggressive industrial expansion and brutal Empire building. Hesitation and Separation. The Civil War had split American in two. *He* might pause, *She* hesitated. Sexual, racial, and geographical separation are at the heart of Definition. (*MED*, 21)

A stutter is, after all, a way of returning speech to a moment of suspension analogous to that of Bartleby. There is a moment of arrest that prevents language flowing through the normal syntactical routes, from one thing to another. A page from the beginning of the poem's second section will serve as an example of the movement of language in the poem:

> Wearied human language
> take me so that I no longer
> am perpetually dispersed
> and appear not to know
> When I wander far off
> roughened and wrought human
> to the matter of fact
> Refuting and chastising
> Love a secret between two
> Certainty decreed to go
> They are always masked (*MM*, 114)

In these lines, there is a repeated threat of blankness. Enjambment is possible with the first four lines but unlikely elsewhere. Nonetheless, a continuation of sense remains a potential that the reader cannot help but explore. Each line stands under threat of effacement by the succeeding line (this effect is more noticeable at a reading). The cumulative effect of this appearance and disappearance of linguistic fragments gives the same prominence to the silent moment at which sense and syntax are disrupted as to the actual words of the text. With "When I wander far off/ roughened and wrought human/ to the matter of fact," for example, the reader has to break off and begin again with each new line-unit. The meaning, moreover, of a line such as "roughened and wrought human" is so elusive that the reader is urged to look outside the line for a the completion of sense that is withheld. The character of Howe's poetry, in *Melville's Marginalia* and elsewhere, is shaped by this dependence on the unsounded shifts in direction that it demands of the reader. It is here that the evanescent presence of the stutter—and Bartleby, in particular, in this poem—is located in the formal contours of the text.

The poetic line in such stanzas is usually not a satisfactorily sense-bearing or syntactical unit. Syntactical parts sometimes occupy more than a line, sometimes less. Enjambment is an option in places and not in others. The dynamism of the poetry consists in its ability to bump up against the line break, without it being clear whether it will stop short or press on. The syntactical units may rest within the line or extend over several lines, or the reader may exercise choice in the matter. The result is a constant questioning of the relation between greater and smaller parts and a repeated deferral of the notional reconciliation of wholeness.

The relation of grammar to line break in these lines can be understood in the light of Lacan's comment on the *Nachträglichkeit* of syntax, a diachronic movement that operates "even if the sentence completes its signification only with its last term, each term being anticipated in the construction of the others, and, inversely, sealing their meaning by its retroactive effect."[51] In Howe's writing, the nature of the line breaks and the play with deferral cause the kind of retrospective closure described by Lacan to be both anticipated and suspended.

With regard to temporality, this might be expressed both as an unfulfilled promise and as a backward look that cannot achieve the comfort of reconciliation. Considered in terms of Laplanche's formulation of *Nachträglichkeit*, neither the forward-falling shadow of the determining moment nor the backward interpretation of the hermeneutic perspective succeeds in imposing intelligibility. The pervasive citation and continual deferral of the meaning-making contract between writer and reader create an effect of suspension. This is both a realization of Bartleby's hesitation and a capture of the moment at which a text has the potential to be otherwise. The line break is experienced as the intervention of an otherness that applies an extraneous, almost arbitrary authority to the broken elements of the language. With prior determination and retrospective interpretation equally in suspension, the enigmatic order of the line break is felt as a foreign structuring element.

* * *

Howe's antinomian understanding of Bartleby's hesitation preserves the dynamism of the moment between two kinds of death—silence and the mediatedness of print. Agamben is again close to Howe when he extends his reading of Bartleby with an analysis of Melville's phrase "On errands of life, these letters speed to death."[52] Noting Bartleby's possible former occupation in the dead letter office, Agamben reads this sentence in the context of Paul: "But now we are delivered from the Law, that being dead where we were held; that we should serve in the newness of spirit, not in the oldness of the letter" (Romans 7:6).[53] This returns us, in Howe's intellectual universe, to Anne Hutchinson's appeal to Paul during her trial, when she criticizes those who are "ministers of the letter and not the spirit."[54]

"Because he stole the light" (*MM*, 146) reasserts the Promethean themes evident earlier in the poem ("The beautiful passage in *Prometheus*" [*MM*, 117], for example, or "Dare I uncreate Prometheus" [*MM*, 120]). In Howe's poem, this light can be understood as a similar refusal of the printed word to that expressed in her *Linebreak* interview: "what Anne Hutchinson is about, being instantly infused with grace so there would be no text—there would be no need for law because this direct experience would come that had no use for print."⁵⁵ This thought finds expression in *Melville's Marginalia* in the line "Printing ruins it" (*MM*, 147).

The opposition between printing and an inspired immediacy represented by such figures as Hutchinson and Dickinson is crucial to the final page (150) of *Melville's Marginalia*. The page opens into a space in which an intense light is perceptible—"Light in which we were rushing" (*MM*, 150)—an echo, perhaps, of Hutchinson's "I think the soule to be Nothinge but Light."⁵⁶ Against the dead letter of the law, Howe offers a term that locates life in immediacy.⁵⁷ The ninth line's "rushing light," taken from Shelley's *Masque of Anarchy*, restates the second line's "Light in which we were rushing." "We" and "he" are unidentified in the poem, but the "rushing light," an indication of spirit, finds its translation into the dead letters of print with "you know print settles it" and "print is sentinel so sages say."⁵⁸ The poem's final two lines—"Obedience we are subjects Susan/ Scared millions and on he rushed"—sketch an impression of subjectedness in language but offer a final escape route located in the kinetic Promethean potentiality that is made available in the closing pages of the poem series.

These perceptions at the end of the sequence are anticipated by the epigraph to "Turning," the first section of the book *The Nonconformist's Memorial*. This passage from Mary Shelley's *Journal* is marked in Melville's edition of *Shelley Memorials*: "The enthusiast suppresses her tears, crushes her opening thoughts, and—all is changed"⁵⁹ (*NCM*, 1). In choosing this passage, Howe is forcing a line to be drawn linking Mary Shelley to Melville. Although *Melville's Marginalia* scarcely engages with Melville's writings, his absence becomes a negative space toward which all other lines tend. For Mary Shelley, the intense seclusion of the enthusiast harbors a generative, law-smashing energy, much as Bartleby's messianic rebellion is characterized by withdrawal. Bartleby's potentiality, suspended between being and non-being, action and passivity, contains a transformative impetus that is anticipated in Mary Shelley's "all is changed." One of the poem's ironies is that the cultural nationalism of Yeats and John Mitchel and the different engagements with liberatory politics of Byron and Shelley are given less prominence than the destabilizing quietism and hesitancy of Bartleby and the vagabond eccentricity of Mangan.

Howe's preface to *Melville's Marginalia* includes a passage by Mangan in which he proudly asserts his vagabond nature. The passage concludes with a description of a stasis that he cannot achieve and a reckless pun: "Other men sojourn for life in the country of their choice; there is a prospect of ultimate repose for most things; even the March of Intellect must one day halt; already we see that pens, ink, and paper are—stationary" (*MM*, 104). What

Howe reads as Melville's extension of Mangan in Bartleby, whose defining desire is "I like to be stationary," allows the Mangan figure to "repose" but, in untying him from his wandering vocation, endows him with a more abstract capacity to roam.[60]

Bartleby, then, represents a 'stationary/ stationery' quality that is pregnant with the possibility of expression. The chaotic figure of Mangan, prolix and hostile to stasis, is captured and his restless energy becomes a kind of potential. When, toward the end of Melville's story, Bartleby is imprisoned in "the Tombs," it is because he is a "vagrant."[61] In the two figures, Howe brings together inertia and wandering, presenting them as two incommensurable sides of the same coin.

Arisbe and The Leisure of the Theory Class (Pierce-Arrow)

When asked in an interview about the role of "non-meaning, sound, the visual aspects of language" in her work, Howe replied, "But that *is* meaning."[62] Her work frequently tests the signifying potential of the visual and the aural, domains that mobilize both the material and the immaterial, two apparently contradictory dimensions of Howe's thought. The enthusiastic desire to bypass print or the letter of the law finds some satisfaction in the immediacy of visual communication. Yet the very emphasis on the mediated quality of the material object—the book, the manuscript page, the visual artwork—seems to propel it into the sphere of direct communication that Howe likes to place alongside the relative fixity of the printed word. This aspect of the work is present in Howe's poetry from the very point at which it separates itself from visual art. *Pierce-Arrow* is a resonant example of this probing of the non-poetic content of poetry, combining some extremely prosaic verse and numerous visual images.

The Pierce-Arrow was a luxury car manufactured in Buffalo. Production ceased in 1938, the year after Howe was born. The car is of no relevance to the text of the poem, although a photo of Howe outside the former factory is displayed on the back cover of the book. The book's title plays on the temptation to misspell and mispronounce the name "Peirce."[63] *Pierce-Arrow* is rooted in a response to another of the eccentric scholars that have so fascinated Howe, this time the scientist, logician, mathematician and philosopher C. S. Peirce.

It was published in 1999—six years after *The Nonconformist's Memorial*. It was the first book of poetry that Howe published after the death of her second husband, the sculptor David von Schlegell, in October 1992.[64] As Peter Nicholls has eloquently argued of the closing *Rückenfigur* sequence, the emotional tenor of *Pierce-Arrow* is loss.[65] The poem contemplates the experience of love from many perspectives, among which the most strongly accented is found in the assertion "Love's sail is black" (*P-A*, 54).[66] As in others of her works, affective states such as mourning and aggression are presented in ways that traverse personal, cultural and historical layers of meaning.[67]

This curious, wide-ranging book occupies an important transitional place in Howe's writing. The first two parts of the book, in particular, mark a shift away from the fractured voice of the 1980s and early 1990s toward a more discursive mode of expression. *Arisbe* is more straightforward prose than her three experimental essays of the mid-1990s, "Ether Either," the preface to *Frame Structures*, and "Sorting Facts: Or, Nineteen Ways of Looking at Marker." In much of the poetry of *The Leisure of the Theory Class*, Howe incorporates prose verbatim, as, for example, in the following stanza:[68]

> In 1898 Theodore Watts
> ("the foremost English
> critic of literature
> since Matthew Arnold"
> — 1910 *Harmsworth Encyclopedia*)
> became Watts-Dunton (*P-A*, 125)

These sections suggest a recoil from the metaphysically charged work of the 1980s and early 1990s and a retreat into a less immediate manner characterized by drily humorous antiquarianism. *Rückenfigur*, which I discuss in the following chapter, inaugurates Howe's late lyric mode and is utterly distinct in style from the first two sections. The poem is less demonstrative than earlier work; the vocabulary is less abstract and theoretical, the disjunctions not so jagged, the aural qualities of the writing smoother. However, these stylistic shifts should not be read as a dilution of the work's qualities of intensity. In *Pierce-Arrow*, the *Rückenfigur* section functions as the poetic receptacle that absorbs and redistributes in lyric form the violence and privation that lie beneath the smoother surfaces of the first two sections. One of the most striking features of these sections of the book is the way in which prose and poetry of relatively even texture is counterpointed by the visual dynamism of the manuscript facsimiles. *Pierce-Arrow* begins with *Arisbe*, a long prose text that examines the later life of Charles Sanders Peirce and his mysterious wife Juliette. The following section, *The Leisure of the Theory Class*, runs to nearly 100 pages of often self-consciously prosaic poetry. Along with Peirce and Juliette, this section's protagonists include the Victorian writers Algernon Swinburne, Thomas Love Peacock, and George Meredith.

Peirce is the only philosophical thinker that Howe has placed at the center of a poem series. Howe's reading of Peirce is bold and idiosyncratic, however, and it skirts the philosophical content of his thought. In Howe's view, the relative failure of scholars to come to grips with Peirce's manuscripts, especially his highly visual existential graphs, is comparable to the disregard that was, until relatively recently, the fate of Emily Dickinson's manuscripts. In an interview, Howe places Peirce in a line that runs from Dickinson to various tendencies in twentieth-century avant-garde art:

> Many of his logical graphs, and also his calculations, are like poems. Some resemble concrete poetry, others prefigure drawings by Paul Klee, Agnes Martin, Robert Smithson, Hanne Darboven. Some remind me of Joseph Beuys' drawings on paper and blackboards, or work by Artaud and Duchamp. That doesn't make the graphs any less philosophy, mathematics and science.... [T]he idea that in late nineteenth century America Emily Dickinson and Charles Sanders Peirce went to similar extremes in their writing practice seems unacceptable to many readers and editors here and abroad.[69]

Pierce-Arrow reflects Howe's continuing interest in the oddness of forms of nineteenth-century writing that have, in her view, not been assimilated or understood by later readers or scholars. In technical terms, Howe's response to the strangeness of this work is, for the first time in her poetry, to combine her own words with manuscript facsimiles depicting the words and images of others. The writing is interspersed with reproductions of Peirce's papers—including symbols, drawings and doodles—and Swinburne's manuscripts. Howe moves away from the typographical experimentation of works such as *Eikon Basilike* or *Thorow* toward a visual aesthetic that depends on actual reproductions of the books and papers of others.[70] What she achieves, therefore, is a new form of visual citation that is distinct in important ways from the modernist tradition of textual citation. Howe pioneers an original form of collage in which printed word, handwriting, and drawing are imbricated in ways that stress paths of association as much as clashes between individual elements.

Rather than focus on the content of Peirce's thought as a logician, Howe treats him as a kind of poet and a kind of artist.[71] This is a form of polemical strong reading, much like her accounts of Emily Dickinson as a proto-modernist and of Mangan as the model for Bartleby.[72] While Howe's interest in immediacy and words as symbols tallies with aspects of Peirce's thought, it is specifically the points at which Peirce's manuscripts exceed themselves, beginning to resemble twentieth-century visual artworks, that interest her.[73]

At the heart of the book, then, is a claim for the importance of latent predictive energies in aesthetic forms that exceed those known or knowable by their authors.

* * *

The most distinctive feature of the first two sections of *Pierce-Arrow* is the use of manuscript facsimiles, which exist in tension with the words on the printed page. Consciousness, for Peirce, is defined by symbolization. In a late 1860s lecture he remarked, "Life is but a sequence of inferences or a train of thought. At any instant then man is a thought, and as thought is a species of symbol, the general answer to the question what is man? is that he is a symbol."[74] When Peirce invented his existential graphs, in 1896, he remained committed to this position on the centrality of the symbol.[75] These graphs were diagrammatic representations of logical statements that developed out of his system of symbolic logic. Often, as in the examples Howe gives in facsimile, text and symbols are combined. In a manuscript remark, Peirce indicates that these visual schemes of the process of reasoning were particularly well suited to expressing the workings of thought, noting, "I do not think I ever *reflect* in words: I employ visual diagrams, firstly because this way of thinking is my natural language of self-communion, and secondly, because I am convinced that it is the best system for the purpose."[76] Peirce suggests, in other words, that the 'language' of mental processes is composed of non-verbal signs. In order to render and communicate the movement of this thought accurately, he uses his existential graphs.

Howe's foreword to *Pierce-Arrow* places a rather different emphasis on the verbal in Peirce's work. She writes, "Perhaps the Word, giving rise to all pictures and graphs, is at the center of Peirce's philosophy. There always was and always will be a secret affinity between symbolic logic and poetry" (*P-A*, ix). Peirce stresses the visual imagination over the word in cognitive processes, whereas Howe stresses the visual aspect of an originary Word. Howe's capitalized Word, "giving rise to all pictures and graphs," might be understood as a synoptic version of the Sign. Although Peirce remains committed to the analysis of signification and the possible relationships between concepts, for Howe there is a pictorial or diagrammatic dimension to thought and writing that exceeds the relationship of a given symbol to a corresponding concept. Symbolic logic, moreover, is unvoiced. Howe's writing repeatedly reminds the reader that the aural characteristics of writing—as well as its gestural features—cannot be suppressed. She confronts symbolic logic with two modes, the visual and the aural, that exceed it as a signifying model.

Pages xii–xiii of *Pierce-Arrow* reproduce for the reader an existential graph: the words "praises to" are shown surrounded by lines and squiggles in twenty-six different permutations. On the facing pages, these are rendered verbally in such formulations as "Somebody praises somebody to his face," "Somebody praises everybody to his face," "Somebody is not praised to his face by anybody," "Somebody does not praise anybody to his face," and so on.[77] The series of minute diagrammatic variations seems designed to remove any possibility of syntactical ambiguity. It is an attempt to produce an ideal clarity by editing out the idiosyncrasies and the sounded qualities of verbal language—what Peirce at the beginning of his "Prolegomena to an Apology for Pragmaticism" called "a system of diagrammatization by means of which any course of thought can be represented with exactitude."[78]

However, in this quasi-Steinian opening-up of the multiple possibilities of the expression "to praise someone to his face," the visual threatens to supplant the symbolic. Peirce's symbols are decipherable to the logician acquainted with his system. To anyone else, however, the diagrams have a quite different effect, drawing attention to their status as images and causing the repeated words "praises to" themselves to be considered as visual figures, rather than meaning-bearing signs. In short, Howe abstracts Peirce's symbolic logic and reads it against the grain, pursuing symbols at the expense of logic. The illustrations from Peirce's manuscripts that she uses in her book are, she writes, "free to be drawings, even poems" (*P-A*, ix).

The first five pages of *Arisbe* contain both words and images: a photograph, two pages of manuscript from Peirce, and poems and prose by Howe. The photograph depicts the house *Arisbe*, where Peirce lived until his death in 1914.[79] In this it looks back to Howe's early installations, in which words and photographs were placed alongside one another.[80] Page two shows an existential graph that contains a line devoted to each of the words "sings" (a pun on signs?) and "thunders," and then several lines devoted to propositions containing the word "kills." In the top right-hand corner are three isolated diagrams containing the word "sings." The graph gains greatly in significance in juxtaposition with the poem on the facing page:

> Phenomenology of war in the Iliad
> how men appear to each other when
> gods change the appearance of things
> Send him down unwilling Captain of
> the Scorned he is singularly doomed
> Mortality is a sign for humanity our
> barbarous ancestors my passion-self

> Each assertion must maintain its icon
> Faith in proof drives him downward (*P-A*, 3)

This first poem of the book contains the first of several references to the *Iliad*.[81] Nicholls (2002) argues persuasively for the importance of Simone Weil's "The Iliad or the Poem of Force" to *Pierce-Arrow*. The essay had long been important to Howe. In a letter to Taggart, she describes it as "central" to *My Emily Dickinson*.[82] Weil, in the context of Nazism, argues for the utter pervasiveness of Homeric violence:

> Force is as pitiless to the man who possesses it, or thinks he does, as it is to its victims; the second it crushes, the first it intoxicates. The truth is, nobody really possesses it. The human race is not divided up, in *The Iliad*, into conquered persons, slaves, suppliants, on the one hand, and conquerors and chiefs on the other. In this poem there is not a single man who does not at one time or another have to bow his neck to force.[83]

Although, as I have argued with relation to "Leaves" and Pearl Harbor, the Second World War was crucial to Howe's formation as a poet, in this period she is particularly interested in the impact of the American Civil War on American intellectual life. In an interview, Howe has referred to the American Civil War as "Our Iliad" and remarked on the impact it had on the Jameses, Peirce, and Dickinson.[84] Howe's notebooks, moreover, show that *Our Iliad* was the working title for *Pierce-Arrow*. Meredith's late translations "Fragments of the Iliad in English Hexameter Verse" serve further to bring *Pierce-Arrow* into this matrix of associations. Thus, a set of reflections on force and literature spanning classical, nineteenth-century, and contemporary instances can be seen in the background of *Pierce-Arrow*.

Placed opposite the page from Peirce's manuscripts, page 3's poem introduces the linked themes of violence, destiny, and poetic speech.[85] Singing—poetic, perhaps—is set against thunder—the gods—and the word "kills." Phenomenology suggests that aesthetic experience needs, or fails, to render the lived experience of war. The phrases "Captain of/ the Scorned" and "Faith in proof" derive from a George Meredith poem entitled "Earth and Man" and prepare an eschatological theme that will reappear later in the book.[86]

Taken as a pair, pages 2 and 3 of the book lay out interwoven messages that refer to poetry and the violence of warfare.[87] The manuscript page urges a reinterpretation of the page-space of the facing page, inviting the reader to reflect on the visual qualities of *all* writing—qualities that are suppressed in our habitual use of words as an unobstructed conduit to concepts. Conversely, a Peircean countercurrent is established as the imprecision of English-language syntax is contrasted to the supposed clarity of his symbolic logic.

Turning the page, the reader is confronted with another page of Peirce in manuscript—this time the opening of his "The first chapter in Logic," dated 6 October, 1907. Beginning with an ironic prayer, the page contains the assertion that the "earliest occupation of man is poetizing, is feeling and delighting in feeling." Peirce goes on to link feeling to dreams and desires and, thence, pragmatically, to actions—the notion that, as Peirce elsewhere observed, "the rational purport of a word or other expression, lies exclusively in its conceivable bearing upon the conduct of life."[88]

Two words are heavily underlined on the manuscript page—Feeling and Action. Howe appears to be problematizing the line that runs from feeling (or poetizing) to action and, by implication, representations, in "poetizing," of action. This warrants, she seems to suggest, some scrutiny. The path from dream to action, whether or not it issues in violence, is one in which poetry is implicated. At the fringes of Peirce's manuscripts, despite themselves, lie aberrant syntax, dream logic, and the relative autonomy of the visual component of verbal signification. These unacknowledged features of the text are disallowed by its ostensible argument but remain, barely suppressed, within its range of meanings. Howe's aim, therefore, is to complicate the path from poetizing to action. She stresses a buried, speculative axis of Peirce's thought at the expense of his emphasis on the teleological line running from feeling to action. Howe chases Peirce's thought backward into the sphere of dream, severing the symbol from its referential function within symbolic logic. Peirce's insistence that the sign is the foundation of consciousness is a radical one. Howe forces Peirce's theory of signification into an accommodation with the non-conceptual penumbra—a space, potentially, of aesthetic experience—that hovers around the sign.

Howe's prose narrative begins on the facing page and quickly modulates into a space of almost mediumistic reverie. She describes her Orpheus-like descent into the "bowels" of Sterling Library in New Haven, where she spent the summer of 1997 studying Peirce's manuscripts in an atmosphere of outdated bureaucratic functionalism. This netherworld is both dull and frightening. The copycard machine has slots over which the word HELLO appears in red electronic lettering. Howe remarks, "In all their minute and terrible detail these five little icons could be teeth" (*P-A*, 5). The threat that the machine embodies might be read as the hostility of the institution to the ill-disciplined contents of the archive or as the creeping malevolence of a technologized learning environment. The machine's encoding of cash values is seen on the following page as a conduit to some sort of communion with the dead. The relationship between feeling and articulation is, once again, important. She writes,

> It is strange how the dead appear in dreams where another space provides our living space as well. Another language another way of speaking so quietly always there in the shape of memories, thoughts, feelings, which are extra-marginal outside of primary consciousness, yet must be classed as some sort of unawakened finite infinite articulation. Documents resemble people talking in sleep. To exist is one thing, to be perceived another. I can spread historical information, words and words we can never touch hovering around subconscious life where enunciation is born, in distinction from what it enunciates when nothing rests in air when what is knowledge? (*P-A*, 6)

The paragraph is an important restatement of her remarks in "Leaves" on the need for recovering the voices of history's victims. Although the idea of poetry as a means of communicating with the dead remains, Howe now places greater emphasis on unconscious experience, particularly dreams—the territory "outside of primary consciousness" in which "enunciation is born." The intangibility of this ideational referent—"nothing rests in air"—is allied to the immateriality of the linguistic sign—"words and words we can never touch." As in *Melville's Marginalia*, this emphasis on a moment of pure intellection runs alongside a commitment to encountering the book or manuscript as a material object. The writing urges us to read material and immaterial, mediated and immediate, simultaneously.

The use of facsimiles is Howe's means of exploring the interplay between embodied and disembodied 'articulation' in *Pierce-Arrow*. Poetry, dream and violence are interwoven, as we have seen, in the manuscript pages used in the *Arisbe* section of the book. In *The Leisure of the Theory Class*, the Peirce manuscript material consists almost entirely of non-textual elements. Here, Howe appears to be interested in the doodle as the graphic expression of daydreaming. The first page of this long poem contains a curious Peirce drawing that depicts people with distorted noses and feet (*P-A*, 31). This is followed, further into the poem, by a drawing of a face and the word "Epistêmy" (*P-A*, 70). There are also two facing pages of mathematical calculations that stretch down their respective pages, curving leftward in a way that emphasizes the visual qualities of the pages (*P-A*, 114–15). The final manuscript page (*P-A*, 117) comprises a set of doodles of such diverse objects as fish, horses, birds, human figures, a hatchet, a pistol, and a cannon. In contrast to the promise of clarity offered by symbolic logic, Howe advances a position that stresses the vagaries of dream logic as symbol metamorphoses into symbol.

The four manuscript pages from Swinburne, all in *The Leisure of the Theory Class*, engage with a different matrix of ideas.[89] The first is an autograph inscription ("with best regards AC Swinburne") in a copy of *Marino Faliero: A Tragedy* (*P-A*, 32). There follow manuscript pages from "Atalanta in Calydon" (43), "A Leave Taking" (45–46) and "A Ballad of Life" (122). The lines from "Atalanta in Calydon" amount to a secular account of the Creation, emphasizing extreme oppositions—life and death, light and dark—that anticipates the beginning of *Rückenfigur*: "Iseult stands at Tintagel/ on the mid stairs between/ light and dark symbolism."

The manuscript pages of "A Leave-Taking" (*P-A*, 45–46) and the beginning of "A Ballad of Life" (122) each show a high degree of visual disturbance, with numerous violent scorings-out and alterations. Text runs in curved lines and even upside down, recalling Peirce's figural play in his doodles. With Swinburne, as with Peirce, writing moves toward gesture. However, the violence present in the pages she extracts from Peirce is replaced by Swinburne's melancholic depiction of death and unachieved romantic love. The reader is made powerfully aware—as in *Birth-mark*'s brief discussion and reproduction of Shelley's manuscripts (*Birth-mark*, 19–25)—of the contrast between the wild flourishes and quasi-pictorial elements of the manuscript pages and the necessarily conventional print realization of literary texts.

In her use of the manuscripts of Peirce and Swinburne, Howe emphasizes the distinctiveness of her own use of the words of others. Placed so close to one another (as with the authors in *Melville's Marginalia*), the examples suggest a kind of literary intersubjectivity, with Howe herself as the mediating point between each of these writers. At the same time, the individual hand of these authors as encountered in manuscript underlines the subjective plane of the process of signification—Howe does, after all, include Swinburne's actual signature. The gestural nature of handwriting, then, holds the texts poised between a kind of linguistic communion and their embodied origins as the inscriptions of individuals. Peirce's doodles and Swinburne's agitated crossings-out represent the point at which a figural style of communication takes over. As Howe suggests of Dickinson's manuscripts, handwriting is a place in which the conscious aims of the writer can be accompanied by less articulable energies: "The visible handwritten sequence establishes an enunciative clearing outside intention while obeying intuition's agonistic necessity" (*Birth-mark*, 136). Howe places herself, therefore, at the meeting point between a collage-based openness to polyphony that is underwritten by the uniformity of print and the absolute monophony of the handwritten manuscript.

* * *

Howe's claims about the visual characterization of manuscripts are accompanied, as we have seen, by the contentious and apparently anachronistic suggestion at the beginning of *Pierce-Arrow* that Pierce's manuscripts anticipate the relationship between verbal and visual in twentieth-century art.[90] For a contemporary poet-artist wrestling with the impossibility of a linguistic abstraction analogous to the visual abstraction of postwar art, one of the key issues at stake is the degree to which a poem retains a purchase on the some sort of referential pattern. Writing to Lyn Hejinian in December 1979, Howe remarks, "I think there is nothing more profound than the most abstract piece when it works. This is as you say, a real problem when it comes to the written word. Because unless one can get the drive of some sort of passion into the words no matter how abstract, they seem limp."[91] *Pierce-Arrow*, which appeared twenty years after the letter was written, pursues this question of the abstract representation of affect, in this case the emotions of love and mourning. Howe's interest in Peirce's manuscripts shows her conviction of the affective range of artworks that have sought to query the boundary between finished object and preparatory work: scribbled notes, penciled marks, diagrams, collections of ephemera.

In the background of *Pierce-Arrow* is an interest in the textual underbelly of some twentieth-century art practices. Howe is especially drawn to Duchamp's notebooks and the use of pencil and lined paper in the work of several artists associated with minimalism or Process Art in the 1960s. In all of these cases, the verbal and the visual exert distinct pressures on the reader or viewer.

Howe has said that Duchamp's work—both sculpture and accompanying notes—was particularly important to her at the time she was making the transition from visual art to poetry.[92] The principal English-language versions of the notes are Arturo Schwarz's 1969 facsimile (mentioned by Howe in her interview with Thomson, n.p.); Richard Hamilton and George Heard Hamilton's 1960 typographical version of the 1934 Green Box; and, most comprehensive of all, Paul Matisse's *Notes* (a full-color facsimile published in 1980). It is the Hamilton and Schwarz editions that are most likely to have influenced Howe's visual poetry. In the 1980s and 1990s, Howe was especially interested in typographical versions of manuscripts—versions, in other words, that brought the order of the typesetter into conflict with the disorder of the manuscript page. In the Hamilton version of Duchamp's

Green Box of 1934, *The Bride Stripped Bare by Her Bachelors, Even*, the chaotic page space of Duchamp's notes—the wavering lines, squiggles, diagrams, deletions, ringed words and so on—is reproduced, as far as is possible in the relatively standard form available to typesetters.

The result is something far more complex than a conventionally set page. Many of the pages resemble examples of post-Olsonian poetry. The Hamilton edition devotes one page to each 'poem,' so some of the shorter notes are isolated on the page, including the one beginning "Make a hinge picture." The opening of "Scattering as Behavior Toward Risk," which draws on the genetic text of *Billy Budd*, is only the most obvious of Howe's texts to be influenced by such renderings of manuscripts. This edition, however, only runs text along the horizontal or vertical axes. The Schwarz edition, which presents the English translation in a typographical version on a page facing the original, includes material run diagonally that is comparable in layout to Howe's visual experimentation in *Thorow* and *Eikon Basilike*.

With their eccentricity and visual dynamism, it is not difficult to see why Peirce's manuscripts might remind Howe of Duchamp. The notes that accompany Duchamp's *Large Glass* were only ever published in limited editions, known as the Box of 1914 and the Green Box. Duchamp's working notes, written mainly in 1913 and 1914, are not a programmatic set of guidelines for decoding the symbolism of the *Large Glass*, which he would begin in 1915 and on which he would continue working until he abandoned it in 1923. The notes are undated, and, when published in limited editions in 1914 and 1934, the leaves were not given a sequential order. Some notes do discuss aspects of the artwork, but others are speculative documents that touch on the fields of science, mathematics, and aesthetics.[93] There are diagrams, sketches, photos, and even musical manuscript. The handwritten pages are covered in crossings-out, lines drawn across the page, and inserted text—precisely the kinds of textual disorder that can be found in Peirce's notes.

The notes and projects for the *Large Glass* are a tangled mass of thoughts and conjectures that stray across disciplines. The contours of the thought cannot be dissociated from the form in which it expressed. The hesitant, fragmentary nature of the mental processes involved is made more apparent when the manuscript pages are made available in facsimile. In the 1914 and 1934 boxes, Duchamp clearly desired to present a processual work, one in which unfinishedness was a fundamental principle. In Howe's versions of Swinburne and Peirce, the two thinkers are presented in a way that accentuates the uncertainty in the compositional process. Doodles, in Peirce's case, show a mind shifting from conscious cognitive activity to representations of visual daydreaming; Swinburne's effulgent aural sculptures are accompanied by the violence of his crossings-out.

A different aspect of the pressure exerted by the verbal on visual art can be found in Howe's relationship to the work of another artist whom Howe has described as crucial to her development as a writer, Agnes Martin:

> Agnes Martin had a show at the Greene Gallery that consisted of a series of small grid drawings in pen, ink and pencil over thin washes of color. As I remember it, they were all the same size. A single word sometimes two or three placed directly underneath each one served as a title. Even the name "untitled" seen in relation to these severely abstract grids acted as an opening, almost the way a scrim does onstage. There, if the light catches it, what you thought was background becomes transparent and you see something new and unexpected that was always there, but hidden.[94]

Howe appears to be drawn, on one hand, to the severe simplicity of this abstract work, and, on the other, by her conviction that a conceptual dimension is opened up as soon as the work is related to a word. The word acts as a conduit to a different experience of the visual. This is especially true when there is no obvious match between word and image. Martin's titles have often included words or phrases that refer to the natural world, such as "Flower in the Wind," "Leaf," "The Cliff," and "Night Sea."

In Martin's work, the word "Leaf," for example, is made present as a verbal sign but withheld as a visual one. Neither mode corresponds to the other. As Rosalind Krauss observes, representation in Martin depends, quite literally, on where you are standing. Martin's faintly penciled grids dissolve the "separation of figure against ground" through the movement of appearance and disappearance as the viewer moves closer to or further away from the canvas.[95] The possibility of representation, then, is acknowledged by the coming into being of the faint grid as the viewer approaches the canvas, but it cannot be realized because of the abstraction of that canvas. The fragility and uncertainty of the penciled lines in Martin's work, moreover, assert the singularity of the individual act of mark-making, a feature of the compositional process that Howe recovers in her facsimiles from Peirce and Swinburne. As Howe observes in relation to Creeley and Duncan, the penciled grid can indicate a point at which the particular creative act encounters a 'universal' potential for expression:

> *A poem—that place Duncan calls a "meadow," occurs in a precinct of relations, recognitions, parallels, mirrors, doublings. The creative imagination, local and universal in its singularity and range, is the "eternal pasture folded in all thought" a poet wanders from, and is permitted to return to. Creeley*

> *emphasized the passive verb form. The creative imagination, while constantly maintaining the specific, thinks itself through penciled grids, points, abstract geometric lines, color field washes Agnes Martin, Hilma af Klint, and Emma Kunz are variously given to use.*
>
> ("Leaf Flower in the Wind Falling Blue
> The Dark River," n.p.; Howe's italics)

The processual aspects of Peirce's manuscripts can certainly, as Howe suggests, be seen to share something with work produced by German artist Hanne Darboven, and text-oriented works by Richard Serra and Robert Smithson. All of these artists were active in New York in the late 1960s, when Howe was also living and working as an artist in the city. In a Darboven work such as "Kleine Konstruktion," for example, there are numerous sheets of ruled paper covered with handwritten scrawls, diagrams and arrangements of figures.[96] Richard Serra, an artist latterly associated with large-scale metallic sculpture, established the conceptual framework for his later work with the late-1960s piece "Verb List" (1967–68). This work is composed of two facing pages, each containing two handwritten columns of infinitives. The verbs used begin "to roll/ to crease/ to fold/ to store/ to bend/ to shorten/ to twist" and continue to list a sequence of methods that Serra himself would use. Robert Smithson's "Heap of Language" (1966), a visual text in which words referring to language (tongue, lingo, vernacular, etc.) are piled in a pyramid shape, is another example of art that uses a relatively simple handwritten text and squared paper.[97] Each of these works presents, in various ways, a critique of the notion that art resides in the well-crafted aesthetic object. In the case of Serra and Duchamp, the works ostensibly function as the prelude to something else; in effect, though, they are works in their own right.

In all of this artistic work, there is a preoccupation with the possible place of text in art. Rather than use the text as a graphic device, in the manner of concrete poetry, these artworks have a provisional, draft-like quality and investigate the uncertain status of penciled jottings. Howe's bold interpretative act in reading Peirce in this context can be seen as a continuation of her impulse to find a different historical frame for her own late-twentieth-century aesthetic dilemmas. She seeks to make manifest a nonconformist aesthetic practice latent in Peirce's manuscript writings. The moment of writing—the transaction between intellection and its material realization—is shown to be a moment that is both unstable and open to the potential for visual figuration. Manuscripts become, in this view, a space in which the dream life of the text is discernible. Howe's attention is particularly drawn to the processual, vagabond, wild, oneiric features of textuality.

The wayward—and arguably indefensible—assertion in *Pierce-Arrow* that there is an aesthetic dimension to Peirce's manuscripts is Howe's realization of her remark that "dead appear in dreams" and that documents "resemble people talking in sleep" (*P-A*, 6).

The first two sections of *Pierce-Arrow*, with their extensive use of facsimiles, are Howe's most sustained attempt at establishing a text that lies somewhere between literature and visual art. It is unsurprising that Howe refers often in interviews to the period when she was making the transition, through such diverse figures as Charles Olson and Agnes Martin, from visual artist to poet; her work has remained suspended between those two fields of activity.[98] *Pierce-Arrow* shows text as it becomes art. It is neither the asignifying abstraction of some concrete poetry, nor a form of ekphrasis, but a mode in which verbal content and visual realization are placed in dynamic juxtaposition. The relative sobriety of tone in *Pierce-Arrow* is combined with an enthusiastic appeal to the marginal components of compositional activity. The materiality of the handwritten manuscript is integral to this project. A writer's handwriting and doodles open a figural window to the unconscious dimension of composition. An unusual form of visual-verbal collage facilitates 'telepathic' correspondences between quite distinct authors and texts. In Howe's work, then, material and immaterial, mediated and immediate are interdependent terms, equally present in Howe's pursuit of "some sort of unawakened finite infinite articulation" (*P-A*, 6)."

CHAPTER 6

The Late Lyric

Much of Howe's recent work is defined by an encounter with lyric. In *Rückenfigur*, the *Bed Hangings* poems, and *Souls of the Labadie Tract* Howe incorporates repetitive structures into brief, short-lined, sound-driven poems that have a remarkable density.[1] Although repetition, as I argued in my discussion of *Thorow*, has long been part of Howe's technique, sound patterning, amplified by the compression of the writing, takes on a new prominence in this late work. These poems push at the edges of what might plausibly be called a lyric poem. This affinity with the lyric mode invites a reading that is oriented around a single voice, yet this notional voice is repeatedly exploded into polyphony by Howe's continuing use of collage as an organizational principle.

The lyric has been a much contested space in innovative writing in recent years, particularly in discussions of what might come in the wake of language writing.[2] One of the poets associated with the supposed renovation of lyric, Elizabeth Willis, has written trenchantly of the "late lyric" and its flexibility, self-awareness, and multiplicity. Willis stresses the overlap between language writing and lyric and is keen to debunk the clichés that have collected around both the avant-garde and mainstream positions. Willis points to the historical openness of the mode: "There has been a shift within contemporary lyric practice, whereby the overall structure and energy of the lyric is overlaid or mixed with other influences, forms and rhetorical sampling, often in significant ways. Anywhere from Aristotle to Dickinson to Lorca to Spicer, it has been acknowledged that the lyric poem comes not strictly from within but from elsewhere; it is not *self*-expressive except to the extent that ideas of self or voice are never entirely absent from the tonal shadings of language."[3]

In this view, the lyric is incorrigibly social, albeit often in ways that are at least implicitly oppositional.[4] Willis cites Stevens's famous description of poetry as an unstable, "destructive force" and "a violence from within that protects us from a violence without."[5] Lyric poetry is, thus, a kind of experiment in consciousness: "In the slipperiness between reality and imagination [the poem] leaves a trace of the apparent impossibility of its own emergence into words."[6]

Although Howe is not affiliated in any way to the 'new lyric' or any other loose tendency of that kind, it is clear that her writing from *Pierce-Arrow* onward engages with short form, sound, and subjective utterance in ways that are comparable to Willis's conception of the late lyric. It is not easy to think of Howe as a lyric poet. Indeed, her long serial poems have often been discussed in relation to the kinds of large cultural upheaval typically associated with epic. She has described herself as a poet of war, and her early writing often has a deep commitment to exploring the aftershocks of colonial and military violence. Yet sound is clearly of central importance from an early stage in her work. When lyric qualities become more prominent in the later writing, it is often in the context of such apparently unlyrical subject matter as textual scholarship, philosophical pragmatism, or home furnishings.

Lyric writing after modernism can be explained by neither an approximation to song; nor brevity; nor the continuity of the lyric subject; nor a passionate, intimate, or even private register. Yet traces of all these features, whether ironically deployed or not, can be found in Howe's writing, despite its formal radicalism. I do not want simply to argue that the disruptive energies of this radicalism somehow coexist with lyric content, although this is sometimes so. It is not the case, in other words, that there is a necessary opposition between disjunctive language and lyricism. Such apparently anti-lyrical impulses as syntactical fragmentation or citation, for example, can have a *specifically* lyric function in this work. It is, paradoxically, in the assault on conventionally lyric attributes that a kind of pathos of attenuation emerges. The wounded syntax and stranded textual fragments of Howe's texts, I believe, contrive a form of lyric effect through their very insufficiency. Textual brokenness itself becomes a lyric motif. One way of viewing this brokenness would be to see it as an index of Stevens's invocation of poetic violence. In Howe's case, however, the boundary between the violence within and that without is porous, and the traffic between the two domains is lively. The evasiveness that Stevens prizes in his "Noble Rider" essay is more directly related in Howe to formal discontinuities.[7]

For Howe, an uncompromised version of epic or an uncomplicated return to lyric is inconceivable. Howe unwrites these forms, much as she unspells the landscape in *Thorow*. Howe's late lyric style is a breaking-down of subjective utterance that nonetheless retains a grasp of the subjective moment in any utterance. The poetry's polyphony and its abstinence from the narrative coherence offered by syntax mobilize a larger notion of lyric affect underwritten by a truncated, elliptical quality and by close attention to the writing's sonic features.

Mutlu Konuk Blasing's monograph *Lyric Poetry* places great stress on the somatic and sonic grounds of poetic utterance, which provide a kind of non-semantic, physical basis for the business of making meaning. "Lyric language," she argues, "presents—to the ear—that which resists communication and the will of an individual 'speaker.'"[8] Blasing develops this notion persuasively in her discussion of Stevens's "pressure of reality":

> The subject in language is an individuated sensibility produced by and resounding a personal and communal history in words. But she is never self-identical because she is an echoic medium. What the 'pressure' of reality threatens and what other, contemporaneous discourses may bracket is the audibility of that subject. Poetry ensures the audibility of the echoic personal/ communal subject—not in what is said but what is heard in the sounds of what is said.[9]

Howe's late poetry and criticism, which shows an intense focus on Stevens and sound, seems much preoccupied with relations between "the sounds of what is said" and the "personal/ communal subject." It locates its lyric qualities in compression, acoustic effects, disjunction, and collage. There should be no contradiction, this poetry seems to say, between the unique experiential unity, conscious and unconscious, that is the distinct preserve of each individual and the insistently social experiencing of that selfhood (even to oneself) through language. It is in the interplay between these domains that voice emerges.

In a 2009 article on Jonathan Edwards and Wallace Stevens in *Chicago Review*, Howe argues that the writing of each of these authors offers an experience of "the granting of grace in an ordinary room, in a secular time" ("Choir Answers to Choir," 58). Focusing on sound and intuitive experiences of reading in ways that have something in common with Blasing's thesis, she remarks, "Delight springs from the sense of fluid sound patterns that phonetic utterance excites in me" ("Choir," 57). Howe opens with essay with a long citation from Edwards that describes how he felt, when reading the Bible on the bank of the Hudson River, "a harmony between something in [his] heart, and those sweet and powerful words" (ibid., 51). In describing the physical composition of Edwards's homemade notebooks, Howe offers a version of poetry that is at once sound-driven, polyphonic and a record of the self's encounter with the world. She writes,

> Grassroots out-of-tune steps and branches, quotations of psalms, dissonant scripture clusters are pressed between coarse cardboard covers with frayed edges. Harmony continues to exist through fact and experience—though there is no reason why it should—nor is there any proof you can read back to the notation of one mind's inner relation with nature's vibratory hum. Lyric poets can't move heaven and earth in order to say things language separates from music through yearning muted rhythmic pulse—through stepwise voice motion—("Choir," 54)

This hesitant and provisional characterization of poetry's acoustic operations, couched of necessity in negative terms, suggests an expanded "harmony" that embraces the dissonant. The equivocal syntax of the sentence in the citation makes obscure the relation between language and music that it announces. It is, as in the opening vignette of Edwards on the Hudson, another of Howe's allegories of the rapturously destabilizing power of the reading process.

Rückenfigur

The German word *Rückenfigur* refers to the typically inscrutable figure with back turned in landscape painting, notably that of Caspar David Friedrich.[10] In *Rückenfigur*, the significance of the phrase "love is in the mind," from the last line of *Pierce-Arrow*'s dedicatory poem to the poet's late husband, David von Schlegell, is explored (*P-A*, 5). The phrase captures the double-edged nature of the book's relationship to love. To say that something is "all in the mind" has, of course, a dismissive ring, suggesting a delusional state, a hypochondriacal fantasy perhaps. Yet the poem clearly desires to communicate the intensity of love and its painful obverse, mourning. Love, Howe might also be saying, is both intensely private and necessarily public, bound up in the shared social experience of language.

The poem contains glancing encounters with German Romanticism, the language of color and perspective, bird imagery, and Greek mythology. However, it is dominated by the medieval legend of Tristram and Iseult. *Rückenfigur* does not commit itself to any one of the many versions of the story, though the version retold by Swinburne seems especially pertinent.[11] In the tale, the two unwittingly drink a magic potion that causes them to fall in love as Tristram accompanies Iseult to Cornwall so she can marry his uncle Mark. After the marriage, Tristram moves to Brittany, where he marries another Iseult, Iseult aux Mains Blanches. He is consoled, perhaps, by the name she shares with his lover, but the marriage remains unconsummated. His love for the first Iseult eventually causes him to fall ill. He requests a servant to fetch Iseult by sea, telling him to fly a black sail on the return journey if Iseult is not on board and a white sail if she is. Iseult boards the ship and returns with the servant, but her jealous namesake, who has learnt of the plan, tells Tristram the ship is flying a black sail. Tristram dies of grief. On landing and finding his body, Iseult dies too, kissing her dead lover's lips.[12]

Howe unpicks the legend in order to present a reflection on romantic love that is at once a rendering of emotion and an appraisal of the cultural meanings borne by that emotion. The key to the Tristram and Iseult story for Howe is the ending, when Iseult encounters the dead body of Tristram and, as elsewhere in her work, a female character in the presence of the boundary between life and death acts as a transfigurative motif. The closing tableau can, thus, be compared to the role of Ophelia's death in *Pythagorean Silence*, to Cordelia and Hedvig in *The Liberties*, and to Mary Magdalene's encounter with the risen Christ in *The Nonconformist's Memorial*. The importance of the ending of the Tristram story is underlined by one of Howe's working notebooks for *Rückenfigur*, which contains a prose version of Iseult's words to the dead Tristram pasted into the beginning. The passage is marked by Howe, "This says it all. It is the poem." Pasted into the back page of the same notebook is the following rendering of the end of the tale: "She embraced him and stretched herself, kissed his mouth and face, and right straightly she clung to him, and stretched her body to his body, and laid her mouth to his mouth. Then she yielded up her spirit and died here beside him for sorrow of her lover. Tristram died for longing, Ysolt for that she came too late. Tristram died for love, and the fair Isolt for pity."[13]

In Swinburne's version, surpassing romantic love is the dominant theme, especially in the poem's extraordinary prelude. The love of Tristram and Iseult is presented sympathetically, despite the transgression of adultery—the breaking of the law referred to by Howe's text as "Mark's moral right to Iseult" (*P-A*, 132). The magic potion they both imbibe is a device that exempts the lovers from the usual judgments and complicates the moral fabric of the tale. In their relationship to law, Tristram and Iseult can be compared to another figure in the poem, Antigone, who desired to bury her dead brother Polynices despite the edict that his corpse should be left unburied because he had rebelled against the city of Thebes. Both stories show the tacit endorsement of love—erotic or maternal—that transcends the law.

Although the form of *Pierce-Arrow* is sui generis, a blend of poetry, prose, and images, it is certainly true that the book hosts the after-echoes of both epic and lyric modes. In other words, the literary modes conventionally associated with the imperatives of the public and private domains are placed alongside one another. The treatment in *Rückenfigur* of the medieval romance, filtered through Swinburne's lyrical post-Romantic voicing, is balanced by references to the epic action of the *Iliad* in earlier parts of the book. The ideology of violence is questioned in Howe's handling of Peirce's manuscripts and the *Iliad*, whereas *Rückenfigur* subjects the ideology of love—of which lyric poetry is an exemplary form—to sympathetic scrutiny. It is significant that, although *Rückenfigur* was the first of the three parts of *Pierce-Arrow* to be published, it is placed at the end of the book.[14]

Although apparently more public in orientation, the evacuated and impersonal style of *Arisbe* and *The Leisure of the Theory Class* is ultimately a response to privation, voiced from the positions of the widowed, that negates the epic shifts of the *Iliad*. In *Rückenfigur*, conversely, personal loss modulates into collective privation, as the painterly *Rückenfigur*—a figure of deathly withdrawal—comes to stand for the fragility of both private memory and public history.[15]

What kind of lyric poetry is Howe writing in *Rückenfigur*? The verse is short-lined. The lines, of roughly similar length, are arranged into fourteen-line stanzas. There are typically between five and eight syllables to a line. The sequence is concerned, however obliquely, with love. Thus, the poem inserts itself awkwardly into a number of poetic histories: the medieval romance and its revoicing in Victorian poetry, the Renaissance sonnet sequence, and the modernist long poem.

Yet Howe's lyricism remains intractably contemporary. For Howe, the provisional nature of the fragment—a sine qua non, of course, of many different kinds of avant-garde writing—allows her to write in a many-voiced and self-qualifying style that always curbs its own totalizing ambitions. It is through this quality of incompletion that a specifically lyric quality emerges. In writing of the late modernist tradition, the fragment is no longer experienced with the full estranging force that would once have been its burden. In Howe's writing, a pervasive sense of insufficiency becomes the formal index of the various barriers that her poetry encounters: the inadequacy of the historical record, the inaccessibility of the dead, the intransigence of the word. The fragment, woven into crisscrossing patterns of associations, is, thus, built into the formal and conceptual layers of the text as an insistent reminder of loss.

A line such as "ruin garland effigy figment" (*P-A*, 142) impels the reader toward a completion; as the line breaks, the words are left stranded and denuded of context. Such textual disjecta assume a lyric quality through the evacuation of subjectivity and the curtailment of sense-making. In other words, the very circumscription of the utterance gives rise to a form of pathos. The quality of arrestedness, always suggestive of a larger whole, constitutes a distilled lyric displacement of narrative that permeates each aspect of verbal utterance. The interplay between syntactical disintegration, aural coherence, and collage lends Howe's work a lyric voice that is paradoxically predicated on the loss of voice.

"Surveillance is a constant/ theme in lyric poetry," writes Howe (*P-A,* 138), lending the poem's thematics of looking a predatory edge. Is she referring to the gaze of the *Rückenfigur* or to the viewer of the painting, unable to view the turned-away figure? Does lyric poetry tend toward the moment of arrest captured in the stasis of painting? With surveillance, the motif of self and other that lies at the heart of the love lyric is invaded by the imperatives of power. Howe's poem is driven by doubles and opposites, as the other disintegrates into projections of the self's desire. Neither identity nor non-identity is sufficient; the poem wrestles with a powerful impulse toward disintegration, notwithstanding its status as a singular utterance.[16]

Such oscillations are discernible from the opening of the poem, which places Iseult at Tintagel, "on the mid stairs between/ light and dark symbolism" (*P-A,* 129). The poem's baldest example of such symbolism is the sail, either white or black—life or death, love or its absence. Iseult, the poem's love object, is double (reminiscent of Howe's treatment of Florimell and her "counterfeit" in *Defenestration*). One page-poem begins with an assertion of Antigone's doubleness, as both daughter and half sister of Oedipus, and then translates the motif to Iseult:

> Antigone bears her secret in
> her heart like an arrow she is
> sent twice over into our dark
> social as if real life as if real
> person proceeding into self-
> knowledge as if there were no
> proof just blind right reason
> to assuage our violent earth
> Ysolt's single vision of union
> Precursor shadow self by self
> in open place or on an acting
> platform two personae meeting
> Strophe antistrophe which is
> which dual unspeakable cohesion (*P-A,* 143)

The paternity of Antigone, daughter of Oedipus's incestuous marriage to Jocasta, is a message relayed twice, into "our dark social." She remains hypothetical, an "as if" that is never fully realized. Despite her self-destruction, she represents a counter to the "blind right reason" of the city-state. The doubleness of Ysolt depends on the other Iseult, Iseult aux Blanches Mains, who consigns Tristram to death by falsely reporting the color of the approaching ship's sail. In this case, an either/ or choice is confounded by the second Iseult's duplicity in describing the event. Despite this preoccupation with doubleness, however, there is, as elsewhere in Howe's poetry, an accompanying interest in what is here called "dual unspeakable cohesion." By this, Howe means the *similarity* in difference, which binds together dualisms, oppositions, and antinomies. It is a combustible motif, in this case a way of expressing both internal division ("shadow self by self") and the knife-edge of significance—the white/ black sail.[17]

This doubling develops the Hector/ Achilles/ Patroclus pairings of the *Arisbe* section (*P-A*, 27–29), in which Patroclus wears the amour of Achilles and is killed by the Trojan Hector.[18] Hector puts on the amour and is then, eventually, slain by Achilles, who now bears the shield of Achilles. Achilles, therefore, kills an impersonation of himself. Howe remarks drily, "Iliadic heroism another situation/ of unstable identity" (*P-A*, 26). Although it is not unusual for fluid subjectivity to be an explicit or implicit feature of twentieth-century poetry, Howe is performing an unusual feat of anachronism when she applies this to Homer. Rather than view epic as a form that narrates conflict with the ultimate aim of social cohesion, Howe uses it to assert a processual notion of identity—even at its most heroic—as a series of phantasmatic feints and masks.

Pierce-Arrow's preoccupation with figures of instability ironizes both epic and lyric as poetic modes. Private and public, love and the social are each invaded by the other. Epic, like the laurels of the poet in "Leaves," is viewed with suspicion and presented as a literary cover for "Ramping brute force" (*P-A*, 29).[19] The lyric potentialities of *Rückenfigur* repeatedly fold into an implicit questioning of lyric as a mask for the tyrannous imperatives of desire: this is love as "dread pull" and "determinist caparison" (*P-A*, 129). All boundaries are porous in this work. When Howe writes, "Assuredly I see division" or "Two thoughts in strife" (*P-A*, 134, 135), her skepticism about totalizing visions appears to extend across representations of both psychic and social wholeness.

"Iliadic heroism" is rejected in favor of a mode of poetic utterance that emerges from the "ruin of philosophy" (*P-A*, 129) and challenges the ideological undertow of both epic and lyric modes. Howe was reading Schlegel at the time of writing *Pierce-Arrow*, and it is possible to discern in the book an alignment with aspects of his thought. Howe's working notebooks cite, among many passages from Schlegel, Critical fragment 65: "Poetry is republican speech: a speech which is its own law and end unto itself, and in which all parts are free citizens and have the right to vote."[20] Poetry, in other words, cannot be legislated for by aesthetics or philosophy, except insofar as it produces an immanent philosophy or aesthetics through the example of its own self-creation.

Romantic poetry, writes Schlegel in his famous Athenaeum fragment 116, is free of the world-capturing representational ambitions of epic. Instead, it can "hover at the midpoint between the portrayed and the portrayer, free of all real and ideal self-interest, on the wings of poetic reflection, and can raise that reflection again and again to a higher power, can multiply it in an endless succession of mirrors."[21] The proliferating ironies of poetic language serve to produce a self-reflexive aesthetic, poised between an object and its non-identical representation, that thrives on instability and an apparently limitless interpretative range. Howe's encounter with nineteenth-century German painting and philosophy in *Pierce-Arrow*, therefore, becomes aligned with those—such as Lacoue-Labarthe and Nancy—who find the origins of modernist aesthetics in early Romanticism.[22]

The last poem from *Rückenfigur* is perhaps its most lyrical:

> Day binds the wide Sound
> Bitter sound as truth is
> silent as silent tomorrow
> Motif of retreating figure
> arrayed beyond expression
> huddled unintelligible air
> Theomimesis divinity message
> I have loved come veiling
> Lyrist come veil come lure
> echo remnant sentence spar
> never never form wherefor
> Wait some recognition you
> Lyric over us love unclothe
> Never forever whoso move (*P-A*, 144)

The poem sounds an Orphic note, with lyre and lyric overseeing a reflection on the "motif of retreating figure." Orpheus's grief (cf *P-A*, 132) is "beyond expression" and "unintelligible." The poem's "Sound" is both aural sound and the Long Island Sound, which is close to the house where Howe has lived since the 1970s, and on which von Schlegell often sailed. "Echo remnant sentence spar" reasserts Howe's reliance on the pun and the fragment, language as flotsam. At the same time, "spar" may refer to the use of wood in von Schlegell's sculpture. There is no hope in the poem's anxious backward glance, no means of finally gaining access to the dead. Yet, if "Documents resemble people talking in sleep" at the beginning of the book (*P-A*, 6), then it is through textual assemblages such as *Pierce-Arrow* that the dead do exert some sort of pressure on the present. The "wide" and "bitter" sound is a way of assigning a form of corporeally identified aural coherence to the textual flotsam that Howe brings together. *Rückenfigur* offers a way out of the stylistic impasse generated by the aridly prosaic textures of parts of *The Leisure of the Theory Class*, regrounding personal trauma in a self-aware lyric style that is both public and responsible.

Bed Hangings

The two *Bed Hangings* books, both of which are dominated by the theme of fabric, mount a lyrically oriented exploration of the notion of poetic relation different from that explored in the *Scare Quotes* parts *The Midnight*. In these poems, the fragment and disjunction have more weight than in the more openly associative writing of the *Scare Quotes* sequences.

The linguistic texture of *Bed Hangings I* is much influenced by a 1961 investigation of the material culture of New England called *Bed Hangings: A Treatise on Fabrics and Styles in the Curtaining of Beds, 1650–1850*.[23] From this source, we learn that, in the average seventeenth-century New England settler's house, there was "a bedstead in every room of the house except the kitchen."[24] These beds were usually surrounded by curtaining, providing Howe with a visual metaphor for maternal self-enclosure as well as theatrical representation. The bed hanging serves, as Howe observes at the beginning of *Scare Quotes I*, as an image for the stage curtain, making it a functional analogue of the interleaf. In *Bed Hangings: A Treatise*, a list of materials that runs to more than twenty pages is devoted to the difficulty of defining such vocabulary for fabrics as moreen or harateen, words that are available to us in textual sources but whose meaning is uncertain to the contemporary reader. Transplanted to the context of Howe's poem, they form part of her long-established interest in the emergence of a distinctively American vocabulary and manner of speech.

In *Bed Hangings II*, lace—an overwhelmingly European decorative fabric—is the dominant motif. In this case, the chief resource is Bury Palliser's

The History of Lace, which provides textual material and two images used at the beginning of *Bed Hangings I*.[25] Lace is 'translated' from European into American cultural life ("1775 landscape America/ blindstitched to French/ edge silk damask cover" [*TM*, 101]), much like the "intercolonial" movement of the preachers of the Great Awakening. Although lace was for centuries a symbol of authority, wealth, and power, Howe appears more interested in its regional accents.[26]

Like the interleaf, lace represents a semi-permeable barrier. The larger part of the fabric, moreover, is intangible. Lace might be taken as representative of Howe's own preoccupations: her interest in the materiality of the book is not an end in itself. Instead it coexists with Howe's equally strong interest in the immaterial: religious belief, grace, and ecstasy—all of these seen as ciphers for the resistant strangeness of poetic language.[27]

The *Bed Hangings* poems are mainly—particularly in the shorter of the two series, *Bed Hangings II*—brief, dense, and highly fractured. Whereas threads of association are readily discernible across the fluent prose sections of *Scare Quotes*, the *Bed Hangings* poems are often impenetrable word clusters that bring to the fore the sheer intractability of their discrete particles of language. Even so, the poems are not devoid of associative logic. They glancingly present tiny pieces of New England history in which the themes of enthusiasm, migration, and craftwork are dominant. The enthusiastical excesses of the Great Awakening are also a feature of the writing, as Howe explores the ways in which human cultures embed the particular in a specific place.

Although in many previous works Howe had focused on the damage effected by the patriarchal and the martial, in the *Bed Hangings* poems, the feminine and domestic are brought into her examination of the development of cultural meaning. Fabrics are relational—techniques and styles of lace move to America from England or France. Now, instead of the top-down model of colonial aggression explored in *Thorow*, Howe writes of less immediately visible ways in which a distinctive culture takes shape. The guiding metaphor is now the network—fabric imagined as an analogue of the visual, verbal, and aural relations in the poem.

If *Scare Quotes* describes the material book as a means of establishing a transitional object that operates at the familial level, the *Bed Hangings* books take bed hangings and lace as the means of making a similar point at the cultural level. The *Scare Quotes* sections emphasize the curious lines of association that books propagate as the bearers of affect. In the *Bed Hangings* poems, the emphasis is on the immateriality and the resistance to capture that the airy substance of lace—"cobweb gossamer ephemera" (*TM*, 93)—represents.

The first page of *Bed Hangings II* stresses something of this intangibility:

> Secrecy let me light you in
> In shadow something other
> echoed and re-echoed only
>
> The dark who can veneer it
> That conjoint abstraction will
> come to snow let us go back (*TM*, 89)

The "secrecy" here is presented as both visual—"dark"—and aural—"echoed and re-echoed." The reader is led into the poem ("let me light you in") by a guide who can shed no light. Instead of intelligibility, the reader is confronted with a hall of mirrors. The phrase "conjoint abstraction" derives from chapter 5 of *The Master of Ballantrae* ("it was strange how we turned to that conjoint abstraction of the family itself, and sought to bolster up the airy nothing of its reputation").[28] In Howe's poem, this abstraction is another one of the mysterious double-faced entities that resist the interpreter's quest to confer meaning. This particular poem does not pursue this quest, turning back on itself as it concludes with a retreat: "let us go back."

Howe places this poem at the end of "Furious Calm," one of two essays on Wallace Stevens that she published in *The Wallace Stevens Journal* in 2004.[29] In these brief pieces, Howe places Stevens in a line of pragmatist thought, with its origin in the Great Awakening-era Puritanism of Jonathan Edwards. In "*The Collected Poems*: The Next Fifty Years" she refers to Stevens's studies at Harvard under Josiah Royce and George Santayana. In "Furious Calm," she cites William James in a way that can be aligned with the preoccupation with "relation" in *The Midnight*. James writes, "Both the sensational and the relational parts of reality are dumb. They say absolutely nothing about themselves. We it is who have to speak for them."[30] Howe identifies this as an apt description of Stevens's working methods:

> In experimental transactions with concrete particularities, he sounds the myriad shifting sensations (pre-discursive, fragmentary, unpredictable) of seemingly simple objects, weathers, hours and events. The fluid interaction among reality, intuition, and imagination is benevolent, relentless vitality of nature and of poetry. ("Furious Calm," 136)[31]

These "experimental transactions with concrete particularities" might serve as a description of Howe's own late style in poems such as that beginning "Secrecy let me light you in." The word "snow," for example, is surrounded by a repetitive verbal texture that asserts the aural qualities of language, not its communicative features. The words "echoed and re-echoed" and "let us go back" similarly draw the reader toward a kind of repetitive non-signification. Such passages are guided as much by the aural signature of rhyme's return of the same as they are by meaning. The decontextualized "Conjoint abstraction" is set against the concreteness of the mini-narrative of the excursion curtailed because of snow.

Howe is, no doubt, also thinking of William James's "conjunctive" and "disjunctive" relations, as expressed in his essay "The Thing and its Relations":

> Radical empiricism takes conjunctive relations at their face value, holding them to be as real as the terms united by them. The world it represents as a collection, some parts of which are conjunctively and others disjunctively related. Two parts, themselves disjoined, may nevertheless hang together by intermediaries with which they are severally connected, and the whole world eventually may hang together similarly, inasmuch as *some* path of conjunctive transition by which to pass from one of its parts to another may always be discernible.[32]

These remarks offer a useful model for framing the greater tendency toward an integrative poetics in Howe's later writing. The emphasis on the fragment in the earlier work is, from the mid-1990s, accompanied by an increasing involvement in ideas of relation. The work remains highly disjunctive, but the impulse to conjoin these disparate fragments is stronger. James's emphasis on the reality of relations finds clear parallels in *The Midnight*, even in the shadowy and often subterranean forms of connection that persist in the *Bed Hangings* books. Howe's writing, then, stretches James' model to accommodate unconscious experience and to encompass both private and collective histories. Of Stevens's recollections of Royce and Santayana, Howe remarks, "Perhaps, looking back, Stevens understood that his calling had always been to address, by way of technical innovation and sound pattern, the same problematic his philosophy teachers had addressed discursively. 'Poetry,' he says in *Adagia*, 'must resist the intelligence almost successfully'" ("*The Collected Poems*: the Next 50 Years," 232). The "light" conferred by poetry in the page-poem from *Bed Hangings II* is grounded in the passage she cites just before it in "Furious Calm," which is from a speech given by Stevens when receiving a medal from the Poetry Society of America in 1951. The passage concludes, "[Poetry] makes itself manifest in a kind of speech that comes from secrecy.... It is to be found beneath the poet's word and deep within the reader's eye in those chambers in which the genius of poetry sits alone with her candle in a moving solitude."[33] Adapting Stevens's use of secrecy and candlelight, Howe, then, finds in the occulted quality of Stevens's description of poetry a precedent for her own late work. In this period, as her teaching indicates, she appears, like thinkers such as Richard Poirier and Joan Richardson, to find a pragmatist framework for the American authors who interest her: Edwards, Emerson, William James, Henry James, and Stevens.[34]

The clustering technique that Howe uses in parts of the *Bed Hangings* poems allows her to accumulate groups of artifacts without specifying the relations between them. In this way, she identifies what she admires in Stevens: "what is secret, wild, double, and various in the near-at-hand" ("Furious Calm," 135). The poems combine the historical ambition of her earlier writing with an ability to address the "near-at-hand"—in this case, private and domestic experience. Yet these concrete details are insistently read back into their collective, social meanings.

At several points, the *Bed Hangings* poems make use of specialist vocabulary drawn from Howe's interest in the material culture of New England. An example is the following:

> Perilous quillwork needlework
> Need wheat for an ogee epigram
> if old Lille silk one ogival sliver
> if miniature bobbin come from
> dark underwood again again if
> reeling wild silk precede reeler (*TM*, 90)

"Quillwork" applies to a style of fabric decoration with porcupine quills used by Native Americans; needlework is part of the Western tradition. The encounter between the two is "perilous." The architectural terms "ogee" and "ogival," referring to an S-shaped curve and a Gothic arch respectively, are part of the vocabulary of lace-making (a later poem [*TM*, 106] also appears to link the architectural with needlework). Silk, bobbin, and reel set the counterposed quillwork and needlework against an image of repetitious industry, with "reeling wild" giving this activity a celebratory quality. The three "if"s in the stanza hold it in suspension, oscillating between wild spinning and stasis.[35]

Other technical terms for decorative work important to *Bed Hangings II* include "strapwork" (plaster representations of curling leather straps in relief) and "turkey work" (a style of knotted embroidery). Phrases such as "Maple of casepiece pine of clock" (*TM*, 95); "green/ leather and japanned gold (*TM*, 96); and "Outswept arm otherwise plain" (*TM*, 107) use the descriptive vocabulary of "decorative art studies" (*TM*, 102, 103). *Bed Hangings I* draws on *Bed Hangings: A Treatise on Fabrics and Styles in the Curtaining of Beds, 1650–1850* for phrases including "Alapeen Paper Patch Muslin/ Calico Camlet Dimity Fustian" (*TM*, 4); "High mahogany bed roods &/ raills do ring loop ties back" (12); "Low adamantine net fringe" (14); "handsome/ cambleteen red curtain" (15); "camblet curtanot/ vallens" (36).

Her search mediated by dictionaries and specialized source texts, Howe appears to be exploring the word as the unlocker of the material world's intrinsic meaningfulness. Fabrics such as calico and dimity do not have a great role to play in our contemporary culture. Such terms have a curious effect in the poetry: they are unambiguous designations of particular kinds of artifact; at the same time, details of shapes, sizes, patterns and colors are withheld, so the object cannot be visualized and the reader is cast back onto the word itself. Thus, alongside *The Midnight*'s concerns with the materiality of the text, and with materials themselves, is an interest in the textuality of material. Materials are not presented in their unvarnished objecthood; rather the words that announce them immediately embed them in networks of verbal, literary, and historical association.

As with other of Howe's texts, the focus on objects is accompanied by a powerful investment in immateriality; the "impalpable" interleaf and lacework are analogues of a readerly-writerly exploration of cognitive phenomena such as hallucination and paradox. Howe's fabrics are emblematic of verbal interlacing and interconnection, but there is in the writing an equal commitment to the airy, non-signifying space between fibers.

In the strangely textured poetic landscape of *The Midnight*, the chief purveyors of a specifically theatrical form of immateriality are to be found amid the religious ferment of the Great Awakening, the wave of religious enthusiasm that swept through the Connecticut River Valley in the 1740s.[36] The *Bed Hangings* poems are a textual enactment of this enthusiastic intellectual vagrancy. The mixture of medieval lyric, material culture, maverick pragmatism, dissenting religion, and literary allusion never settles in either of the sequences into a satisfactorily settled matrix of ideas. The "savage pattern" (*TM*, 8) of the work is such that a degree of textural integrity is maintained across the dissonant array of vocabularies on which Howe draws. The writing departs from her sources and emerges reconfigured in the witty, alert, lyric voice that Howe had initiated in *Rückenfigur*. When Howe writes of "inviolate love knots" (*TM*, 28), she assimilates the affective and the material in a way that summarizes the activity of *The Midnight*. Whereas the prose sections show words and objects organized and reorganized in intelligible—if surprising—patterns, the peculiar resistances and difficulties of the *Bed Hangings* poems leave the relationships between word, object, and perceiver in a space of conjecture and irresolution, caught in a network of historical and cultural associations that is continually on the point of unraveling.

The preoccupation with the raw experience of Peirce's secondness in *Pierce-Arrow* gives way in *The Midnight* to the relational vocabulary of James's radical empiricism. However, to seek the ultimate ground for the writing in such exemplars would be as misleading. Material details such as Jonathan Edwards's tendency to sew his own booklets are, after all, as important to Howe as his theology. In the endless play of doubles set in motion by the restless writing of *The Midnight*, the concrete is ever apt to give way to the immaterial, the tangible to the affective: "the Double/ of the object is that I desire it" (*TM*, 12).

Souls of the Labadie Tract

The twin epigraphs to the book *Souls of the Labadie Tract*, from Jonathan Edwards and Stevens, both refer to the activity of the silk worm. Howe thus builds on the fascination with threaded connections evidenced in *Bed Hangings* and, before that, *Eikon*. It is clear from her 2009 essay "Choir answers to Choir" and from the two short texts entitled "Errand," in *Souls of the Labadie Tract*, that Howe wishes to draw a parallel between the two writers' modes of composition. Edwards would jot notes as he was riding and pin the pieces of paper to his clothing; Stevens would scribble notes on envelopes and scraps of paper on his daily walk to work (*SLT*, 9, 73). From these combinations of material would devolve trains of associative thought that "Choir answers to Choir" images as tree branches and rivers (60–61). Collage, Howe seems to be saying, is an American idiom.

The book *Souls of the Labadie Tract* also contains another prose text, *Personal Narrative*, two serial poems—*Souls of the Labadie Tract* and *118 Westerly Terrace*—and a short visual poem that is as radical as anything produced by Howe in the 1980s.[37] In more or less explicit ways, these texts reflect on the late work of Wallace Stevens. The poem *Souls of the Labadie Tract*, on which my discussion of the book will be focused, has the most oblique and also the richest relation to Stevens's example.[38] A series of forty-four short page-poems, its point of departure is a dissident Calvinist sect that was founded in Holland but maintained a community in Maryland between 1684 and 1722.[39] The sect is another of the obscure nonconformist sects that gathers in Howe's American writing. The Labadists believed, she reports, in "inner illumination, diligence and contemplative reflection" (*SLT*, 24).

The group was founded by the Jean de Labadie, who died before the founding of the American community. Labadie was notable for his wanderings, both physical and theological. According to Michel de Certeau, his itinerancy sprang from his belief in "the founding myth that there was somewhere a place of truth," even though he was repeatedly disappointed in his attempt to find a physical place that coincided with this "place of truth."[40] The increasing sense that a "sacramental" sense of place was no longer possible fed his wandering, both in space (Guyenne, Paris, Amiens, Montauban, Orange, Geneva, Utrecht, Middleburg, Amsterdam, and Denmark) and theological conviction (Jesuit, Jansenist, Calvinist, Pietist, Chiliast, and Labadist). In Certeau's view, Labadie's wayward spiritual journey is a kind of processual collage:

> His writing developed essentially as a way of walking. There is not, properly so called, a Labadie 'doctrine'. It is a patchwork, weaving together references and theoretical fragments from all sources. His books were formed from day to day, or rather from 'religion' to 'religion', out of elements he drew from the religion in which he was received against the one he was leaving, or vice versa. Traces of the soil through which he passed stuck to his shoes. He did not create a work constituting his own place. He composed a kind of *junk mystics*, just as there is today a kind of *junk music*.[41]

This description provides a ready way into the patchwork of place and mystical inquiry that characterizes *Souls*.

As ever, for Howe, such a meeting of concerns is filtered through her interest in the vicissitudes of the American language as it becomes modern. Howe notes in her brief foreword that she "found the term 'Labadist' in reference to the genealogical research of Wallace Stevens and his wife Elsie Kachel Moll during the 1940s" (*SLT*, 23). Stevens had a Pennsylvania Dutch background and, in a typical act of strong reading, Howe imputes a link between the poet and the nonconforming sect.[42] In this she is pursuing an otherness to American usage—the European accent that she detects in Stevens. The American language itself becomes a patchwork of overlapping voices and distinct cultural imperatives. In the second "Errand" text, which she places between *Souls of the Labadie Tract* and *118 Westerly Terrace*, Howe cites a Stevens letter to Henry Church in which the poet describes the Pennsylvanian German of Conrad Weiser: "It has been like having the past crawl out all over the place. The author has not corrected his spelling. When he speaks of pork he spells it borck. This is pure Pennsylvania German and, while it might bore anyone else to shreds, it has kept me up night after night wild with interest" (*SLT*, 74). Howe thus conceives of the Labadists and the background of Stevens's ancestors as a network of unrealized cultural potential. Aberrant spellings, vanished dialects, and distant European traces exert a pressure on Stevens's texts, much as they do on *Thorow*. The poem contains other marks of the past. It is, in some respects, in dialogue with *Defenestration of Prague*. There are several citations from Thomas Campion's masques, notably "America in a skin coat/ the color of the juice of/ mulberries" (*SLT*, 70) of the concluding page.[43] Howe is playing with the preoccupation with dissembling in *Defenestration* but anchoring it in more physical metaphors. Mixed with the Campion material are many references to the concordance to Henry James's *The Awkward Age*—another example of Howe drawing on the scholarly paraphernalia of literary study for her source material.[44]

It is, however, by means not of the estranging maneuvers of collage but of self-estrangement that I wish to explore the poem's play with lyric voicing. The epigraph to *Souls* is from Wallace Stevens's "The Hand as a Being": "The wind had seized the tree, and ha, and ha" (*SLT*, 25). The words "ha, and ha" are of particular concern to me. *Souls of the Labadie Tract* is studded with such little cries: "Oh—but of course of course"; "Oh—but how would you know"; "Crying out 'Oh, oh'" on facing pages; the three "oh"s on pages 50–51; and, finally, the "Oh I wouldn't I wouldn't" of page 67.

How do these interjections function within the lyric economy of the poem? Do they signify rapture? anger? pain? Or is it a question merely of the ironic use of polite conversational markers—"Oh—but of course of course" (*SLT*, 50)? In a characteristically scrupulous essay on the role of the word "oh" in English poetry, J. H. Prynne probes the history and meanings of this interjection. He notes a range of incidences of "oh," making a distinction between outward-facing "apostrophe" (to a deity or public figure, for example) and inward-facing "exclamation" (an "oh" of private emotion).[45] These tendencies, he argues, are not mutually exclusive—they may coexist in the same "oh." Prynne notes that such interjections stand to one side of the "coded frameworks of sentence structure."[46] Heavily scarred with the marks of earlier poetic occurrences, the "oh" can mark the "boundary of one discourse where it is momentarily exceeded by another."[47] "[T]he word," he further remarks, "may convoke the currencies of previous usage by quoting recursively the power of poetic speech itself, calling it in evidence to locate a dialectic convergence of outward and inward sense."[48]

In Howe's poem, the "oh"s seem to mark such discursive boundaries in complicated ways. These ultimately place a notion of lyric interiority alongside the social implications of collage. What could be more intimate, whatever the cause, than "Crying out, 'oh, oh'"?

The three "oh"s on pages 50–51 are of particular interest. All of these come from the concordance to James's *The Awkward Age*.

Aren't we the very same as we long ago saw and little by little thought of it	Oh I see—I have to see you fresh as those rough streams are as power is
Oh partly—not altogether	Caught and wide awake
it isn't as if long ago—No I mean the secret between my age or any age—you	Oh—we are past saving Aren't odd books full of us What do you wake us for

(*SLT*, 50–51)

Howe, as so often in her previous work, is using collage to subtract speakers from their utterances. James's novel is almost entirely composed of dialogue. This typically follows the rules of polite social convention, although the characters are often duplicitous. The technique of citation does not detract from the immediacy of these utterances. Levered out of context, the polite-sounding phrases are placed in the precarious situation envisaged, in a quite different context, by Prynne's discussion of inward- and outward-facing interjections. Encountered at a remove—through the research tool of the concordance—Howe's "oh"s play scholarly frame against the directness of speech, rapture against politeness, private utterance against rhetoric, the occasional against the voids of non-meaning that such interjections open in the text.

How does the reader understand, "Oh—we are past saving"? It may have a slyly Beckettian ring, folding an echo of Last Things into a snippet of light conversation. But what work does that redundant "oh" do, besides signaling colloquial speech? The strained sociability of the interjection gives way to a less easily situated affective register. The blank and pliable sound "oh" can absorb meanings of private loss, pain, and rapture that tug at the ostensibly sociable exterior. In this way, a text composed largely of found material manages to convey an atmosphere of interiority. It is helpful to turn here to a conventional distinction between feeling and affect. Howe's usage levers emotion out of purely subjective experience and into the more fluid interpersonal domains of affect. The boundedness of lyric convention thus opens into a more porous and uncertain form of poetic speech.

As well as these proliferating "oh"s, *Souls of the Labadie Tract* makes surprisingly frequent use of "I"s and "you"s. Again, the effect is of a teasing and testing of lyric boundaries. This feature of the writing both explodes and reaffirms the convention of lyric address. Indeed, looking again at the facing pages discussed above, it is possible to read the entire sequence as a glancing encounter between an "I" and a "you."

The poem on page 51 begins with an "I" that "has to" see a "you," a covert invocation, perhaps, of a lyric dyad. At the bottom of page 50 and the top of page 51, "we" and "us" suggest common cause between the "I" and the "you"—perhaps even a larger collectivity. Memory, or perhaps history, intrudes at this point: on the right-hand page, an unapproachable or even hypothetical "long ago" may be recovered, "little by little," "partly," "not altogether." Yet the "secret between" the two ages remains undisclosed. The poem ends with a suspended "you," a perilously positioned other. There is no achieved relation between the I and the you, but rather the poems, although almost entirely composed of cited material, move within a vestigial lyric frame. This is notable further into *Souls of the Labadie Tract* with the chiasmic play of "I see you and you see I see you" (*SLT,* 66). This is an example of the concentrated use of repetition in Howe's later work. Similar play with subject pronouns can be found in *118 Westerly Terrace*—"I want my own house I'm/ you and you're the author/ You're not all right you're" (*SLT,* 78).

Moments of subjective density, then, persist in this writing, which, almost despite itself, does not let go of a notion of the lyric subject. In *Souls of the Labadie Tract,* interjections and personal pronouns bring an intimacy that belies the use of citation. It is not that the lyric mode is itself merely 'cited' in some sort of affectless play with genre. Howe retains the affective contours of lyric while at the same time turning it outward from subjective intensities toward a mode of transpersonal hallucinatory reverie.

This quality of reverie owes something to the background presence of Stevens's strange late poem "The Souls of Women at Night" (which Howe lists in her acknowledgements at the end of the book). In Stevens's short poem, the speaker is abroad at night and has "gained" a "metaphysical blindness" that amounts to a "fantastic irruption." Attended by owls, this speaker speculates, as she wanders, that she might be able to "keep a rendezvous,/ Of the loftiest amour, in a human midnight."[49] The suggestion of an amorous encounter reinforces the suggestion of cuckoldry in the phrase "muchhorned." The speaker is "one-sensed," but this sense is "not one of the five." There is a suggestion of an encounter with the dead, with a community of dead souls—the "cata-sisters" or titular "women at night." The poem's mixture of furtive sensuality and death places it on the border between physical and metaphysical.

The links between Howe's poem and Stevens's are on the surface barely evident, aside from references to "screech-owl feather" (SLT, 33) and "owls and honor" (*SLT,* 64). One reading, admittedly speculative, would be to read the speaker of the Stevens poem as Minerva or, in her Greek variant,

Pallas Athena. This is a goddess to whom numerous attributes are attached but who often represents wisdom when accompanied by owls. She is also a goddess of war and of peace, of weaving (in book 6 of Ovid's *Metamorphoses* she has a spinning contest with Ariadne), and of the arts in general.[50] The helmet Minerva often wears might be understood as a version of the mantilla (or lace scarf) to which Stevens alludes in "The Souls of Women at Night" and the horns sometimes attached to the helmet (as in some translations of the *Iliad*) as a precedent for Stevens's "much-horned night." In paintings since the Middle Ages, notably Rembrandt's famous *Minerva in her Study* (1635), moreover, the Athena/ Minerva figure has been depicted wearing a crown of laurels.[51]

The oblique associative connections active in the background of Howe's poem (whether or not actually intended) lead us back to the preoccupations of much earlier work. In "THERE ARE NOT LEAVES ENOUGH TO CROWN TO COVER TO CROWN TO COVER," of course, Stevens, by means of the title citation, is the starting point for reflections on war and poetic speech that, for many, are the defining statement of Howe's intentions. The play between the crown of laurels, femininity, martial conquest, and poetic speech in *Pythagorean Silence*—"Bark be my limbs my hair be leaf// Bride be my bow my lyre my quiver" (*PS*, 17) and "their words are weeds wrapped around my head" (*PS*, 32)—resonates in this text and continues to haunt Howe's work. As in *Pythagorean Silence*, the plasticity of language and the dynamism of collage are offered as attributes that are inimical to the logic of violent conquest.

Owls are a recurrent theme in "Choir Answers to Choir." Howe writes of her admiration for Stevens's "The Owl in the Sarcophagus," which produces in her an "intuitive" "feeling of union and bliss" ("Choir," 57). Such poetry, she writes, invoking a Stevensian Supreme Fiction, runs "parallel to religious faith" (ibid.). Howe also cites the "Sounds" chapter of *Walden*, where the hooting of screech owls represents "a vast and undeveloped nature that men have not recognized" (ibid., 56–57). As a prelude to a paragraph on Edwards's habits as a reader and writer, Howe also quotes from the Book of Job: "I cried in the congregation, brother to dragons companion to owls" (ibid., 58).

This cluster of references, read alongside "The Souls of Women at Night," calls forth Minerva's wisdom, not her martial attributes. However, as in "Leaves," the two are necessarily intertwined in ways that impede the poet's access to speech. The Stevens poem acts as an absent point of orientation that binds the poem to a notion of poetic speech that Howe describes in prose as "Melodic fragments balance at an indifferent point approaching nothingness" ("Choir," 59).[52]

In this late work, although warfare is a muted presence in comparison to earlier poems, and the "pressure of reality" differently registered, we can find the persistence of themes that have long haunted Howe's writing. The world opened up by "The Souls of Women at Night" is comparable to the field of unknowing and not-saying that lies at the fringes of a poetry notably marked by a countervailing commitment to both knowledge and speech. In *Souls of the Labadie Tract*, Howe transposes a vestigial Stevens poem suggestive of both metaphysical speculation and sensual delight to a space that is equivocally American, a space traversed by the shape-shifting transformations of the masque, the integrative pathways of the weaver, the wanderings of the itinerant mystic, the tenuous politesse of displaced Henry James dialogue, the ambiguous gasps of "ah" and "oh," and the violence compacted within any conception of New England geography. In these spaces of uncertainty, Howe's voice finds its own precarious place.

Notes

Introduction

1. There is a substantial critical literature on language writing. See, e.g., books by Hartley, Perloff (1991), Perelman, Reinfeld, and Nerys Williams.
2. See Silliman, ed. (1986). Howe's work was also included in Douglas Messerli's anthology of language writing.
3. The Hejinian, Taggart, and Hamilton Finlay letters are at Special Collections at UCSD, the Brown correspondence at Santa Cruz.
4. Nicholls (1999), 155.
5. Ibid., 155–56.
6. See Richardson.
7. See, e.g., letter of 3 December 1981 to Hejinian, where Howe writes of her love of late Stevens.
8. Originally published as "Statement for the New Poetics Colloquium" in the magazine *Jimmy and Lucy's House of 'K'* in 1985.
9. This is a version of a passage from William Carlos Williams's *In the American Grain*: "The land! don't you feel it? Doesn't it make you want to go out and lift dead Indians tenderly from their graves, to steal from them—as if it must be clinging even to their corpses—some authenticity" (89).
10. While the use of historical material tends to shift from public toward private in her more recent work, in *Pierce-Arrow* she writes of the language of the dead, and in *The Midnight* of the legacy of "European memory" in New England.
11. Examples of the diverse thinkers that critics have aligned with Howe's poetry include Kristeva and Wittgenstein (see Middleton); Lacan and Derrida (Nicholls, 1996); Heidegger (McCorkle, Taggart); Benjamin (Naylor); Serres (Adamson); and Adorno (Reinfeld).
12. All concepts that have come under attack from many of Howe's peers among the late-twentieth-century American poetic avant garde.
13. The term "similitudes" derives from the King James Version of Hosiah 12:10 ("I have also spoken by the prophets, and I have multiplied visions, and used similitudes, by the ministry of the prophets"). The phrase "I have used similitudes" is

cited on the title page of the first edition of Bunyan's Pilgrim's Progress; Howe rings the phrase on a facsimile that she appends to a 19 December 1988 letter to Norman O. Brown. To the typescript of a letter of 28 December 1988 to Brown, she adds in longhand, "similitudes. That's what the puritans spoke in. That's what it's all about. Poetry."

14. Beckett interview, 26.
15. Bernstein interview, n.p.
16. Howe's allusion is to Adorno and Horkheimer's analysis of the development of rationalism in *The Dialectic of Enlightenment*.
17. Howe is linking contemporary events with early American history, when predestination was a given of the intellectual environment. See my first and final chapters for further discussion of the idea of 'relation'.
18. In an interview with the author, in June 2001, Howe remarked: "Sacrificial daughter, that's a big sacrifice. When I was 10 I played Astyanax. That was the first part I had in an Upper School play (I was then in the Lower School). Astyanax is sacrificed when the Trojans are defeated. A year later I played Iphigenia who was also sacrificed." See my discussion of *Liberties* and *Eikon* for treatment of the sacrificial victim in Howe's work.
19. See Perloff (1999), n.p.
20. "The Captivity and Restoration of Mrs Mary Rowlandson," collected in *Birth-Mark*.
21. The phrase "geopolitical chain of violence" comes from Howe's 1996 essay on the work of documentary film-maker Chris Marker, "Sorting Facts; or Nineteen Ways of Looking at Marker" (318).
22. The reader is referred to articles by Kaplan Harris, Brian Reed, and Fiona Green for accounts of this period.
23. See Ma (1994) and Quartermain for discussion of "Scattering as Behavior Toward Risk"; see Martin for "Kidnapped."
24. The work is available on the archival Web site Eclipse (<http://english.utah.edu/eclipse/>).

1   The Maternal Disinheritance

1. Falon interview, 37.
2. Howe mentions Yeats directing her mother in a letter to Norman O. Brown dated 25 August 1987.
3. O'Hara's early play *Try! Try!* was performed at the theater in 1951 (with a set designed by Edward Gorey); the poet had a six-month residency at the theater in 1956 (the same year in which John Ashbery's *The Compromise* was performed). John Weiners was involved in the theater as an actor and stage manager in the 1960s.
4. See Keller, 198.
5. See Back, 61–106; Golding, 168–81.
6. Golding, 173.

7. C.f. the seventeenth-century lyric "Kilcash," which begins "What shall we do for timber?"
8. These letters gained their title posthumously. They were ostensibly sent to both Johnson and her friend Rebecca Dingley, but the frequent use of a private language of intimacy—"Stellakins" and so on—makes it hard to not see them as pertaining to Swift's relationship with "Stella."
9. Early drafts of *Pythagorean Silence*, preserved at the UCSD archive, contained a dramatized section; Howe also dramatized aspects of Anne Hutchinson's speech in her *Birth-mark* essay "Incloser."
10. The tripartite theme is reinforced by the lines quoted in section II from St Patrick's hymn: "I bind unto myself today/ The strong Name of the Trinity,/ By invocation of the same,/ The Three in One and One in Three" (*Liberties*, 189). The Swift/ Stella/ Vanessa trio is converted to a Swift/ Stella/ Cordelia trio.
11. The city of Dublin was founded at the confluence of two rivers, the Liffey and the Poddle (which now runs underground). The references in the word-grid to "wattled dwellings" and "Thingmount" come from an early twentieth-century history of Dublin by Samuel A Ossory Fitzpatrick. Other phrases that Howe takes from this text include "Ioe, a blaze" (*Liberties*, 165) and "John the Mad or Furious fought like a true beserker" (*Liberties*, 167).
12. See Deane for discussion of the co-option of the Celtic mode by the Anglo-Irish literary elite (28–29). As has been noted by Back, the "God's spies" section has a Beckettian cast (91).
13. During the question and answer session following a 1988 reading, Howe remarked on how she came to feel the necessity of providing a basic level of prefatory information for the reader: "Some things the reader *has* to know" (reading at UCSD, 22 November 1988). The term preface does not do justice to the curious texts with which Howe begins some of her poems, most of which can be regarded as prose or prose-poetry components of the poems themselves.
14. See, e.g., *Eikon*.
15. *Liberties*, 157. See Swift ([1784] 1948), vol. 1, 291. Back also discusses the passage (67).
16. Conroy is "ready to carve a flock of geese, if necessary" (187). In Ireland, "to go west" encompasses meanings both of exile and of death.
17. Yeats, ed. ([1888, 1892] 1977.), 255. The version of the story that Yeats uses is by Patrick Kennedy.
18. Swift ([1765] 1973), 391. Howe alludes to the phrase in her preface and cites it, without the "in," later in the poem (*Liberties*, 163). During the playlet, Stella reinforces the link with: "her snowy flesh" (*Liberties*, 187).
19. Howe is citing a letter to Wallis, 12 February 1723 (Swift, 1963, 450).
20. Vanhomrigh, like Esther Johnson a student of Swift's, fell in love with her tutor and corresponded with him. Swift's "Cadenus and Vanessa" was a by-product of the friendship.

21. Compare, e.g., Howe's treatment of the figure of Pamela (from Sidney's *Arcadia*) in *Eikon Basilike*.
22. Letter dated 28 April 1978.
23. Some of these motifs appear at the end of a letter of 27 May 1991 to Norman O. Brown: "That's why you hear the wind howling on the heath. I heard it on the day of Pearl Harbor. It has been howling ever since. I have always been Cordelia. 'The weight of this sad time we must obey;/ Speak what we feel, not what we ought to say.' We are God's spies."
24. See Foster interview, 166: "in the cathedral, Stella is buried under the floor near the entrance, or that's where her grave marker is. You walk over it as if there were a dog buried there. Swift's pet dog. At the same time, considering that Swift was the dean of the cathedral, it seems a flagrant gesture. A swipe at respectability."
25. Figures of three recur throughout the poem.
26. Fraser, 186.
27. Duncan, cited in Fraser, 186.
28. See "Sorting Facts" for reflections on poetry, history, and montage.
29. See *Birth-mark*, 18.
30. This idea will be discussed more fully in my next chapter.
31. Letter dated 25 September 1983. See also "Sorting Facts" for more recent reflections on *Hamlet*, especially the Laurence Olivier film, important to Howe since she first saw it as a child.
32. The indirect references are combined with such direct quotations as "We are left darkling" (*Liberties*, 176) or "Enter Bastard, solus with a letter" (*Liberties*, 217).
33. The couplet is from Swift's "To Stella, Who Collected and Transcribed My Poems."
34. As Howe notes in her preface, Stella's relation to Swift, her former tutor, is akin to that of daughter and father. Stella was the daughter of a steward on the estate of Swift's patron, Sir William Temple, but she was rumored to have been Temple's daughter. It has also been suggested that Swift was the son of Temple. This speculation, which Howe alludes to in her preface, is dismissed by Swift's biographer Ehrenpreis, but it seems possible that Swift himself may have considered himself to be related to Stella and to be unable for that reason to marry her. See also Nokes, 19.
35. Letters of 11 and 24 May 1982.
36. Letter to Taggart, 22 May 1983.
37. With "ester*snowe*" (*Liberties*, 205, my italics), Howe aligns herself with Esther/Stella. She, Howe, like Stella, doesn't have access to the literary establishment of her day. Howe's correspondence contains many references to her isolation as a woman writer. Taken in conjunction with the poem's sympathy with Cordelia's experience of paternal neglect and with Howe's identification with Swift, discussed above, it is possible to read the poem's trinity of characters as projections of Howe.
38. An uncertain paternity, then, hovers over Hedvig, Swift and Stella.

39. See the earlier exchange:
    Stella: Tangle and Seaweed—
    Cordelia: In history people are all dead. (*Liberties*, 187)
40. See the Andersen tale cited above. Apollo's chariot, moreover, was harnessed to seven white swans. See Yeats's "Nineteen Hundred and Nineteen": "Some moralist or mythological poet/ Compares the solitary soul to a swan; I am satisfied with that." The lines also echo Yeats's "Wild Swans at Coole": "All suddenly mount/ And scatter wheeling in great broken wings/ Upon their clamorous wings."
41. Letter of 11 May 1982. Heidegger's essay "What are Poets For?" meditates on Hölderlin's question "what are poets for in a destitute time?" When Hedvig is lying dead, Old Ekdal says, "The forest has taken its revenge" (Ibsen, 214).
42. See Yeats's "The Madness of King Goll": "And now I wander in the woods/ When summer gluts the golden bees."
43. In a working journal entry dated 14 May 1985 Howe writes: "But my father I am here to hold onto you—the daughter you really did not like very much. This mystery of birth."
44. See Foster interview, 166, and Howe's remarks to Taggart, both cited above.
45. *Macbeth* II, iii, 137.
46. *The Midnight* includes, often in substantially revised form, material that had been published in small press editions, in the dialogue with Cole Swensen in *Conjunctions* 35 (Fall 2000), and the essay "Ether Either."
47. This short text explores Noh Theatre (via Yeats and Pound) and Patrick Brontë's Irish background. See Martin.
48. See Fredman. See also chapter 8 of Marjorie Perloff's *Dance of the Intellect* and her essay "Lucent and Inescapable Rhythms" for discussion of lyric and its postmodern others.
49. Howe's rough working notes include the jottings, "The only touchable element of the dead is their letters and poems. Explore *this via Ma's books*" (Howe's emphasis).
50. Thompson interview, n.p.
51. The Coracle book *Kidnapped* contains a physical interleaf.
52. Howe acknowledges such sources at the end of *The Midnight*. Passages from *Macbeth* provide epigraphs to each of *The Midnight*'s five sections, and Lady Macbeth appears to have a strong maternal resonance for Howe.
53. Winnicott, 14.
54. C.f., Foster interview, 179, in which Howe refers to the description in Melville's journal of a woman beside a new grave, calling "to the dead."
55. C.f. the role of Ariadne and Arachne in *Eikon*.
56. C.f. Howe's exploration of fictiveness in *Defenestration*.
57. Stevenson, 192.
58. Ibid., 15.
59. Ibid., 69.

2 The Ghost of the Father

1. Letter dated 4 August 1982.
2. Letter to Taggart, 13 July 1986. Howe's emphases (added freehand to the typescript). Howe is referring to Heidegger's essay "What are Poets For?" The lines "blood and water streaming/ swift to its close/ ebbs out/ out/ out/ of/ my pierced side/ *not in my native land*" (*Liberties*, 212) provide a clear alignment of the speaker with Christ and another motif of paternal abandonment.
3. The *History* and *Secret History* were not published until 1841 and 1929 respectively.
4. See the lines "westward and still westward/ matches coughing like live things" (*Secret History*, 95). As Green notes, this adaptation of words from *The Mystery of Edwin Drood*, changes "eastward" to "westward."
5. See introduction to the Dover edition, xix. See also passages such as: "My landlord had unluckily sold our Men some brandy, which produced much disorder, making some too Cholerick, and others too loving. (So that a damsel who came to assist in the kitchen would have been ravish't, if her timely consent had not prevented the Violence.)... Firebrand and his servant were the most suspected, having been engag'd in those kind of Assaults before" (147–49).
6. Another Mark, who died at the age of two, was the half brother of Howe's grandfather. *Secret History* contains the dedication: "*for Mark my father, and Mark my son*" (*Secret History*, 91).
7. See the introduction to *Frame Structures*, 16–17, where Howe implies that overwork led to his premature death at the age of 60.
8. The term "library cormorant," also cited at the head of the essay "Submarginalia" in *Birth-mark*, 27, is Coleridge's.
9. See also *Birth-mark*, 18: "Thoreau said, in an essay called 'Walking', that in literature it is only the wild that attracts us. What is forbidden is wild. The stacks of the Widener Library and all the great libraries in the world are still the wild to me.... I go to libraries because they are the ocean."
10. See Green, 82, 83, 99. See also Back, 19–37, for an extended reading of this poem.
11. Although, as Green notes, Howe herself in a journal entry writes that she somehow laid her father "to rest" in the poem, *Secret History* shares formal attributes and a preoccupation with father-figures that will be apparent in many of her later poems (95).
12. The lines "crucified by ordinance" (*Eikon*, 56, 57) and "of Gold of Thorn of Glory" (*Eikon*, 63) draw attention to this association with Christ.
13. See also Madan.
14. See also Foster interview, 176: "Charles, the king, is murdered by those who bowed down to him. He was God's representation on earth. People still believed a king was holy. And this was a culmination of violent deaths on the scaffold in England during the sixteenth century. Raleigh was executed; before him, Thomas More, Mary Queen of Scots, Lady Jane Grey, Essex, just a stream of women and men, powerful ones, religious heretics, biblical translators even,

who ended their lives as sacrificial victims. These men and women in power had to be performers. They acted until the moment of death. So executions were staged but they were real."
15. DuPlessis refers to Howe's texts as "matted palimpsests" (126); Davidson applies the coinage "palimtext" (64ff).
16. In her Foster interview, 175, Howe remarks on Hawthorne's story "Roger Malvin's Burial," which she reads as a portrayal of the guilt of the regicides.
17. Nicholls (1999), 155. Nicholls is citing Lyotard's *Heidegger and "the jews"* (1990), 10.
18. See also Nietzsche's "On the Uses and Disadvantages of History for Life" for a related discussion of the "monumental," "antiquarian," and "critical" species of history. Howe discusses antiquarianism in her preface to *Frame Structures*, 17–18. See also Bruns (2009), 18–19.
19. Lyotard (1990), 10.
20. Nicholls is not representative of this tendency.
21. Macherey, 27. Howe misquotes slightly: Macherey's phrase begins "sealed and intermin*able*, completed." Macherey's book is also cited in *Birth-mark*, 46.
22. Howe links her father and Butterick, both scholars working in the shadow of what she calls "commanding and prolific figures" (Foster interview, 174).
23. Foster interview, 175. In an autumn 1988 letter to Taggart, Howe explained the background to a paper she had given at Buffalo that had been critical of Olson: "I think I was shattered by [Robert] Duncan's death, George's sickness, David's sickness, the ghost of my father in Buffalo, and it all gathered into a striking out at fathers."
24. See Beckett interview, 24.
25. In a letter dated 1 November 1993 Howe writes to Taggart that she admires de Certeau's "writing about writing," and in particular his *Heterologies* (1986).
26. Howe devotes a considerable portion of her *My Emily Dickinson* to a discussion of the idea of sovereignty.
27. De Certeau (1986), 110–11.
28. An analogy might also be drawn to the nexus of ideas on law and sovereignty to be found in Carl Schmitt's *Political Theology*, Walter Benjamin's essay "Critique of Violence," Jacques Derrida's essay "Force of Law: 'The Mystical Foundation of Authority,'" and Giorgio Agamben's *State of Exception*.
29. Reading at UCSD, 22 November 1988.
30. Howe's correspondence with Norman O. Brown contains several approving references to John Cage.
31. Foster interview, 175
32. See pp. 54, 56–57, 58–59, 73, 78–79, and 82.
33. Reading at UCSD, 22 November 1988. Howe's "scattering" comment also recalls the gendering of antinomian speech at the end of her interview with Foster: "History has happened. The narrator is disobedient. A return is necessary, a way for women to go. Because we are in the stutter. We were expelled from the Garden of the Mythology of the American Frontier. The drama's done. We are the wilderness. We have come on to the stage stuttering" (181).

34. Howe would develop this idea in her *Bed Hangings* poems. Arachne the weaver produced a cloth so faultless that the goddess Athena tore it apart in frustration; Arachne then tried to hang herself, but Athena loosened the rope, and Arachne became a spider and the rope a cobweb. Ariadne fell in love with Theseus and gave him the thread with which he found his way out of the Minotaur's labyrinth; Ariadne was deserted by Theseus in Naxos, where she was married to Dionysus, who placed among the stars the diadem he gave her at their wedding. The two figures are closely linked for Howe.
35. Milton ([1649] 1962), 362. Howe glosses this as "the prayer of a pagan woman to an all-seeing heathen Deity" (*Eikon*, 49). The phrase "all-seeing deity" derives from the editor's discussion of Pamela's prayer in the Hughes edition of *Eikonoklastes*, 153.
36. For a summary of the correspondence on this point between Empson and other scholars in the *Times Literary Supplement* see Milton ([1649] 1962), 154, n14.
37. Back, 130.
38. A scrip is an archaic term for a wallet or purse. Pseudomisus is the name adopted by the pseudonymous author of a 1654 pamphlet on enclosure legislation.
39. Foster interview, 176–77. Her reference to the masque is an allusion to Milton's critique of the form in *Eikonoklastes*: "quaint Emblems and devices, begg'd from the old Pageantry of some Twelf-nights entertainment at *Whitehall*, will doe but ill to make a Saint or Martyr" (Milton, [<1649> 1962], 342).
40. Howe's strange polemic about Harvard and Milton appears to be indebted to the work of René Girard, particularly his book *The Scapegoat*, which Howe has said had "a big effect" on her (e-mail correspondence with author, 6 August 2002). *The Scapegoat*, like its predecessor *Violence and the Sacred*, argues that violence is the repressed origin of human culture. The persecution of the victim, or scapegoat, is a means of bringing about the "cure" of a social crisis. See Girard, 44.
41. Howe might almost be reiterating Sidney's praise in the *Defense of Poesy* of the "perfect picture" painted by the poet against the mere "wordish description" of philosophical prose. The line "The Foundation of hearsay" (*Eikon*, 66) is a quotation from *The Defense of Poesy*. *Defenestration*'s "peerless poesie" (*Defenestration*, 108) also echoes this source.
42. *Birth-mark*, 19–20. The phrase beginning "the subject" is from Foucault's essay and is acknowledged by Howe. The phrase "What matter who's speaking," from Beckett, and the idea of 'indifference' are also both imported from Foucault's essay, 115, 138. See also *MED*, 13: "My voice formed from my life belongs to no one else. What I put into words is no longer my possession."
43. Collis, 19.
44. Ibid., 10, 18.
45. There is an equivocation in Howe's work on this point. See *My Emily Dickinson*, 138: "Poetry leads past possession of self to transfiguration beyond gender."
46. Milton ([1649] 1962), 342.

47. By Edmund Calamy. Calamy's 1702 version of a historical narrative written by Richard Baxter was revised and abridged by Samuel Palmer in 1775 and published as *The Nonconformist's Memorial*.
48. Bernstein interview, n.p.
49. Letter to Norman O. Brown of 3 March 1989.
50. Letter to Taggart, 13 July 1986 (cited at greater length in my discussion of *The Liberties*).
51. "Four-Part Harmony," 22.
52. Beckett interview, 21. Howe's language echoes the language of Puritan sermons—the "unbeaten way" comes from the Puritan cleric Thomas Hooker, who founded the town of Hartford, Connecticut, near Guilford, where Howe has lived since the 1970s. Howe's working journal for the period 30 December 1987 to 21 June 1988 contains the source quote: "The secresie of God does drive men to much trouble, it is like an unbeaten way to the seamen, they must sound every part of it."
53. Quartermain, 194.
54. See Nicholls, 597.
55. The lines on page 32 allude glancingly to Hopkins's "The Blessed Virgin compared to the Air we Breathe" and "To seem the stranger, lies my lot, my life." The line "bereft of body" derives from Aristotle's *Physics*.
56. See Jenkins for a recent and ethically oriented reading of *The Nonconformist's Memorial*.
57. The first printing was a limited edition artist's book, a collaboration with Robert Mangold.
58. Letter dated 24 February 1989 (Howe's emphases).
59. Letter to Norman O. Brown, 15 February 1989.
60. See also *MED*, 129: "the unsaid words—slavery, emancipation and eroticism."
61. See *MED*, 35: "'My Life had stood—a Loaded Gun'... carefully delineates and declines all aspects of the 'Will to Power' nearly 20 years before Nietzsche's metaphysical rebellion." "Touch Shakespeare for Me," an unpublished paper written after *My Emily Dickinson*, also discusses Dickinson and Nietzsche.
62. Hart, 175.
63. Bernstein interview, n.p. Haskins notes that Pope Gregory the Great in the sixth century linked Mary Magdalene with the sinful woman of Luke and the woman who, in Mark, has seven devils thrown out of her. She was also often identified with the Mary of Bethany (the brother of Lazarus) and the woman taken in adultery in John. Thus the dominant Western representation of Magdalene was as a reformed prostitute. See Haskins, 16; 96.
64. Bernstein interview, n.p.
65. Haskins, 407, n62.
66. Back, 178.
67. Ibid, 180, 164.
68. Letter to Norman O. Brown, 15 February 1989.
69. Williams, 9.
70. Letter dated 24 February 1989. Howe's emphasis.

71. Keller interview, 11.
72. See Braine, 759:
    > The pre-Christian idea of a name as a means of control over what is names, bringing it within reach of human science and manipulation, is echoed in the negative emphasis both in the Old Testament and the Greek Fathers, who said that God 'has no name,' or is 'ineffable.' This negative perspective was reinforced by Exodus 33:18–23, which represents Moses as unable to see God's face, but only his back, and is echoed in the Gospels: 'no man has seen God at any time' (John 1:18).... later Eastern tradition developed the idea that we never say anything positive of God's 'essence' (God as he is in himself), but only about his 'uncreated energies.'
73. Pseudo-Dionysus, 141.
74. Keller interview, 6, 9, 22.
75. The Hamilton Finlay correspondence is held at UCSD.
76. Harris, 449.
77. See Hart and essays in Berry and Wernick, eds.; Budick and Iser, eds.; Coward and Foshay, eds.; and Scharlemann, ed. Derrida's fullest treatment of the subject, "How to Avoid Speaking: Denials," can be found in Budick and Iser's book.
78. Derrida (1982), 6.
79. However accurate that critique may itself be: Hart, 202, points out that Derrida's critique of Pseudo-Dionysius is based on a mistranslation of "superessentiality," which should be rendered by a more negative term.
80. See Keller interview, 9–16, for Howe's discussion of the ways in which opposing voices speak in *The Nonconformist's Memorial*. These lines are sometimes printed upside down (as in 6–7), but page 10 allows the voice of exegetical commentary and the insistent voice of "I" to run alongside one another. For Jesus's "I am" statements (also noted by Back, 166), see, respectively, John 6: 35; 9:5; 10:7; 10:11; 14:6; 15:5.
81. In her letter to Taggart of 5 June 1993, written eight months after the death of David von Schlegell, Howe remarks of Melville's graveside description, "I am that woman.... That woman knows there is no consolation. Melville knew there was no consolation. I know there is no consolation."
82. Back, too, discusses these lines in relation to the "dramatic scriptural events as experienced by Mary," suggesting that Howe is attempting to restore the "absent I" of the "acting individual" to "tradition" (167).
83. "A predicate nominative" may also be taken from a scholarly account of the grammar of the prologue. See Colwell.
84. Keller interview, 29.

3 Susan Howe's Renaissance

1. See, e.g., the letter to Hejinian dated 28 December 1981: "I have lost all interest in LANGUAGE MAG concerns. ALL." Howe goes on to say how much more interested she is in the later poetry of Stevens—an interest that would find its fullest expression in her late work.

2. Letter of 27 December 1985.
3. See, however, McHale's discussion of Howe's use of Shakespeare in *Pythagorean Silence* and Spenser in *Defenestration of Prague*.
4. Silliman, Harryman, Hejinian, Benson, Perelman, Watten (1988), 264.
5. See *Souls of the Labadie Tract* for Stevens and Edwards. In her letter of 3 December 1981 to Hejinian, Howe talks of combining elements of Duchamp's *Large Glass* with books II and IV of Spenser's *Faerie Queene*.
6. Letter to Silliman, 4 August 1982. Howe makes this point with reference to a passage from Alastair Fowler's book *Spenser and the Numbers of Time*. In a letter of 28 December 1988 to Norman O. Brown, Howe asserts the importance of the work of Frances Yates, G Wilson Knight's *The Crown of Life*, and Walter Benjamin's *The Origin of German Tragic Drama* to both *Pythagorean Silence* and *Defenestration*. Knight's *Wheel of Fire* was important to *The Liberties*.
7. Letter to Silliman, 4 August 1982.
8. Ibid.
9. Letter dated 6 November, 1985.
10. See Howe's comments in her Foster interview, 168–69.
11. See Iamblichus, in K. S. Guthrie, 82. See also Sendler, 144–45.
12. See Beckett interview, 19, in which Howe discusses Melville: "The first nameless avatar of *The Confidence Man* possibly comes from the East. Like Pythagoras he dresses in white and remains apart." The *Life of Pythagoras* of Diogenes Laertius describes him as dressed in white; see Guthrie, KS, 146.
13. The teachings of Pythagoras are virtually impossible to disentangle from those of his followers. Such attributes of Pythagoreanism as asceticism, dietary regulations, a theory of number, a related musical theory that extends to the doctrine of the harmony of the spheres, geometry, the theory of opposites, and the doctrine of the transmigration of souls can be grouped around his name, but Pythagoras remains an elusive presence. See Cornford, K. S. Guthrie, W. K. C. Guthrie, Kahn, and Riedweg.
14. See W. K. C. Guthrie, 167: "Silence and secrecy were prominent features of [the Pythagoreans'] behavior." According to Iamblichus, in K. C. Guthrie, 74, Pythagorean initiates were required to be silent for five years.
15. Emerson ([1838] 1983), 106.
16. See Beckett interview, 21: "I can't get away from New England. It's in my heart and practice. The older I get the more Calvinist I grow.... I am at home with them."
17. The Heideggerean readings of Howe's poetry offered by McCorkle and Taggart have much to offer in this regard. See also Bruns (1989), 11: "I understand the later Heidegger as opening us up to the ancient and discredited tradition that figures poetry in terms of the darkness of speech, that is, the *ainigma* or dark saying that reduces us to bewilderment and wonder and exposes us to the uncontrollable."
18. Beckett interview, 18. Howe is clearly thinking of the critique of such hierarchized oppositions in the work of some feminist theorists. See, for example, Cixous's "Sorties: Out and Out."

19. See Schultz (1994), n.p.
20. Letter of 1 April 1986.
21. *Oxford English Dictionary.*
22. Letter of 13 November 1981. One of Howe's source may have been Norman O. Brown, "Daphne, or Metamorphosis," in his book *Apocalypse and/or Metamorphosis*. The essay reflects on parallels with the Apollo and Daphne tale in texts by authors including Petrarch, Bacon, Rilke, Yeats, Joyce, and Gide, among many others. In the 1991 edition, Brown appends the lines that open *Pythagorean Silence*. In her letter to Brown of 6 November 1985, Howe writes,
    "Women can return with Daphne who is running to meet them in a place of Peace or play of Place where they will be and have been unremembered and sovereign. A place outside standard grammatical and historical Control. Your writing and Robert Duncan's in its de-centering of issues, its fracturing of messages and meanings offers the best hope for women who are interested in Change which is after all mutability."
23. In Ovid, trans. Arthur Golding, 288–89. The extent of Ovid's Pythagoreanism is a matter of some dispute and modern commentators see Golding's reading on this point as inadequate. See Lyne, 25 and 52.
24. Ovid, trans. Golding, XV 188–92.
25. Ibid. I, 694.
26. Ovid, *Metamorphoses*, trans. Dryden, I, 554–57. See below for discussion of Ophelia's "coronet."
27. Duncan, iv, 7.
28. See Howe's dialogue with Creeley, "Four-Part Harmony," 22: "I do feel my models would be people like Pound or Eliot. A modernist list of models. That there are so few women in any list is very problematic to me."
29. Pound (1948), 31 [1910].
30. Ibid., 75 [1912].
31. Ibid., 175, 180 [1920].
32. Pound (1917, 238n).
33. HD, 47–55 [1913–1917].
34. Eliot ([1922] 1972) II, 98–103; III, 203–6. See Tomlinson 152–62, especially 158ff for analysis of the Tereus/ Philomela tale in the Cantos. See also Sarah Annes Brown, chapter 10. See my note 53 below for Howe's use of motifs from *The Waste Land*.
35. This may betray the influence of Nietzsche's *Philosophy in the Tragic Age of the Greeks*, a key work for Howe at the time, according to her letters to Hejinian (12 February 1978) and Taggart (7 March 1982). *Pythagorean Silence* contains many references to pre-Socratic thought.
36. It is important to emphasize the centrality of theatrical performance to Howe's writing. Discussing her work in her interview with Lynn Keller, she remarks, "the pages in Eikon and in Nonconformist's Memorial we have been talking about are in my head as theater. I hear them one particular way. I think that comes from my childhood and very directly from my mother" (Keller interview, 13).

37. Berry, 71, makes the *Ros marinus* suggestion.
38. Ibid., 27, 71.
39. *Hamlet* 4.7.173–84.
40. Berry, 27, notes the sexual connotations of mermaid, a term applied to prostitutes in Shakespeare's time.
41. Ibid.
42. See also page 23, in which Hamlet 1.4 is mined and in which, with "scatters flowers," Howe links an early speech by Polonius to Ophelia's flowers.
43. Beckett interview, 24.
44. In her letter to Norman O. Brown of 6 November 1985, Howe remarks of her title,

    I used it...for many reasons aside from the fact of the beauty of the word DEFENESTRATION. It goes back to Spenser by strange paths through Sidney and John Dee, and wandering English players through Masques and echoes of *The Tempest* and *Cymbeline*...but it's all very tenuous how all the connections meet and part and lead on through the poem. Rilke and Kafka were born in Prague. Czech was dismembered by all the European powers at Munich when I was one, and spending the summer in Ireland with my mother and her family who are Irish. Ireland is in all my poetry because I have spent a lot of time there. But we are Anglo-Irish as was Spenser and Yeats.

    Some of these remarks point to Howe's interest in Frances Yates's work. *The Rosicrucian Enlightenment* contains reference to the defenestration (18), Sidney, and John Dee. *The Tempest*, *Cymbeline*, and Jonson's masques are discussed in *Shakespeare's Last Plays: A New Approach*. See *A Study of Love's Labours Lost* for discussions of Pythagoras (97–99) and revelry (152ff) that seem pertinent to *Pythagorean Silence* and *Defenestration*, respectively.
45. See *Defenestration*, 93–94, and Spenser's *A View of the Present State of Ireland* ([1633] 1997). The *View*, begun three years before Spenser's death in 1599, argues that a strong hand should be used against those in this "most barbarous Nation in Christendome" who opposed English rule (172).
46. The theme of the mask is discussed in relation to Yeats in Bruns (2009).
47. Beckett interview, 25 (Howe's emphasis).
48. C.f. the epigraph, from Dr. Johnson, of *Cabbage Gardens* (*FS*, 74), discussed above, and the preface to *Thorow*, 41–42.
49. Spenser ([1596] 1970), IV, xii: 2.
50. Ibid., III, vii, 26.
51. Beckett interview, 25–26.
52. Ibid., 26.
53. Howe may also have *The Waste Land*'s "sylvan scene" (II, 98) in mind (the phrase derives, in turn, from *Paradise Lost*). Eliot's poem also contains reference to Tristan and Isolde (I, 31; see *Defenestration* 99–100), Ophelia's farewell (II, 170–71), overhanging boughs (III, 172–73), and Psalm 137 (III, 182; see *Pythagorean Silence*, 44). In her 2004 article "Furious Calm," on Wallace Stevens, Howe points to the way Thoreau linked the word "savage"

to "salvage" and, thus, to "sylvan" in his journals. Writing of the "old books" of the early settlers, Thoreau observes, "there is some of the wild wood and its bristling branches still left in their language" (cited in "Furious Calm, 135).

54. Swensen interview, 376; *TM*, 63; "Ether Either," 125.
55. This quality of elusiveness is also, for Howe, a property of the author and speaker of "My Life had stood a—Loaded Gun": "Like Edgar/Tom...she escapes the violence of definition, blood of the hunt—by camouflage and cunning. Anonymous dramatic monologue, figment revealing only its disguising, we will never capture Dickinson in one interpretation" (*MED*, 105–6).
56. Letter of 17 March 1983.
57. This particular masque was, of course, a post-Jacobean one.
58. See Howe's letter to Taggart of 13 November 1981, in which she writes of "a sort of holy trinity of music/ word/ object."
59. See Adams, 315.
60. The cover of Howe's *Secret History* contains an illustration from an eighteenth-century book on perspective.
61. The one-off ritual was followed by the destruction of the entire apparatus, lending each event the character of potlatch.
62. Orgel (1973), 7.
63. See Beckett interview, 24.
64. Jonson, in Adams, ed., 350.
65. Ibid., 350–51.
66. *The Tempest* 4,1.148–50. In these lines, as both the Orgel and the Kermode editions of *The Tempest* note, Shakespeare is extending a figure that derives from Latin poetry and from Job 20:6–8. Orgel (1987), 180–81, observes that Prospero's phrase "insubstantial pageant" is comparable to Jonson's statements on the ephemerality the masque and, furthermore, that his references to "towers" and "gorgeous palaces" recall the fabulous settings of the courtly masques themselves.
67. C.f. *As you Like It*'s "Are not these woods/ More free from peril than the envious court?" (2.1.3–4).
68. Milton ([1645] 1968), ll 177–81.
69. See *The Vision* and the conclusion to "Ego Dominus Tuus": "I call to the mysterious one who yet/ Shall walk the wet sands by the edge of the stream/ And look most like me, being indeed my double,/ And prove of all imaginable things/ The most unlike, being my anti-self,/ And standing by these characters disclose/ All that I seek" (Yeats, 1994, 212). Daniel Albright, the editor of the Everyman edition, comments (584n), "From his earliest poems Yeats was preoccupied with the concept of an anti-world, a faeryland in which every desire was gratified, an artificial domain related to the ordinary world as presence is to absence."
70. The first account of Irish mumming dates from 1685 and features Cromwell as a character. However the tradition is thought to date back at least to the previous century. See Gailey, 8. Cromwell, St. George, and St. Patrick were common characters in the plays' comic enactment of political conflict.

71. Gailey notes that it was unique among ritualized folk celebrations in that women were allowed to take part (84). Gailey also points to various parallels between Irish mumming plays and the English masque.
72. Orgel (1973), 5.
73. Beckett interview, 25.

4 The Poetics of American Space

1. Ma (1995), 471; Back, 56; Perloff (1989), 9, 10; Reinfeld, 124; Schultz (2005), 157.
2. See Schultz (2005), 144: "History in Howe's work is dependent on the procedures of language; her authority as historian is based on her authority as a poet, not vice versa."
3. Howe is citing the Thoreau of the essay "Walking," a key text for her own *Thorow*.
4. See Back, Collis, Frost, and Nicholls (1996) for accounts of Howe's reading of antinomianism.
5. This remark comes from the transcription of a question and answer session with Howe that is appended to "Encloser," an early version of her essay "Incloser" (revised and republished in *Birth-mark*).
6. Hall, David, 318.
7. See my discussion of letter and spirit in *Melville's Marginalia*.
8. Hall, David, 337; 338.
9. Ibid., 338.
10. Bernstein interview, n.p.
11. Caldwell's essay on the antinomian controversy is cited by Howe in the opening acknowledgements to *Birth-mark*. Howe makes the point that American antinomianism is, first, distinct from its European counterpart, and, second, gendered feminine (*Birth-mark*, ix–x). Caldwell writes that Hutchinson "was intolerable to [her examiners] because she called attention to the failure of language to operate according to their expectations. Anne Hutchinson's loosening of the form of language, her ambiguities and arbitrariness, must have seemed a threat to the very foundation of things" (359). Howe cites Caldwell's contention that Hutchinson was speaking "a different language" that had "serious literary consequences in America" (see Caldwell, 347). See also Kibbey.
12. Hall, David, 381.
13. Ibid., 342.
14. See Back, 40.
15. See, e.g., George W Bush's State of the Union address, 28 January 2003: "We must... remember our calling as a blessed country is to make this world better."
16. See, however, "Federalist 10" (1987) and "Heliopathy" (1990) for roughly contemporaneous American poems that Howe chose not to reprint in book form.

17. See Nicholls (1996) for commentary on the source material for the second section of the poem, George Sheldon's *A History of Deerfield, Massachusetts*.
18. The first section did not appear in the original Awede edition.
19. What Howe calls Hope's "epicene name" is, of course, only a consonant away from her own. In her letter of 29 May 1987 to Taggart, Howe notes James Joyce's use of the word epicene to describe his own name.
20. See Scott Howard for discussion of the "seldom opened book" on Hope Atherton that was source material for Howe.
21. Schultz (2005), 153.
22. See Bercovich (1975), 62 and 218, n28.
23. See Scott Howard for reference to the typological ambitions of Atherton's narrative.
24. Bercovitch (1978), 15.
25. Letter of 29 May 1987.
26. Ibid. This observation, in turn, echoes the "Cashel has fallen/ trees are turf" of *Cabbage Gardens*, 75.
27. See Keller (1997) and Fraser for feminist readings of Howe that place her in the context of Pound and Olson's long poems.
28. See Rogin, 72–75. Rogin links O'Sullivan's political nationalism to the literary nationalism of Melville's "Hawthorne and his Mosses."
29. See Nicholls (1999), 156.
30. From Cotton Mather's *Magnalia* (c.1725), excerpted in Heimert and Delbanco, 333–34. *Magnalia* is frequently cited in *Birth-mark*.
31. An ultra-violet coronal spectrometer is a device which allows analysis of the sun's corona rather than the sun itself.
32. Genesis 2:23 "This is now the bone of my bones and the flesh of my flesh: she shall be called Woman because she was taken out of man."
33. "Incloser" (*Birth-mark*, 43–86) is closely concerned with Shepard's use of the parable.
34. Back, 49, notes several maternal references in "Taking the Forest."
35. Howe has written relatively little on twentieth-century poetry, but she has published essays on Olson and two other Black Mountain poets, Robert Creeley and Robert Duncan.
36. Fraser, 176.
37. See Mellors, 105–6. Howe is explicit about her antipathy to Olson's misogyny in a letter to Norman O. Brown dated "20 something" September 1988:

    The fact is that the violent and ugly language toward women that Olson used is on a par with Pound's talk about kikes and Olson went on very righteously about that. Pound on that subject was genuinely cracked, Olson was not cracked. I can't think of another poet who uses such violent language towards a part of the human race. I could never never dictate what should be said. Language must never be ruled by anyone—but I can at least state my hurt and shock at it. Olson's view of American history reflects this lack in him, and ultimately destroys his view of Melville—though *Call Me I* is one of the finest things written on the subject because of its *love*. But later Melville is lost on Olson and he says its because of M's Christianity—I think it's something else that has to do with the feminine that Olson is blind to. As to history—his American history is the story of the Patriarchs. Liberal though he was. Careful study of the Captivity Narratives and conversion narratives and the history that goes along with it just shows me how strident and narrow his view was.

38. Keller interview, 20.
39. This essay, published in 1987, expands themes addressed in *Call Me Ishmael* and announces itself as a "preliminary exploration of the hidden feminine in Melville and Olson" (although femininity is not explicitly addressed until the closing paragraphs). Howe's essay is concerned with teasing out the affinities between Melville and Olson through an examination of their shared preoccupation with the deep logic of American culture. See also Howe's comment in her essay "Charles Olson: A Dialogue There Is": "For me, Olson gave birth to Melville, and *Call Me Ishmael* gave birth to *My Emily Dickinson*" (167).
40. See Michael André Bernstein, 235, on myth as counter-myth in *Maximus*.
41. Olson ([1947] 1967), 97. Howe does much to disrupt lines "drawn straight ahead," often returning to motifs of drifting or errancy.
42. C.f. Howe's discussion of the word "whale" in Melville, cited below.
43. See *Moby-Dick*, chapter 32: "But I have swam through libraries and sailed through oceans." The phrase forms the epigraph to the preface of *Melville's Marginalia*.
44. Melville's "white doe" comment, from "Hawthorne and His Mosses" (408), is cited in *Call Me Ishmael* (43). The image recalls Howe's characterization of Florimell in *Defenestration*. See DuPlessis for discussion of the tropes of hunting in Howe's work (128–29).
45. Middleton, 93.
46. Olson (1970), 23.
47. For her friend George Butterick, etymology was the pathway to a point of pristine linguistic origin: "Etymology... is [Howe's] true genealogy.... She instinctively seeks to possess language to its roots, pre-family, pre-historical, even before language semanticizes itself" (313).
48. Melville [1850], 407.
49. Swensen interview, 381.
50. The Awede edition allocates a page to each poem, whereas the Wesleyan reprint occasionally doubles them up.
51. Interview with the author, June 2001. Johnson was a powerful fur trader and landowner who gave the lake the name of the English king in 1755 and, during the French and Indian War of 1754–63, oversaw the British forces in the Battle of Lake George. The lake had earlier been named Lac St Sacrément by the French. The French and Indian War is also known as the Seven Years' War, referring to the years 1756–63. Johnson was, like other historical figures that have interested Howe, a kind of border crosser: an intermediary between the

colonialists and Native Americans, responsible for overseeing trade between the English settlers and various Native American tribes. See Steele, viii. Jenny White makes a strong case for the importance of Fenimore Cooper's *The Last of the Mohicans* and *The Pioneers* to *Thorow*.
52. Back, 56.
53. Susan Howe and David Grubbs, *Thiefth* (Blue Chopsticks, 2005).
54. *Thiefth* was issued by Blue Chopsticks, an offshoot of Drag City records, which is a label normally associated with experimental rock music.
55. Grubbs makes use of material recorded by Swedish saxophonist Mats Gustafsson and the Greek cellist Nikos Veliotis, both of whom have collaborated with him on other projects.
56. Grubbs (2009), n.p.
57. These are published in a fourteen-volume edition.
58. Later in *Thorow*, a poem that begins "Walked on Mount Vision" ends at the foot of the page with "my whole being is Vision" (*Thorow*, 49); again, Howe assimilates herself to the landscape.
59. "God and grammar" alludes to a passage from Nietzsche's *Twilight of the Idols* ([1889]1968): "I fear we are not getting rid of God because we will still believe in grammar" (38).
60. See, e.g., her introduction to *Frame Structures*.
61. Howe gives a machine-age gloss to the words of another American Romantic, Emerson, on the mobility of poetic language: "But the quality of the imagination is to flow, and not to freeze.... Here is the difference betwixt the poet and the mystic, that the last nails a symbol to one sense, which was a true sense for a moment, but soon becomes old and false. For all symbols are fluxional; all language is vehicular and transitive, and is good, as ferries and horses are, for conveyance, not as farms and houses are, for homestead" (Emerson [1844] 1990, 211).
62. See the notion of the wild sketched in Thoreau's "Walking."
63. See Back, 18 and 51, on the importance of Todorov's *The Conquest of America: the Question of the Other* to understanding Howe's American work. Although distinct in its ambitions from the writing of thinkers that Howe mentions by name in her preface, Todorov's book's emphasis on power as a phenomenon of signification brings it within the orbit of *Thorow*'s preoccupations.
64. Todorov, 27.
65. Bercovitch (1975), 38–44, discusses the "redemptive history" of Cotton Mather's biography of John Winthrop.
66. See also Howe's remark: "Maybe [Robert Duncan] could have explained why, for me, Lake Erie is an allegory of elemental irrationality" ("Then *He* is in Range," 54).
67. Beckett interview, 21.
68. Nicholls (1996), 589.
69. In "Ktdaan," Thoreau writes of the woods of Maine: "These are not the artificial forests of an English king—a royal preserve merely. Here prevail no forest laws,

but those of nature. The aborigines have never been dispossessed, nor nature disforested...the country is virtually unmapped and unexplored, and there still waves the virgin forest of the New World" (Thoreau [<1864> 1988], 111).
70. Thoreau [1862], 277–78.
71. Ibid., 281.
72. C.f. Freud's belief that ontogeny recapitulates phylogeny: that the infant's development repeats the movement from savage to civilized human. See, for example, Freud [1915], 195: "The content of the Ucs. may be compared with an aboriginal population in the mind."
73. See Sayre for an extended treatment of Thoreau's relationship to "savagism," which Sayre describes as "the complex of theories about Indians held by nearly all Americans of Thoreau's time" (3). Howe's "under a spell of savagism" adapts Sayre's description of the younger Thoreau as "under the spell of savagism" (18).
74. Thoreau writes in *Walden*, "Thus it seemed that this one hillside illustrated the principle of all the operations of Nature. The Maker of this earth but patented a leaf. What Champollion will decipher this hieroglyphic for us, that we may turn over a new leaf at last?" (Thoreau [<1854> 2008], 207). Champollion was a Frenchman who in the 1820s deciphered Egyptian hieroglyphics (see Irwin's *American Hieroglyphics*). Bercovitch notes the religious origins of Romantic attempts to read the scripture of nature:

> All Romantics regarded nature as the temple of God. All of them, that is, were the heirs of natural theology—the traditional Christian view, shared by Catholics and Protestants alike, that Creation is God's 'other book', a Holy Writ of living hieroglyphs. The tradition leads forward to Romantic naturalism through a process of redefinition which, for our present purpose, may be simply stated. As the Bible gradually lost its authority after the Renaissance, *sola scriptura* became *sola natura*." (Bercovitch, 1975, 152)

75. Comment made after reading at UCSD, 22 November 1988.
76. Lyotard (1984), 13.
77. Marsh, 251.
78. Howe is citing Deleuze and Guattari's *A Thousand Plateaus*, 42. See also Todorov on naming and the natural world:

> Proper names form a very particular sector of the vocabulary: devoid of meaning, they serve only for denotation, but not directly for human communication; they are addressed to nature (to the referent), not to men; they are, in the fashion of indices, direct associations between aural sequences of sounds and segments of the world. The share of human communication that occupies Columbus's attention is therefore precisely that sector of language which serves, at least in an initial phase, only to designate nature." (28)

79. Thoreau [1862], 268.
80. Howe, thereby, transposes the notion of westward movement from the particularly Irish associations that she had explored in *The Liberties*. For discussion of the compass see Elisabeth Joyce.

81. The early settlers saw the land as a blend of "unmitigated harshness and tremendous potential fertility," according to Richard Slotkin's *Regeneration Through Violence* (19). Thoreau's vision, at least in "Walking," gives pre-eminence to the wild as the source of a cultural renewal. At one point he simply writes: "In short, all good things are wild and free" (Thoreau [1862], 279).
82. Freud [1920], 35.
83. See Beckett interview, 21: "Sometimes I think my poetry is only a search by an investigator for the point where the crime began."
84. Freud [1920], 21.
85. Ibid., 21–23.
86. Howe uses the term "transference"—although in a different sense—when she describes her encounter with Thoreau: "When I wrote *Thorow* I was staying several months alone on a lake in the Adirondacks and I surrounded myself with books by and about [Thoreau], so I reached some kind of transference" (Keller interview, 16).
87. Beckett interview, 24.
88. See Lacan, 49: "The unconscious is that part of the concrete discourse, in so far as it is transindividual, that is not at the disposal of the subject in reestablishing the continuity of his conscious discourse."
89. Thoreau [1862], 264.
90. Ibid.
91. Freud [1915], 195.
92. Howe is referring to the widely reported slaughter of the defenders of Fort William Henry, a fort Johnson himself had had constructed. The massacre by Mohawks of surrendered British and Americans became notorious as an illustration of Indian brutality and French duplicity. See Steele for a skeptical account that suggests that the extent of the violence was exaggerated.
93. Johnson, vol. 2, 780.
94. Ibid., vol. 7, 652. The second poem on page 47 also includes excerpts from vol. 11, 726. *Thorow* also cites Thoreau. The line "squadrons of clouds" (*Thorow*, 51) is from a journal entry, August 5, 1851 (Thoreau, [<1906> 1962], vol. 2, 374), and the line "A sort of border life" (*Thorow*, 50) comes from "Walking" (Thoreau [1862], 284). Mt Vision (*Thorow*, 49), Erebus (*Thorow*, 54), and Shelving Rock (ibid.) are all place names from the immediate area. Johnson had a house nearby at "Sacandaga vläie" (*Thorow*, 58).
95. Writing as late as the mid-1950s, Perry Miller could still describe wildness as a fundamental characteristic of the American artist: "The American, or at least the American artist, cherishes in his innermost being the impulse to reject completely the gospel of civilization, in order to guard with resolution the savagery of his heart" (Miller [<1955> 1967], 207).

5 Enthusiasm, Telepathy, and Immediacy

1. See Harris and Reed for excellent discussions of Howe in this period, in particular her relationship with the work of Ad Reinhard and Ian Hamilton Finlay.

2. See Swensen interview, 386: "It would take a book for me to go on about what *The Large Glass* means to me." Howe goes on to align Duchamp with Henry James.
3. From Duchamp's "Note for the Green Box."
4. Keller interview, 6. Howe worked with Greenwald at the St Mark's poetry workshop.
5. Harris, 456, n.15.
6. Thompson interview, n.p.
7. Fraser 184–87; Reed, n.p.
8. Megan Williams, 127.
9. See Drucker (1998) and McGann (1993).
10. Reed, n.p.
11. See Davidson for a sympathetic account of Howe's thought on materiality and the act of reading.
12. See also Ashton, 23–24. Ashton's book attacks "literalism" in language writing (of which she considers Howe's poetry to be an example).
13. Keller interview, 22. Howe seeks to distinguish her influences among artists from those—Russian Formalism and Frankfurt School Marxism—that she attributes to Language writers: "I suppose I got some of these ideas because they were all around, but I got them first through artists' writings—through people like Reinhardt, Finlay, Judd, Smithson."
14. See Michaels, 1–18. Michaels suggests, somewhat misleadingly, that Howe argues for the reproduction in facsimile of the 86 blank pages between the entries in the front and back of the notebook (1–2). Although Howe argues that later editions of the autobiography neglect the "structural paradox of the material object," she goes no further than the assertion that "[n]either editor saw fit to point out" the material features of the notebook (*Birth-mark*, 60). Howe's observation that the booklet contains two different narratives separated by an "empty center" might more productively be read in relation to her interest in antinomies—"problematical type and antitype" (*Birth-mark*, 61)—and the preoccupation with points of origin in her poetry.
15. Michaels, 3.
16. Michaels's position on intention misconstrues Howe (5). See Howe's partial dismissal, with regard to Dickinson, of Foucault's argument on intentionality in his essay "What is an Author?" (*Birth-mark*, 19–20).
17. This is specifically related to a paternal injunction. See Howe's account of being excluded by her father from the Widener stacks at Harvard in *Birth-mark*, 18; see also *Pierce-Arrow*, 5; and *The Midnight*, 120–28.
18. Letter of 14 July 1992, Howe's emphasis.
19. See Davidson for discussion of the ways in which Howe's textual collage "destroys the force of Arnold's condescending rhetoric and reveals its class biases" (88).
20. See Swensen interview: "Perhaps I'm obsessed with the spirits who inhabit a place because my mother brought me up on Yeats. Before I could read, I heard 'Down by the Salley Garden' as a lullaby" (375).

21. Yeats ([1891] 1970), 27. Yeats is citing the judgment of John Mitchel, a leader of the Young Ireland movement and the editor of the collection of Mangan poems that Melville owned.
22. Yeats ([1887] 1970), 25–26.
23. James Joyce wrote two papers on Mangan; a translation of the second of these, originally written in Italian and delivered in Trieste in 1907, is cited by Howe in the first section of her poem.
24. For Jacques Derrida, telepathy is itself an alien formation within psychoanalysis: "Psychoanalysis...resembles an adventure of modern rationality set on swallowing *and* simultaneously rejecting the foreign body named Telepathy, for assimilating it and vomiting it without being able to make up its mind what to do with it" (Derrida [1988] 38).
25. Letter of 29 June 1851, in *Correspondence*, ed. Horth, 195. See also Melville's 1 May 1850 letter to Richard Henry Dana: "I am especially delighted at the thought, that those strange, congenial feelings, with which after my first voyage I for the first time read 'Two Years Before the Mast', and while so engaged was, as it were, tied & welded to you by a sort of Siamese link of affectionate sympathy" (ibid., 160).
26. Melville [1850], 346. The passage, from his "Hawthorne and His Mosses," is cited in Cowen's preface, xiii. See also Wilson, ed., for the relationship between Melville and Hawthorne.
27. See Howe's description of her technique in the Keller interview, 25: "What I did was to randomly go through [Cowen's] book and light on something—sort of chance operation without discipline. I would pull a line from one of the portions he had marked and then use it to make a poem."
28. Freud ([1900] 1953–74), 531.
29. Cowen, vol. 1, xxxiii.
30. See James Joyce ([1902] 2000), 57 "In 'Dark Rosaleen,' [Mangan's poetry] does not attain to the quality of Whitman indeed, but is tremulous with all the changing harmonies of Shelley's verse."
31. James Joyce ([1907] 2000), 136. The editor of this text, Kevin Barry, 300, points out the links between Joyce's Mangan and the character Davin in *Portrait of the Artist as a Young Man*. Mangan's description of his father as a "human boa-constrictor" in his "Fragment of an Unfinished Autobiography" (Mangan, xxxvi), reappears in *Finnegans Wake*'s "mynfadher was a boer constructor."
32. Mitchel, 30.
33. Cowen reproduces the pages from Mitchel's edition of Mangan that Melville annotated.
34. James Joyce ([1907] 2000), 136.
35. Bollas, 143. See Nicholls (2002) for a different construction of the role of *Nachträglichkeit* in Howe's work.
36. Laplanche, 261.
37. Ibid.
38. Ibid., 265.

39. Foster interview, 174.
40. The phrase is discussed in Lloyd, 123–24. Lloyd's book makes a persuasive case for attaching certain postmodern motifs to Mangan. Lloyd remarks on the coexistence in George Moore's *Lalla Rookh* of the "parallel fashions of Orientalism and Celticism" (123). Lloyd's book is cited in the first part of Howe's poem. The words "Araby," "Lalla," and "Rookh" occur in a poem in *The Midnight*.
41. Lloyd notes the importance to Irish cultural nationalism of Orientalist and philological theories that gave "a scientific orientation and therefore credibility to the tradition that placed the Eden of human origins in the Middle East" (121). Mangan published 'translations' from tongues of which he had no knowledge.
42. Cited in Clifford, 95.
43. Ibid., 94.
44. See, e.g., Shelley's "Alastor, or the Spirit of Solitude" (1816) and Byron's "The Corsair" (1814). The young protagonist of Joyce's "Araby" falls for a girl who is known as Mangan's sister; the word "Araby" casts an "Eastern enchantment" over him.
45. In the French edition of the book, Howe reproduces texts from Melville's edition of Mangan that identify "the Poet" as "Cain-like" (*Marginalia de Melville*, 84) and Mangan as having a "grand Byronic soul" (*Marginalia de Melville*, 85). Mangan wrote of "the veil of Sais," an image of veiled beauty prominent in the German Romantic tradition (see Lloyd, 125); he described himself as "the Man In The Cloak" (see Sheridan, 59); his 'translations' were often pure invention; and he described the mind as "a Cain that may build cities, but can abide in none of them" (cited in Clifford, 94). There are also links between Mangan and Byron's poetry in the figure of Cain. See Lloyd, 194, and *Melville's Marginalia*, 140, for further reference to Cain.
46. Translated in *Potentialities* (1999). Agamben imputes a Pauline preference for spirit over the letter of the law to Bartleby. Agamben's essay was first published alongside an Italian translation of Gilles Deleuze's "Bartleby; Or, the Formula," collected in English in *Essays Critical and Clinical* (1998). Deleuze's Bartleby also provoked a response from Jaques Rancière: his "Deleuze, Bartleby, and the Literary Formula."
47. Bernstein interview, n.p.
48. Agamben, 257. This is clearly a different conception from that of the negative, operative in much of Howe's work. Often, however, the category of nothing and the aporetic guarantor of the law in Howe are generative.
49. Ibid., 253–54.
50. See my discussion of *Articulation*.
51. Lacan, 303.
52. Agamben, 269.
53. Ibid. See also *Eikon*'s "Paul also was Romans 7" (*Eikon*, 76).
54. See my discussion of *Articulation*. Agamben, 269, notes this phrase, too.
55. Bernstein interview, n.p.

56. David Hall, 356.
57. See Howe's question in *Birth-mark*, 16—"What is the nature of epistolary enthusiasm?"—for a different kind of letter.
58. The twinning of rushing light and grace also appears in *Birth-mark*, 47: "A poem can prevent onrushing light going out. Narrow path in the teeth of proof. Fire of words will try us. Grace given to few. Coming home through bent and bias for the sake of why so."
59. Cowen, volume 2, 508. The choice of this epigraph may also be related to the death of Howe's husband, David von Schlegell, in 1992.
60. Melville (1853), 126. "I like to be stationary" is the epigraph to the second, "Conversion" section of *The Nonconformist's Memorial* collection (43).
61. Melville ([1853] 1993), 127.
62. Interview with author, June 2001.
63. See "Ether Either," 121–22, for Howe's interest in the pronunciation of the 'ei' diphthong.
64. Howe remarks in an e-mail,
    The whole of Nonconformist [i.e., the book] has the coming death of David hanging over it. I identified his treatment in the art world with Melville's treatment in the literary one. I identified David's war experience with Melville's whaling voyage. I identified his love of the sea with Melville. For four years we knew he was going to die. He designed sculptures for memorials and was constantly entering contests for them. The famous Vietnam one by Maya Linn was during that time—she was around the sculpture dept at Yale when he was teaching there—memorials were in the air. I mean as sculptural objects. So it all tied into David. The intensity and the sense of terror that is in both Non CM and MM was lurking around in my mind— (email to author, 6 August 2002).
    In an interview with Lyn Keller conducted in March 1994, Howe remarked that she had been unable to write poetry following the death of her husband.
65. Nicholls (2002), 442ff. C.f. the mourning for Howe's father in *Secret History* or Howe's own suggestion that the deaths of her mother and her Uncle John were the "catalyst" that set *The Midnight* in motion (Thomson interview, n.p.).
66. In Swinburne's "Tristram of Lyonesse" it is the words "Ah, the ship comes surely; but her sail is black" that cause Tristram to die of a broken heart.
67. Howe cites Peter Sacks's book *The English Elegy* in her working notes: "The movement from loss to consolation requires a deflection of desire—with the creation of a trope both for the lost object and for the original characters of the desire itself" (7). She remarks, "But if Sacks says castration lies at the core of the work of mourning what about women elegists?"
68. This technique occurs in more muted ways in other of her works, notably *Melville's Marginalia*.
69. Swensen interview, 379–80.

70. Howe developed this technique in *Birth-mark*, with its use of manuscript material from Emily Dickinson and Shelley. The front cover of *The Nonconformist's Memorial* displays an image from a Shelley manuscript.
71. Howe would later develop her interest in the relationship between American poetry and pragmatism, co-teaching with her third husband, Peter Hare, the module Poetry and Pragmatism in 2002. The course reads pragmatist texts alongside the work of modernist poets such as Williams, Stein and Stevens. See http://wings.buffalo.edu/epc/authors/howe/syllabi/poetry&pragmatism.html.
72. See *Birth-mark*, 1, for Howe's remarks on Dickinson as proto-modernist.
73. See also "An Exchange between Joan Jonas, Susan Howe and Jeanne Heuving," n.p. in the online journal *How2*:
    I reached Peirce's existential graphs through my interest in Emily Dickinson's late manuscripts. I felt that his logical graphs were poetry and drawing at the same time they were logic, and that they need to be seen in facsimile rather than transcription. People were accustomed to seeing William Blake's manuscripts in that way. I feel that the same editorial approach should be taken to Dickinson and Peirce, and I would like to see some of the manuscripts displayed as art objects in a gallery.
74. Peirce, "Consciousness and Language," 351. Burks, the editor, dates the lecture to 1866 or 1867.
75. Roberts, 11.
76. MS620, 8. Cited in Roberts, 126.
77. Presented in this way, the sentences bring to mind the iterative sequences of Gertrude Stein, who worked with Peirce's friend William James.
78. Peirce ([1906] 1991), 249.
79. Howe suggests that the name came from Peirce's reading of Pope's translation of the *Iliad*.
80. See, again, Keller interview, 8.
81. See also Howe's conversation with Joan Jonas and Jeanne Heuving: "War in this century ushered in modernism and disrupted classical syntax. *The Iliad*, in particular, unlike many other texts about war, in its brevity and brutality, is very resonant in our lifetime." n.p.
82. Letter of 13 July 1986.
83. Weil, 191.
84. Swensen interview, 380–381. The link that Howe draws between literary form and politics is revealing:
    CS: It's too easy to draw parallels between social upheaval and artistic upheaval, between a disruption of daily space and a disruption of expressive space, so I won't but…
    SH: But I will. I insist on it. The Civil War is our Iliad.… There is no way of overstating the importance of this war to the American psyche.
85. See Howe's conversation with Jonas and Heuving: "The blank space between two poems in a series invites contingencies."

86. See the material cited from Swinburne's "Atalanta in Calydon" or the *Rückenfigur* section.
87. See Thompson interview, n.p.: "I like to lay the pages out on the table so one speaks to and almost mirrors the other. I finish one and answer it with the next."
88. Peirce ([1905] 1998), 332.
89. As Brian Reed points out, there are antecedents for the prominence of Swinburne in *Pierce Arrow*: see the preface to *Frame Structures* (12) and "Ether Either" (122; 126–27).
90. See Harris for discussion of Howe's early critical writing on art.
91. Letter of 13 December 1979.
92. Keller interview, 9.
93. See Dalrymple Henderson.
94. Thompson interview, n.p. A scrim is a thin sheet of material used on stage in a theatre. When lit from behind, it becomes transparent, revealing what it had previously screened from the audience. The word appears in *The Midnight* (57). See Keller interview, 7: "I can't express how important Agnes Martin was to me at the point when I was shifting from painting to poetry. The combination in Martin's work, say, of being spare and infinitely suggestive at the same time characterizes the art I respond to. And in poetry I am concerned with the space of the page apart from the words on it." See also Howe's remark in an essay published in *Jacket 31* that Agnes Martin's 1960s and 1970s work had "been an inspiration for all my writing life," http://jacketmagazine.com/31/rc-howe.html.
95. Krauss, 164. Krauss cautions that Martin's choice of titles has led—or rather misled—critics into reading Martin's work as a version of "abstract sublime," another artistic representation of transcendence. See also Reed for discussion of Krauss, Martin, and Howe.
96. See, e.g., Giesen and Westheider.
97. The Smithson piece is discussed in relation to Howe in chapter 2 of Dworkin (32–49).
98. See *Birth-mark*, 152, where Howe talks of how the formal and material aspects of Dickinson's work contribute to the meaning.

6 The Late Lyric

1. There has been a concurrent renewal of the visual and material dimensions of her activity. See *Fragment of the Wedding Dress of Sarah Pierpont Edwards*, *Poems Found in a Pioneer Museum*, and *Frolic Architecture*.
2. See Nerys Williams, Rankine and Spahr, Jeffries, *PMLA*, and anthologies edited by Shepherd, Mengham and Kinsella, and Swensen and St John.
3. Willis, 228. Willis studied with Howe at Buffalo in the early 1990s. Her position on the poem "from elsewhere" has something in common with Susan Stewart's suggestion that "poetry involves being spoken through as well as speaking" in her article "Lyric Possession" (38)—a text to which Willis refers.
4. See Vanderborg's discussion of Howe's "communal lyric" (101).

5. See Stevens (1997) 178, 665 [1942].
6. Willis, 229. See also Moxley for an essay on contemporary lyric that is colored by Adornian perspectives. For Moxley, too, impossibility is an important category.
7. Stevens (1942), 664: "Nothing could be more evasive and inaccessible."
8. Blasing, 27–28.
9. Ibid., 136.
10. See Nicholls (2002) for a detailed discussion of this aspect of the poem. The pun on "reconfigure" is inescapable.
11. Swinburne used twelfth-century French versions as his models, unlike Tennyson and Arnold, who based their poems on Malory. See McGann and Sligh, eds., 485.
12. The story has a Homeric analogue, also mentioned in the poem (*Rückenfigur*, 137)—Aegeus in the *Odyssey* commits suicide on seeing his son Theseus's ship flying a black sail as Theseus returns from his encounter with the Minotaur.
13. Undated working notebook.
14. *Rückenfigur* was first published in *Conjunctions* 30, Spring 1998.
15. Adorno's suggestion that the most valuable lyric works "are those in which the subject, with no remaining trace of mere matter, sounds forth in language until language itself acquires a voice" has been the most useful for the present discussion. See Adorno, 43.
16. Howe has said that she encountered Klein's work on mourning, preferring it to Freud, in the aftermath of David von Schlegell's death (Interview with the author, June 2001). Reflections on primal ambivalence and splitting inform her "Sorting Facts" essay, written during this period.
17. As in *Defenestration* and *Eikon*, a theatrical metaphor—"on an acting/platform"—accompanies the language of dissimulation.
18. W. J .T. Mitchell has discussed the description of Achilles' shield as a moment in the *Iliad* when ekphrasis becomes a means of exposing the ideological underpinnings at work in a literary text (179–80).
19. The word "brute" occurs three times on 28–29 and again—"actual brute/predestined fact" on the first page of *Rückenfigur* (129). The phrase "actuality is something brute" (*P-A*, 29) seems to refer to Peirce's notion of secondness, described in one of his letters to Lady Welby in the following terms: "Generally speaking genuine secondness consists in one thing acting upon another,—brute action. I say brute, because so far as the idea of any *law* or *reason* comes in, Thirdness comes in (Burks, ed., vol. 8, 330 [Peirce's italics]). Howe uses material from the letters to Welby on 81–83 of *Pierce-Arrow*.
20. Schlegel, 150. The fragment appears, among several other from Schlegel's Critical and Athaeneum fragments, in Howe's working notes to *Pierce-Arrow*.
21. Schlegel, 175.
22. See Lacoue-Labarthe and Nancy's *The Literary Absolute* (also cited in Howe's working notes).

23. By Abbott Lowell Cummings. Poems from pages 7, 10, 12, 15, 16, 36, and 37 of *The Midnight* contain material from this book, which is acknowledged on the first page of *Scare Quotes I*.
24. Lowell Cummings, 2.
25. See *TM*, 93: "The shirt worn by William/ the Silent when he fell by/ an assassin is still preserved/ at the Hague," comes from page 221 of Palliser's book. Other references to lace and fabric production show the influence of the Palliser history.
26. Palliser's book devotes thirty-six pages to the kinds of lace produced in different English regions. Lace, notes Palliser, was banned altogether by Edward IV in 1463; the sumptuary laws of Henry VIII forbade the wearing of lace by anyone below the rank of a baron or a knight's wife (Palliser, 251); measures were sometimes taken to forbid the use of lace produced abroad.
27. The illustrations of lace from Palliser's book reproduced on pages 2 and 111 of *The Midnight* recall Howe's comparison between Peirce's intricate doodles and late twentieth-century artworks.
28. Stevenson, 121.
29. The issue of the *Wallace Stevens Journal* collects the proceedings of a conference on Stevens held at the University of Connecticut in April 2004. Howe's had long admired Stevens. In a letter of 3 March 1989 to Norman O. Brown, she writes: "the Stevens of *Harmonium* doesn't interest me. That's the Stevens most people like. It's the late Stevens I adore. 'Auroras,' 'Notes,' 'Credences of Summer,' 'To an Old Philosopher,' 'The Rabbit as King of the Ghosts,' among many many many short poems. I love his essays; To me he has that dark vision of America that you speak of. I think that he is being done a dis-service by Vendler, Bloom, Hollander, etc and that seems to throw more radical poets off the trail. One doesn't mention Stevens in Language poetry circles etc. But that's so wrong. I think the language is wildly experimental in the sense that he is experimenting with the power of words as emblems, as charged and mysterious entities."
30. "Furious Calm," 136. See James ([1907] 1978), 118. See also Stevens [1952], "the interrelation between things is what makes them fecund" (867).
31. See "Incloser," *Birth-mark*, 51, for a comparable assimilation of landscape and poetics:
    > During the 1850s, when the Republic was breaking apart, newly exposed soil from abandoned narratives was as rich and fresh as a natural meadow.
    >
    > Emily Dickinson and Herman Melville are bridge builders. Their writing vaults the streams. They lead me in nomad spaces. They sieve cipherings, hesitations, watchings, survival of sound-meaning associations: the hound and cry, track and call. So much strangeness from God. What is saved to be said.
    >
    > Once dams, narratives are bridges.
32. See James ([1912] 1996), 107.

33. "Furious Calm," 136. The passage is taken from "On Receiving the Gold Medal from the Poetry Society of America," in Stevens, 834.
34. All writers of longstanding interest to Howe. *My Emily Dickinson* describes Edwards as "the most astute and original American philosopher to write before the age of James, Peirce and Santayana" (*MED*, 48). His practice of sewing booklets together is compared to Dickinson's work with fascicles. See also *The Midnight*, 58: "Jonathan Edwards was a paper saver. He kept old bills and shopping lists, then copied out his sermons on the verso sides and stitched them into handmade notebooks. When he was in his twenties, Ralph Waldo Emerson cut his dead minister father's sermons in manuscript out of their bindings, then used the bindings to hold his own writing. He mutilated another of Emerson senior's notebooks in order use the blank pages. Stubs of torn off pages show sound bites." See also Howe's description of Emerson's desire to "put on eloquence like a robe" in *The Midnight* (*TM*, 46).
35. "If" is an important word in *The Midnight*—see, e.g., page 45, "Coulds are iffy," or page 134 for Howe's interest in counterfactuals and conditions.
36. See Timothy D. Hall, especially 19–20, for material on the Great Awakening that may have informed *The Midnight*'s depiction of the American reception of European thought. Another eighteenth-century dissenting movement that appears in the pages of *The Midnight* is Sandemanianism. This sect had its origins in a revolt against the Church of Scotland. Its founder, Robert Sandeman, visited the United States in 1764, and several congregations were established in New England. The largest of these was in Danbury, Connecticut (about 40 miles from Howe's home in Guilford), where Sandeman died in 1771 (see Cantor, 24.). The Sandemanians are comparable as European exports to the fabric and lace designs of Europe, the English preachers of the Great Awakening, and the two brothers of *The Master of Ballantrae*, who die far from home in the wilderness of the Adirondacks in upstate New York.
37. "Fragment of the Wedding Dress of Sarah Pierpont Edwards" combines text relating to the documentation of a scrap of material held at the Beinecke Rare Book and Manuscript Library (*Souls*, 114, 116) and the *Transactions of the Connecticut Academy of Arts and Sciences* of December 1949. The *Transactions* details proceedings of the academy's thousandth meeting, for which Stevens composed and read "An Ordinary Evening in New Haven" (*Souls*, 117, 119). An early version of *118 Westerly Terrace* was published by Belladonna Books in 2005.
38. A recording of *Souls of the Labadie Tract*, made with David Grubbs, was issued as a CD before the poem appeared in book form.
39. See Saxby, 309 and 388n70. Howe uses the text for her reference to the "lappadee poplar" in a 1790s map of Maryland and as her source for the quotations from "a Swedish pastor" and Samuel Bownas in her introduction.
40. Certeau (1992), 280.
41. Ibid.

42. Stevens's father grew up in Bucks County. "Dutch Graves in Bucks County" is one of the poems about which Howe chose to speak when addressing students in a course on poetry and sound run by Charles Bernstein at the University of Pennsylvania (http://writing.upenn.edu/bernstein/syllabi/sound.html).
43. Howe uses the masques written for *The Lord Hay's Masque* and *The Somerset Masque*. See Campion, ed. Davis, 212, 217, 271–72. Campion's introduction to his *Somerset Masque* certainly echoes the concerns of *Defenestration* and *Souls*: "I grounded my whole Invention upon Inchauntments and several transformations" (268).
44. See Bender. See also *Eikon*'s use of Edward Almack's work on editions of the *Eikon Basilike* and the use of the genetic text of *Billy Budd* in "Scattering as Behavior Toward Risk".
45. Prynne, 141, 142. The essay concludes with brief discussion of a poem Wallace Stevens addressed to George Santayana, "To an Old Philosopher in Rome."
46. Ibid, 168.
47. Ibid.
48. Ibid.
49. Stevens, 458.
50. See Ilie for an account of the ambiguous figure of Minerva's significance to the Enlightenment. For Ilie, the eighteenth century is the Age of Minerva:

> This is the goddess who symbolized the wisdom and knowledge that reaches beyond empirical experience into a transcendent reality where Reason and Unreason fuse into the One. The Minerva of this proposition is not the mythological goddess but the mediating mind between spirit and matter. She is the figure in Ancient Philosophy whose dispersed remnants persisted in the eighteenth century. (23)

51. See Manuth and de Winkel, 13–14.
52. Stevens's long poem "Owl's Clover" was originally published in *The Man with the Blue Guitar* (1937) and "The Owl in the Sarcophagus" in *The Auroras of Autumn* (1950).

Bibliography

By Susan Howe

Poetry

The Western Borders. Tuumba, 1976. Available in facsimile form at the Eclipse Web site, http://english.utah.edu/eclipse/authors.html.
Defenestration of Prague [and *The Liberties*]. New York: Kulchur Foundation, 1983.
"Federalist 10." *A.bacus* 30. Elmwood, CT: Potes and Poets Press, 1987.
Articulation of Sound Forms in Time. Windsor, VT: Awede. 1987.
"Heliopathy." *Temblor* 4 (1990).
The Europe of Trusts (containing "THERE ARE NOT LEAVES ENOUGH TO CROWN TO COVER TO CROWN TO COVER" [first published in 1985 as "Statement for the New Poetics Colloquium" in *Jimmy and Lucy's House of 'K'* 5 (November 1985), 16–17]; *Pythagorean Silence* [1982]; *Defenestration of Prague* [1983]; and *The Liberties* [1980]). Los Angeles: Sun and Moon Press, 1990.
Singularities (containing *Articulation of Sound Forms in Time* [1987]; *Thorow*; "Scattering as Behavior towards Risk"). Hanover, NH: Wesleyan University Press, 1990.
The Nonconformist's Memorial. New York. Grenfell Press, 1992.
The Nonconformist's Memorial (containing *The Nonconformist's Memorial* [1992]; *Silence Wager Stories*; *A Bibliography of the King's Book, or Eikon Basilike* [1989] and *Melville's Marginalia*). New York: New Directions, 1993.
Frame Structures: Early Poems 1974–1979 (containing *Hinge Picture* [1974]; *Chanting at the Crystal Sea* [1975]; *Cabbage Gardens* [1979]; *Secret History of the Dividing Line* [1978]). New York: New Directions, 1996.
Marginalia de Melville, trans. Bernard Rival. Courbevoie: Théâtre Typographique, 1997.
Pierce-Arrow [containing *Arisbe, The Leisure of the Theory Class*, and *Rückenfigur*]. New York: New Directions, 1999.
Bed Hangings. New York: Granary Books, 2000.
Bed Hangings II. Ballybeg, Co. Wicklow: Coracle, 2002.
Kidnapped. Ballybeg, Co. Wicklow: Coracle, 2002.

The Midnight [containing *Scare Quotes I* and *II* and *Bed Hangings I* and *II*]. New York: New Directions, 2003.
118 Westerly Terrace. New York: Belladonna, 2005.
Souls of the Labadie Tract [containing "Errand," *Personal Narrative, Souls of the Labadie Tract*, "Errand," *118 Westerly Terrace* [2005], and *Fragment of the Wedding Dress of Sarah Pierpont Edwards*]. New York: New Directions, 2007.
Poems Found in a Pioneer Museum. Ballybeg, Co. Wicklow: Coracle, 2009.
Frolic Architecture (with James Welling). New York: Grenfell Press, 2010.

Criticism and Prose

"The End of Art." *Archives of American Art Journal* 14, no. 4 (1974): 2–6; reprinted in *The ABCs of Robert Lax*, ed. David Miller and Nicholas Zurbrugg. Exeter, UK: Stride, 1999): 80–91.
My Emily Dickinson. Berkeley, CA: North Atlantic Books, 1985.
"Statement for the New Poetics Colloquium." *Jimmy and Lucy's House of K* 5 (November 1985), 16–17. [Republished in *The Europe of Trusts* as "THERE ARE NOT LEAVES ENOUGH TO CROWN TO COVER TO CROWN TO COVER."]
"Where Should the Commander Be," *Writing* 19 (November 1987): 3–20.
"Then *He* Is in Range" *American Poetry* 6, no. 1 (1988): 54–57.
"Charles Olson: A Dialogue There Is." *Acts* 10 (1989): 166–73.
"Encloser," in *The Politics of Poetic Form*, ed. Charles Bernstein. New York: Roof, 1990: 175–196.
The Birth-mark: Unsettling the Wilderness in American Literary History. Hanover, NH: Wesleyan University Press, 1993.
"Sorting Facts: Or, Nineteen Ways of Looking at Marker." *Beyond Document: Essays on Nonfiction Film*. Ed. Charles Warren. Hanover, NH: Wesleyan University Press, 1996: 295–343.
"Ether Either." *Close Listening: Poetry and the Performed Word*, ed. Charles Bernstein. New York and Oxford: Oxford University Press, 1998: 111–27.
"Furious Calm." *The Wallace Stevens Journal* 28, no. 2 (Fall 2004): 133–37.
"*The Collected Poems*: The Next 50 Years." *The Wallace Stevens Journal* 28, no. 2 (Fall 2004): 231–34.
"Leaf Flower in the Wind Falling Blue The Dark River." *Jacket* 31, http://jacketmagazine.com/31/rc-howe.html.
"Choir Answers to Choir: Notes on Jonathan Edwards and Wallace Stevens" *Chicago Review* 54, no. 4 (2009): 51–61.

Interviews

Beckett, Tom. "*The Difficulties* interview." *The Difficulties* 3, no. 2 (1989): 17–27.
Falon, Janet Ruth. "Speaking with Susan Howe." *The Difficulties* 3, no. 2 (1989): 28–42.

Bernstein, Charles. "Interview." *Linebreak*. Radio program recorded in summer 1995 and archived as an audio file. http://writing.upenn.edu/pennsound/x/LINEbreak.html.

Foster, Edward "*Talisman* interview." *The Birth-mark: Unsettling the Wilderness in American Literary History*; Hanover, NH: Wesleyan University Press, 1993: 165–81. [originally published in *Talisman* 4 (Spring 1990)].

Creeley, Robert, and Susan Howe. "Four-Part Harmony: Robert Creeley and Susan Howe Talk it Out," *Village Voice* Literary Supplement, 12 April 1994.

Keller, Lynn. "An Interview with Susan Howe." *Contemporary Literature* 36, no. 1 (Spring 1995): 1–34.

Swensen, Cole. "A Dialogue: Susan Howe and Cole Swensen." *Conjunctions* 35 (Fall 2000): 374–87.

Montgomery, Will. Unpublished interview, June 2001 [cited as "interview with author"].

Thompson, Jon. "Interview with Susan Howe." *Free Verse* (Winter 2005). 8 June 2008, http://english.chass.ncsu.edu/freeverse/Archives/Winter_2005/interviews/S_Howe.html.

Heuving, Jean, Susan Howe, and Joan Jonas. "An Exchange between Joan Jonas, Susan Howe and Jeanne Heuving." *How2* 2, no. 3 (Spring 2005).

Audio Recordings

Thiefth (with David Grubbs). Blue Chopsticks BC15, 2005.
Souls of the Labadie Tract (with David Grubbs). Blue Chopsticks BC17, 2007.

Other

E-mail to author, 6 August 2002.

Archival Material

Material Held at the Archive for New Poetry, Mandeville Department of Special Collections, University of California, San Diego (UCSD)
Letters to Charles Bernstein, Lyn Hejinian, John Taggart, Ron Silliman.
Miscellaneous drafts, working notebooks and journals, mid-1970s to late 1980s.
Audiocassette recording of a reading at UCSD, 22 November 1988.

Material Held at the Special Collections, University of California, Santa Cruz (UCSC)
Letters to Norman O. Brown.

Material Held at the Beinecke Rare Book and Manuscript Library, Yale
Miscellaneous working notebooks, drafts, and journals relating to *Pierce-Arrow* and *The Midnight* (consulted July 2007 courtesy of Susan Howe prior to the acquisition of the papers by the Beinecke).

By Other Authors

Adams, Robert M. "The Staging of Jonson's Plays and Masques." In *Ben Jonson's Plays and Masques*, ed. Robert M. Adams, 311–17. New York: Norton, 1979.

Adamson, Gregory Dale. "Serres Translates Howe." *SubStance* 26, no. 2 (1997): 110–124.

Adorno, Theodor. "On Lyric Poetry and Society," trans. Shierry Weber Nicholsen. In *Notes to Literature*, vol. 1, 37–54. New York: Columbia University Press, 1991.

Adorno, Theodor, and Max Horkheimer. *The Dialectic of Enlightenment*, trans. John Cumming. London: Verso, [1944] 1986.

Agamben, Giorgio. "Bartleby, or On Contingency," in *Potentialities*, ed. and trans. Daniel Heller-Roazen, 243–71. Stanford, CA: Stanford University Press, 1999.

———. *State of Exception*. Trs. Kevin Attell. Chicago, IL; London: University of Chicago Press, 2005.

Almack, Edward. *A Bibliography of the King's Book; or, Eikon Basilike*. London: Blades, East & Blades, 1889.

Ashton, Jennifer. *From Modernism to Postmodernism: American Poetry and Theory in the Twentieth Century*. Cambridge: Cambridge University Press, 2005.

Back, Rachel Tzvia. *Led by Language: The Poetry and Poetics of Susan Howe*. Tuscaloosa, AL: University of Alabama Press, 2002.

Bender, Todd K. *A Concordance to Henry James's* The Awkward Age. New York: Garland, 1989.

Benjamin, Walter. "Critique of Violence", trans. Edmund Jephcott, eds Marcus Bullock and Michael Jennings, in *Selected Writings* Volume 1, 236–52. Cambridge: Harvard University Press, 1999.

Bercovitch, Sacvan. *The Puritan Origins of the American Self*. New Haven, CT: Yale University Press, 1975.

———. *The American Jeremiad*. Madison, WI: University of Wisconsin Press, 1978.

Bernstein, Michael André. *The Tale of the Tribe*. Princeton, NJ: Princeton University Press, 1988.

Berry, Philippa. *Shakespeare's Feminine Endings: Disfiguring Death in the Tragedies*. London: Routledge, 1999.

Berry, Phillipa, and Andrew Wernick, eds. *The Shadow of Spirit*. London: Routledge, 1992.

Blasing, Mutlu Konuk. *Lyric Poetry: The Pain and the Pleasure of Words*. Princeton, NJ: Princeton University Press, 2007.

Bollas, Christopher. *Cracking Up: The Work of Unconscious Experience*. London: Routledge, 1995.

Braine, David. "Negative Theology." In *The Routledge Encyclopedia of Philosophy*, vol. 6, ed. Edward Craig, 759–66. London: Routledge, 1988.

Brown, Sarah Annes. *The Metamorphosis of Ovid from Chaucer to Ted Hughes*. London: Duckworth, 1999.

Brown, Norman O. *Apocalypse and/or Metamorphosis*. Berkeley, CA: University of California Press, 1991.
Bruns, Gerald. *Heidegger's Estrangements*. New Haven, CT: Yale University Press, 1989.
———. "Voices of Construction: On Susan Howe's Poetry and Poetics (A Citational Ghost Story)." *Contemporary Literature* 50, no. 1 (Spring 2009): 28–53.
Budick, Sanford, and Wolfgang Iser, eds. *Languages of the Unsayable: The Play of Negativity in Literature and Literary Theory*. New York: Columbia University Press, 1989.
Bush, George W. State of the Union address, 28 January 2003. http://www.americanrhetoric.com/speeches/stateoftheunion2003.html/.
Butterick, George. "The Mysterious Vision of Susan Howe." *North Dakota Quarterly* 55 (1987): 312–21.
Byrd, William. *William Byrd's Histories of the Dividing Line*. New York: Dover, [1841, 1929] 1967.
Calamy, Edmund. *The Nonconformist's Memorial*. Ed. Samuel Palmer. Two vols. London: W. Harris, 1775.
Caldwell, Patricia. "The Antinomian Language Controversy." *Harvard Theological Review* 69 (1986): 345–67.
Campion, Thomas. *The Works of Thomas Campion*, ed. Walter R. Davis. London: Faber, 1969.
Cantor, Geoffrey. *Michael Faraday: Sandemanian and Scientist: A Study of Science and Religion in the Nineteenth Century*. Basingstoke: Macmillan, 1991.
Cixous, Hélène. "Sorties: Out and Out: Attacks/ Ways Out/ Forays." In *The Newly Born Woman*, trans. Betsy Wing, 63–132. Minneapolis: University of Minnesota Press, 1986.
Clifford, Brendan. *The Dubliner: The Lives, Times and Writings of James Clarence Mangan*. Belfast: Athol, 1988.
Collis, Stephen. *Through Words of Others: Susan Howe and Anarcho-Scholasticism*. Victoria, BC: English Literary Studies Editions, 2006.
Colwell, Ernest Cadman. "A Definite Rule for the Use of the Article in the Greek New Testament," *The Journal of Biblical Literature* 52 (1933): 12–21.
Connecticut Academy of Arts and Sciences. *Transactions of the Connecticut Academy of Arts and Sciences* 38 (December 1949).
Cornford, Francis Macdonald. "Mysticism and Science in the Pythagorean Tradition." In *The Pre-Socratics*, ed. Alexander P. D. Mourelatos, 135–60. New York: Anchor, [1974] 1993.
Coward, Harold, and Toby Foshay, eds. *Derrida and Negative Theology*. Albany, NY: SUNY Press, 1992.
Cowen, Wilson Walker. *Melville's Marginalia*. 2 vols. New York: Garland, 1987.
Dalrymple Henderson, Linda. *Duchamp in Context: Science and Technology in the Large Glass and Related Works*. Princeton, N.J.: Princeton University Press, 1998.
Davidson, Michael. *Ghostlier Demarcations: Modern Poetry and the Material World*. Berkeley: University of California Press, 1997.

De Certeau, Michel. *Heterologies*. Manchester: Manchester University Press, 1986.

———. *The Mystic Fable*, trans. Michael B. Smith. London: University of Chicago Press, 1992.

Deane, Seamus. *A Short History of Irish Literature*. London: Hutchinson, 1986.

Deleuze, Gilles. "Bartleby; Or, the Formula," in *Essays Critical and Clinical*, trans. Daniel W. Smith and Michael A. Greco. London: Verso, 1998, 68–90.

Deleuze, Gilles and Felix Guattari, *A Thousand Plateaus: Capitalism and Schizophrenia*. Trs. Brian Massumi. London, Continuum: 2004.

Derrida, Jacques. *Margins of Philosophy*, trans. Alan Bass. Chicago: University of Chicago Press, 1982.

———. "Telepathy," trans. Nicholas Royle. *Oxford Literary Review* 10 (1988): 3–41.

———. "How to Avoid Speaking: Denials." In *Languages of the Unsayable: The Play of Negativity in Literature and Literary Theory*, ed. Sanford Budick and Wolfgang Iser, 3–70. New York: Columbia University Press, 1989.

———. "Force of Law: The 'Mystical Foundation of Authority.'" Trs. Mary Quaintance. In *Acts of Religion*. Ed. Gil Anidjar. New York: Routledge, 2002. 230–298.

HD [Hilda Doolittle]. *Collected Poems 1912–1944*. New York: New Directions, 1983.

Drucker, Johanna. *Figuring the Word: Essays on Books, Writing, and Visual Poetics*. New York: Granary Books, 1998.

Dworkin, Craig. *Reading the Illegible*. Evanston, IL: Northwestern University Press, 2003.

Duchamp, Marcel. *The Bride Stripped Bare by her Bachelors, Even. A Typographic Version by Richard Hamilton of M. Duchamp's Green Box*, trans. George Heard Hamilton. London: Percy Lund, Humphries, 1960.

———. *Notes and Projects for the Large Glass*, ed. Arturo Schwarz, trans. George H. Hamilton, Cleve Gray and Arturo Schwarz. London: Thames & Hudson, 1969.

———. *Notes*, ed. Paul Matisse. Paris: Centre national d'art et de culture Georges Pompidou, 1980.

Duncan, Robert. *Bending the Bow*. New York: New Directions, 1968.

DuPlessis, Rachel Blau. *The Pink Guitar: Writing as Feminist Practice*. Tuscaloosa, Alabama: University of Alabama Press, [1990] 2006.

Eliot, T. S. "The Waste Land." In *The Waste Land and Other Poems*, 25–51. London: Faber, [1922] 1972.

Emerson, Ralph Waldo. "The Poet." In *Ralph Waldo Emerson*, ed. Richard Poirier, 197–215. Oxford: Oxford University Press, [1844] 1990.

———. "Literary Ethics." In *Essays and Lectures*, 93–112. New York: Library of America, [1838] 1983.

Fitzpatrick, Samuel A. Ossory. *Dublin: A Historical and Topographical Account of the City*. London: Methuen, 1907.

Foucault, Michel. "What Is an Author?" In *Language, Counter-memory, Practice*, trans. Donald F. Bouchard and Sherry Simon, 113–38. Oxford: Basil Blackwell, 1977.

Fowler, Alastair. *Spenser and the Numbers of Time*. London: Routledge, 1964.
Fraser, Kathleen. *Translating the Unspeakable: Poetry and the Innovative Necessity*. Tuscaloosa: University of Alabama Press, 2000.
Fredman, Stephen. *Poet's Prose: the Crisis in American Verse*. Cambridge: Cambridge University Press, 1983.
Fried, Michael. *Art and Objecthood: Essays and Reviews*. Chicago: University of Chicago Press, [1967] 1998.
Freud, Sigmund. *The Interpretation of Dreams. The Standard Edition of the Complete Psychological Works of Sigmund Freud*, vols. 4 and 5. London: Hogarth Press, [1900] 1953–74.
———. "The Unconscious." *Standard Edition*, vol. 14 [1915], 166–215.
———. *Beyond the Pleasure Principle*. *Standard Edition*, vol. 18 [1920], 7–64.
Frost, Elisabeth Ann. *The Feminist Avant-Garde in American Poetry*. Iowa City: Iowa University Press, 2003.
Gailey, Alan. *Irish Folk Drama*. Cork: Mercier Press, 1969.
Giesen, Sebastian, and Ortrud Westheider, eds. *Hanne Darboven: das Frühwerk* (Hamburger Kunsthalle [catalogue]). Berlin: Kulturstiftung der Länder in Verbindung mit der Hamburger Kunsthalle, 2004.
Girard, René. *The Scapegoat*, trans. Yvonne Freccero. London: Athlone Press, 1986.
Golding, Alan. "Authority, Marginality, England and Ireland in the Work of Susan Howe." In *Something We Have but They Don't: Anglo-American Literary Relations since 1925*, ed. Steve Clark and Mark Ford, 168–81. Iowa: Iowa University Press, 2004.
Green, Fiona. "Plainly on the Other Side: Susan Howe's Recovery." *Contemporary Literature* 42, no. 1 (Spring 2001): 78–101.
Grubbs, David. "Shadowy Hush Twilight: Two Collaborations with Susan Howe" (2009). http://www.pores.bbk.ac.uk/issues/issue5/poetry-and-music/davidgrubbs.
Guthrie, Kenneth Sylvan, ed. *The Pythagorean Sourcebook and Library*. Grand Rapids: Phanes, 1987.
Guthrie, William Keith Chambers. *History of Greek Philosophy*, vol. 1. Cambridge: Cambridge University Press, 1971.
Hall, David. *The Antinomian Controversy 1636–1638*. Durham, NC: Duke University Press, 1990.
Hall, Timothy D. *Contested Boundaries: Itinerancy and the Reshaping of the Colonial American Religious World*. Durham, NC: Duke University Press, 1994.
Harris, Kaplan P. "Susan Howe's Art and Poetry, 1968–1974." *Contemporary Literature* 47, no. 3 (2006).
Hart, Kevin. *The Trespass of the Sign: Deconstruction, Theology and Philosophy*. Cambridge: Cambridge University Press, 1989.
Hartley, George. *Textual Politics and the Language Poets*. Bloomington: Indiana University Press, 1989.
Haskins, Susan. *Mary Magdalene: Myth and Metaphor*. London: HarperCollins, 1993.

Heimert, Alan, and Andrew Delbanco, eds. *The Puritans in America: A Narrative Anthology*. Cambridge, MA: Harvard University Press, 1985.

Holmes, Oliver Wendell. *Touched with Fire: The Civil War Letters and Diaries of Oliver Wendell Holmes Jr., 1861–1864*, ed. Mark DeWolfe Howe. Cambridge, MA: Harvard University Press, 1946.

Hopkins, Gerard Manley. *Poems and Prose*, ed. W. H. Gardner. Harmondsworth, UK: Penguin, 1985.

Howard, W. Scott. "Literal/ Littoral Crossings: Re-Articulating Hope Atherton's Story After *Susan Howe's Articulation of Sound Forms in Time*," *Reconstruction* 6, no. 3 (2006), http://reconstruction.eserver.org/063/howard.shtml.

Ibsen, Henrik. *The Wild Duck*. *Plays: One*, trans. Michael Meyer. London: Methuen, [1884] 1980.

Ilie, Paul. *The Age of Minerva: Counter-rational Reason in the Eighteenth Century*. Philadelphia: University of Pennsylvania Press, 1995.

Irwin, John T. *American Hieroglyphics*. New Haven: Yale University Press, 1980.

James, William. *Pragmatism*. In *Pragmatism* and *The Meaning of Truth*. London, Cambridge, MA: Harvard University Press, [1907] 1978, 9–166.

———. "The Thing and Its Relations." In *Essays in Radical Empiricism*. Lincoln: University of Nebraska Press, [1912] 1996, 92–122.

Jeffries, Mark. *New Definitions of Lyric: Theory, Technology and Culture*. London: Routledge, 1998.

Jenkins, G. Matthew. *Poetic Obligation: Ethics in Experimental American Poetry after 1945*. Iowa City: Iowa University Press, 2008.

Johnson, William. *The Papers of Sir William Johnson*. 14 vols. Albany: SUNY Press, 1921–1965.

Joyce, Elisabeth. "'Thorowly' American: Susan Howe's Guide to Orienteering in the Adirondacks." *Electronic Book Review* 10 (Winter 1999–2000), http://www.altx.com/ebr/ebr10/10joy.htm.

Joyce, James. "James Clarence Mangan" [1902 and 1907 versions]. In *Occasional, Critical and Political Writing*, ed. Kevin Barry, 53–60, 127–136. Oxford: Oxford University Press, [1902, 1907] 2000.

———. "The Dead," in *Dubliners*, 167–214. Cambridge: Cambridge University Press, [1914] 1995.

Kahn, Charles H., *Pythagoras and the Pythagoreans: A Brief History*. Indianapolis, IN: Hackett, 2001.

Keller, Lynn. *Forms of Expansion: Recent Long Poems by Women*. Chicago: University of Chicago Press, 1997.

Kermode, Frank. Editor's notes to William Shakespeare's *The Tempest*. London: Methuen, 1954.

Kibbey, Ann. *The Interpretation of Material Shapes in Puritanism*. Cambridge: Cambridge University Press, 1986.

Krauss, Rosalind. "The /Cloud/." In *Agnes Martin*, ed. Barbara Haskell, 155–67. New York: Whitney Museum of American Art, 1992.

Lacan, Jacques. *Ecrits: A Selection*, trans. Alan Sheridan. London: Routledge, 1977.

Lacoue-Labarthe, Philippe, and Jean-Luc Nancy. *The Literary Absolute: The Theory of Literature in German Romanticism*. Albany: SUNY Press, [1978] 1988.
Laplanche, Jean. "Notes on Afterwardsness." In *Essays on Otherness*, ed. John Fletcher, 260–65. London: Routledge, 1998.
Lloyd, David. *Nationalism and Minor Literature: James Clarence Mangan and the Emergence of Irish Cultural Nationalism*. Berkeley: University of California Press, 1987.
Lowell Cummings, Abbot. *Bed Hangings: A Treatise on Fabrics and Styles in the Curtaining of Beds, 1650–1850*. Boston: Society for the Preservation of New England Antiquities, [1961] 1994.
Lyne, Raphael. *Ovid's Changing Worlds: English Metamorphoses, 1567–1632*. Oxford: Oxford University Press, 2001.
Lyotard, Jean-François. *Driftworks*. New York: Semiotext(e), 1984.
———. *Heidegger and "the jews,"* trans. Andreas Michel and Mark S. Roberts. Minneapolis: University of Minneapolis Press, 1990.
Ma, Ming-Qian. "Poetry as History Revised: Susan Howe's 'Scattering as Behavior toward Risk.'" *American Literary History* 6, no. 4 (Winter, 1994): 716–37.
———. "Articulating the Inarticulate: Singularities and the Counter-method in Susan Howe." *Contemporary Literature* 36, no. 3 (1995): 466–89.
Macherey, Pierre. *A Theory of Literary Production*. London: Routledge, 1978.
Madan, Francis Falconer. *A New Bibliography of the Eikon Basilike of King Charles the First*. London: Oxford Bibliographical Society, 1950.
Mangan, James Clarence. *The Poets and Poetry of Munster: A Selection of Irish Songs by the Poets of the Last Century with Poetical Translations by the Late James Clarence Mangan*, ed. C. P. Meehan. Dublin: James Duffy, [1849] 1901.
Manuth, Volker, and Marieke de Winkel. "Rembrandt's *Minerva in her Study* of 1635: The Splendor and Wisdom of a Goddess." New York: Otto Naumann, 2002 (accessed at www.dutchpaintings.com/Rembrandt.pdf, October 2010).
Marsh, Nicky. "All Known—Never Seen: Susan Howe, Samuel Beckett and an Indeterminate Tradition." *Samuel Beckett Today/Aujourd'hui* 9 (2000): 239–54.
Martin, Catherine. "'Double Play of Double Meaning': Dreams, Repetition and the Importance of Noh in Susan Howe's *The Midnight*." *Textual Practice* 20, no. 4 (December 2006), 759–75.
McCorkle, James. "Prophecy and the Figure of the Reader in Susan Howe's *Articulation of Sound Forms in Time*." *Postmodern Culture* 9, no. 3 (1999), http://pmc.iath.virginia.edu/text-only/issue.599/9.3mccorkle.txt.
McGann, Jerome. *Black Riders: The Visible Language of Modernism*. Princeton, NJ: Princeton University Press, 1993.
McGann, Jerome, and Charles L. Sligh, eds. *Algernon Charles Swinburne: Major Poems and Selected Prose*. New Haven: Yale University Press, 2004.
McHale, Brian. *The Obligation toward the Difficult Whole: Postmodernist Long Poems*. Tuscaloosa: Alabama University Press, 2004.
Mellors, Anthony. *Late Modernist Poetics: From Pound to Prynne*. Manchester: Manchester University Press, 2005.

Melville, Herman. "Hawthorne and His Mosses" [1850]. In *Nathaniel Hawthorne's Tales*, ed. James McIntosh, 337–50. New York: Norton, 1987.

———. *Moby-Dick*. Harmondsworth, UK: Penguin, [1851] 1986.

———. "Bartleby the Scrivener," in *Billy Budd and Other Stories*, 95–130. London, Vermont: Everyman, [1853] 1993.

———. *Correspondence*. The Writings of Herman Melville, vol. 14, ed. Lynn Horth. Evanston and Chicago: Northwestern University Press and The Newberry Library, 1993.

Mengham, Rod and John Kinsella, eds. *Vanishing Points: New Modernist Poems*. Cambridge: Salt, 2004.

Messerli, Douglas, ed. *"Language" Poetries: An Anthology*. New York: New Directions, 1987.

Michaels, Walter Benn. *The Shape of the Signifier: 1967 to the End of History*. Princeton, NJ: Princeton University Press, 2004.

Middleton, Peter. "Julia Kristeva, Susan Howe and Avant Garde Poetics," in *Contemporary Poetry Meets Modern Theory*, ed. Anthony Easthope and John O. Thompson, 81–95. Toronto: University of Toronto Press, 1991.

Miller, Perry. "The Romantic Dilemma," in *Nature's Nation*. Cambridge, MA: Harvard University Press, [1955] 1967.

Milton, John. *Comus*. In *Comus and Other Poems*, ed. F. T. Prince. London: Oxford University Press, [1645] 1968: 35–82.

———. *Eikonoklastes*. In *Complete Prose Works of John Milton*, vol. 3, ed. Merrit Y. Hughes. New Haven, CT: Yale University Press, [1649] 1962.

Mitchel, John. "James Clarence Mangan, His Life, Poetry and Death." In *Poems by James Clarence Mangan, with a Biographical Introduction by John Mitchel*, 7–31. New York: Haverty, 1859.

Mitchell, W. J. T. *Picture Theory: Essays on Verbal and Visual Representation*. Chicago: University of Chicago Press, 1994.

Moxley, Jennifer. "Lyric Poetry and the Inassimilable Life." *The Poker* 6 (2005), 49–58.

Naylor, Paul. *Poetic Investigations: Singing the Holes in History*. Evanston, IL: Northwestern University Press, 1999.

Nicholls, Peter. "Unsettling the Wilderness: Susan Howe and American History" *Contemporary Literature* 37, no. 4 (Winter 1996): 586–601.

———. "Beyond *The Cantos*: Pound and American Poetry," in *The Cambridge Companion to Ezra Pound*, ed. Ira Nadel, 139–60. Cambridge: Cambridge University Press, 1999.

———. "'The Pastness of Landscape': Susan Howe's *Pierce-Arrow*." *Contemporary Literature* 43, no. 3 (Fall 2002): 441–60.

Nietzsche, Friedrich. "On the Uses and Disadvantages of History for Life." In *Untimely Meditations*, trans. R. J. Hollingdale, 57–123. Cambridge: Cambridge University Press, [1874] 1997.

———. *Philosophy in the Tragic Age of the Greeks*, trans. Marianne Cowan. Chicago: Gateway, 1962.

———. *The Twilight of the Idols*, trans. R.J. Hollingdale. Harmondsworth, UK: Penguin, [1889] 1968.

Nokes, David. *Jonathan Swift, a Hypocrite Reversed*. Oxford: Oxford University Press, 1985.

Olson, Charles. *Call Me Ishmael*. London: Jonathan Cape, [1947] 1967.

———. *The Special View of History*. Berkeley, CA: Oyez, 1970.

Orgel, Stephen. "The Poetics of the Spectacle." In *Inigo Jones: The Theatre of the Stuart Court*, vol. 1, ed. Stephen Orgel and Roy Strong, 1–14. London, Berkeley, CA: Sotheby Parke Bernet/ University of California Press, 1973.

———. Editor's notes to William Shakespeare's *The Tempest*. Oxford: Clarendon, 1987.

Ovid. *Metamorphoses*, trans. Arthur Golding, ed. John Frederick Nims. New York: Macmillan, [1597] 1965.

———. *Metamorphoses*, trans. Dryden et al. ed. Samuel Garth. Ware, Hertfordshire: Wordsworth, [1717] 1998.

Palliser, Bury. *The History of Lace*. New York: Scribner, 1902.

Peirce, Charles Sanders. "Consciousness and Language." In *The Collected Papers of Charles Sanders Peirce*, vol. 7, ed. Arthur W Burks. Cambridge, MA: Harvard University Press, 1958: 347–58.

———. "Letters to Lady Welby." In Burks, ed., vol. 8.

———. "Prolegomena to an Apology for Pragmaticism." In *Peirce on Signs: Writings on Semiotic by Charles Sanders Peirce*, ed. James Hoopes, 249–52. Chapel Hill, NC, and London: University of North Carolina Press, [1906] 1991.

———. "What Pragmatism Is." In *The Essential Peirce*, vol. 2 [1893–1913], 331–45. Bloomington and Indianapolis: Indiana University Press, [1905] 1998.

Perelman, Bob. *The Marginalization of Poetry: Language Writing and Literary History*. Princeton, NJ: Princeton University Press, 1996.

Perloff, Marjorie. *The Dance of the Intellect*. Cambridge: Cambridge University Press, 1985.

———. "Collision or Collusion with History: The Narrative Lyric of Susan Howe." *Contemporary Literature* 30, no. 4 (Winter 1989): 518–33.

———. "Language Poetry and the Lyric Subject: Ron Silliman's Albany, Susan Howe's Buffalo," (1999) http://epc.buffalo.edu/authors/perloff/langpo.html.

———. "Lucent and Inescapable Rhythms." (1988) http://epc.buffalo.edu/authors/perloff/metrical.html.

———. *Radical Artifice: Writing Poetry in the Age of Media*. Chicago: University of Chicago Press, 1991.

PMLA. *The New Lyric Studies*. PMLA 123, no. 1 (March 2008): 216–22.

Pound, Ezra. *Selected Poems*, ed. T. S. Eliot, rev. edition. London: Faber, 1948.

———. "Notes on Elizabethan Classicists." In *Literary Essays of Ezra Pound*, 227–48. London: Faber, [1917] 1954.

Prynne, J. H. "English Poetry and Emphatical Language." *Proceedings of the British Academy* 74 (1988): 135–69.

Pseudo Dionysius. *The Complete Works*, trans. Colm Lubheid. London: SPCK, 1987.
Quartermain, Peter. *Disjunctive Poetics*. Cambridge: Cambridge University Press, 1992.
Rancière, Jacques. "Deleuze, Bartleby, and the Literary Formula." In *The Flesh of Words: The Politics of Writing*, trans. Charlotte Mandell, 146–64. Stanford, CA: Stanford University Press, 2004.
Rankine, Claudia, and Juliana Spahr, eds. *American Women Poets in the 21st Century: Where Lyric Meets Language*. Middletown, CT: Wesleyan, 2002.
Reed, Brian. "'Eden or Ebb of the Sea': Susan Howe's Word Squares and Post-linear Poetics." *Postmodern Culture* 14, no. 2 (2004), http://pmc.iath.virginia.edu/text-only/issue.104/14.2reed.txt.
Reinfeld, Linda. *Language Poetry: Writing as Rescue*. Baton Rouge and London: Louisiana State University Press, 1992.
Reinhardt, Ad. "Art as Art." In *Art in Theory, 1900–1990*, ed. Charles Harrison and Paul Wood, 806–809. Oxford: Blackwell, 1992.
Richardson, Joan. *A Natural History of Pragmatism: The Fact of Feeling from Jonathan Edwards to Gertrude Stein*. Cambridge: Cambridge University Press, 2007.
Riedweg, Christoph. *Pythagoras: His Life, Teaching and Influence*, trans. Steven Rendall. Ithaca, NY: Cornell, 2002.
Roberts, Don D. *The Existential Graphs of Charles S. Peirce*. The Hague: Mouton, 1973.
Rogin, Michael Paul. *Subversive Genealogy: The Politics and Art of Herman Melville*. Berkeley, CA: University of California Press, 1983.
Sacks, Peter. *The English Elegy: Studies in the Genre from Spenser to Yeats*. Baltimore, MD: Johns Hopkins University Press, 1985.
Saxby, T. J. *The Quest for the New Jerusalem: Jean de Labadie and the Labadists, 1610–1744*. Dordrecht: Martinus Nijhoff, 1987.
Sayre, Robert F. *Thoreau and the American Indians*. Princeton: Princeton University Press, 1977.
Scharlemann, Robert, ed. *Negation and Theology*. Charlottesville, VA: University Press of Virginia, 1992.
Schlegel, Friedrich. *Friedrich Schlegel's Lucinde and the Fragments*, trans. Peter Firchow. Minneapolis: University of Minnesota Press, 1971.
Schmitt, Carl. *Political Theology*. Trs. George D. Schwab. Cambridge, Mass.; London: MIT Press, 1985 [1922].
Schultz, Susan. "Exaggerated History." *Postmodern Culture* 4, no. 2 (January 1994), http://www.iath.virginia.edu/pmc/text-only/issue194/review_5.194.
———. "The Stutter in the Text: Editing and Historical Authority in the Work of Susan Howe," in *A Poetics of Impasse in Modern and Contemporary American Poetry*. Tuscaloosa, AL: University of Alabama, 2005.
Sendler, Egon. *L'Icone, image de l'invisible*. Paris: Desclée de Brouwer, 1981.
Shepherd, Reginald, ed. *Lyric Postmodernisms: An Anthology of Contemporary Innovative Poetics*. Denver, CO: Counterpath Press, 2008.

Sheridan, John Desmond. *James Clarence Mangan*. Dublin: Talbot Press, 1937.
Sidney, Sir Philip. *The Defense of Poesie*. London: Dent, [1595] 1999.
Silliman, Ron, ed. *In the American Tree*. Orono, ME: National Poetry Foundation, 1986.
Silliman, Ron, Carla Harryman, Lyn Hejinian, Steve Benson, Bob Perelman, and Barrett Watten. "Aesthetic Tendency and the Politics of Poetry: A Manifesto." *Social Text* 19–20 (1988): 261–75.
Slotkin, Richard. *Regeneration Through Violence*. Middletown, CT: Wesleyan University Press, 1973.
Spenser, Edmund. *The Faerie Queene*. *Poetical Works*, ed. J.C. Smith and E. de Selincourt. Oxford: [1596] 1970.
———. *A View of the Present State of Ireland*, ed. Andrew Hadfield and Willy Maley. Oxford: Blackwell, [1633] 1997.
Steele, Ian K. *Betrayals: Fort William Henry and the "Massacre."* New York: Oxford University Press, 1990.
Stevens, Wallace. *Collected Poetry and Prose*. New York: Library of America, 1997.
———. "The Noble Rider and the Sound of Words" [1942]. In *Collected Poetry and Prose*, 643–65.
———. "A Note on 'Les Plus Belles Pages'" [1952]. In *Collected Poetry and Prose*, 867.
———. "On Receiving the Gold Medal from the Poetry Society of America" [1951]. In *Collected Poetry and Prose*, 832–34.
Stevenson, Robert Louis. *The Master of Ballantrae*. Oxford: Oxford World's Classics, [1889] 1983.
Stewart, Susan. "Lyric Possession." *Critical Inquiry* 22, no. 1 (Autumn 1995): 34–63.
Swensen, Cole and David St John. *American Hybrid: A Norton Anthology of New Poetry*. New York: WW Norton, 2008.
Swift, Jonathan. *Journal to Stella*. 2 vols, ed. Harold Williams. London: Oxford University Press, [1784] 1948.
———. *Correspondence*. Vol. 2, 1714–1723. Ed. Harold Williams. Oxford: Clarendon Press (1963).
———. "On the Death of Mrs. Johnson." In *Swift's Satires and Personal Writings*, ed. William Alfred Eddy, 389–402. Oxford: Oxford University Press, [1765] 1973.
Taggart, John. *Songs of Degrees: Essays on Contemporary Poetry and Poetics*. Tuscaloosa, AL: University of Alabama Press, 1994.
Thoreau, Henry David. *Journals*. 2 vols, ed. Bradford Torrey and Francis H. Allen. New York: Dover, [1906] 1962.
———. "Ktdaan." *The Maine Woods*. London: Penguin, [1864] 1988: 1–111.
———. *Walden*, in *Walden, Civil Disobedience and Other Writings*, ed. William Rossi. New York, London: Norton, [1854] 2008: 5–226.
———. "Walking," in *Walden, Civil Disobedience and Other Writings* [1862]: 260–287.

Todorov, Tzvetan. *The Conquest of America: The Question of the Other*, trans. Richard Howard. New York: Harper, [1984] 1992.

Tomlinson, Charles. *Poetry and Metamorphosis*. Cambridge: Cambridge University Press, 1983.

Vanderborg, Susan. "The Communal Lyric: Palimpsest in the Corpus of Susan Howe." In *New Definitions of Lyric: Theory, Technology and Culture*, ed. Mark Jeffreys, 99–126. New York and London: Garland, 1998.

Weil, Simone. "The Iliad or the Poem of Force," trans. Mary McCarthy. In *Simone Weil: An Anthology*, ed. Sîan Miles. London: Virago, [1945] 1986, 182–215.

White, Jenny L. "The Landscapes of Susan Howe's *Thorow*." *Contemporary Literature* 47, no. 2 (2006), 236–60.

Williams, Megan. "Howe Not to Erase(Her): A Poetics of Posterity in Susan Howe's *Melville's Marginalia*." *Contemporary Literature* 38, no. 1 (Spring 1997): 106–32.

Williams, Nerys. *Reading Error: the Lyric and Contemporary Poetry*. New York: Peter Lang, 2007.

Williams, William Carlos. *In the American Grain*. Aylesbury: Peregrine, [1925] 1971.

Willis, Elizabeth. "The Arena in the Garden: Some Thoughts on the Late Lyric." In *Telling It Slant: Avant-garde Poetics of the 1990s*, ed. Mark Wallace and Steven Marks, 225–35. Tuscaloosa: University of Alabama Press, 2002.

Wilson, James C., ed. *The Hawthorne and Melville Friendship: An Annotated Bibliography and Critical Essays, and Correspondence between the Two*. Jefferson, NC: McFarland, 1991.

Winnicott, D. W. *Playing and Reality*. London: Routledge, [1971] 1991.

Yates, Frances. *The Rosicrucian Enlightenment*. London: Routledge, 1972.

———. *Shakespeare's Last Plays: A New Approach*. London: Routledge, 1975.

———. *A Study of Love's Labour's Lost*. Cambridge: Cambridge University Press, 1936.

Yeats, W. B. "Clarence Mangan." In *Davis, Mangan, Ferguson*, W. B. Yeats and Thomas Kinsella, 21–26. Dublin: Dolmen, [1887] 1970.

———. "Clarence Mangan's Love Affair" [excerpt]. *Davis, Mangan, Ferguson*. W. B. Yeats and Thomas Kinsella. Dublin: Dolmen, [1891] 1970: 26–27.

———, ed. *Fairy and Folk Tales of Ireland*. Gerrards Cross: Gerard Smythe, [1888, 1892] 1977.

———. *The Poems*, ed. Daniel Albright. London: Everyman, 1994.

General Index

absence, 6, 12, 16, 28, 29, 30, 34, 37, 40, 42–43, 45–47, 48, 50, 52, 58, 84, 129, 151, 180
Agamben, Giorgio 125–26, 128, 189
Almack, Edward 31, 196
Andrews, Bruce, ix, 55
Anglo-Irishness, xi, 1–3, 5–8, 16–18, 68–69, 169, 179
Antigone, xii, xx, 149, 151–52
antinomianism, x, 40, 46, 81–85, 87, 114–15, 119, 125, 128–29, 173, 181
Arnold, Matthew, 118, 124, 131, 187, 193
Ashbery, John, 1, 18
associative poetics, xvi–xviii, xix, 3, 4, 10, 17–22, 25–26, 36, 40, 58–59, 75, 81, 82, 87, 93, 113, 115, 120, 124–25, 132, 150, 154, 155, 160, 165, 194
Atherton, Hope, 19, 86, 88, 89, 91, 93, 94, 98
authority, xiii, xv, 9, 12–13, 16, 27–41, 46–47, 50, 63, 69, 73, 77–78, 82, 85, 87, 97–98, 155

Back, Rachel Tzvia, x, 2, 37, 47, 52, 80, 85, 98, 101, 169, 172, 176, 182, 184
Bartleby, xiii, 59, 97, 118, 119, 120–21, 125–30, 189
Beckett, Samuel, 2, 29, 163, 169, 174

Bercovitch, Sacvan, 87, 89, 184, 185
Bernstein, Charles, ix, x, 55, 172, 196
see also Bernstein interview in works index
Bible, the, xv, xvi, 32, 44–53, 56, 78, 87, 147, 188
Blasing, Mutlu Konuk, 147
Bollas, Christopher, 121–23
Brown, Norman O., x, 32, 42, 45, 47, 58, 60, 117, 168, 170, 173, 177, 178, 179, 182–83, 194
Bruns, Gerard, 114, 177, 179
Buffalo Zoo, xvii, 16, 22, 29, 58
Butterick, George, 33, 173, 183
Byron, Lord George Gordon, 118, 121, 122, 124, 129, 189

Cage, John, 80, 99, 173
Certeau, Michel de, 34, 53, 161, 173
Charles I, 30–41, 98, 172
Citation, xi, xiii, 17, 20, 30, 67, 114, 119, 124, 128, 132, 146, 163–64
Collage, xi, xviii, xxii, 5, 10, 17, 20, 22, 25, 40, 50, 93, 105, 113, 115, 132, 138, 143, 145, 147, 151, 160–63, 165, 187
Collis, Stephen, x, xxii, 40
colonialism xx, 2–3, 69–70, 77, 79–111, 155
Cordelia, 4, 8, 10–16, 27, 149, 169, 170, 171

Cowen, Wilson Walker 117, 118, 121, 124, 188
Creeley, Robert, 42, 141

H.D. (Hilda Doolittle), x, 45, 63, 88
Daphne, 8, 10, 45, 59, 61–69, 78, 178
Darboven, Hanne 132, 142
Davidson, Michael, x, xxii, 173, 187
Deleuze, Gilles, 100, 106, 185, 89
Derrida, Jacques, 40, 49–50, 53, 176, 188
Dickens, Charles, 29, 32, 36
Dickinson, Emily, xi, xv, xvi, 20, 29, 33, 39, 42, 43, 44–47, 61, 82, 88, 92, 97, 103, 114, 115, 116, 125, 126, 129, 132, 135, 138, 145, 175, 180, 187, 191, 192, 194, 195
displacement, 2, 6, 8, 9, 10, 16–17, 18
doubleness, 2, 18, 19, 23, 24–25, 69–71, 87, 95, 123, 151–52, 156, 158, 160, 163, 180
dreams, 22, 70, 75–76, 136–38, 140, 142–43
drifting, xiii, 35, 36, 37, 40, 105–7
Dryden, John, 57, 62
Duchamp, Marcel, xi, 56, 113, 132, 139–40, 142, 177, 187
Duncan, Robert, x, 11–12, 35, 63, 88, 114, 141, 173, 178, 182, 184
DuPlessis, Rachel Blau, x, 114, 173, 183
duplicity, 19, 24, 25, 152

ecstasy, 26, 29, 42, 47, 83, 114, 115
Edwards, Jonathan, xi, 56, 147–48, 156, 158, 160, 165
Eliot, T.S., xv, 18, 63, 88, 179
Emerson, Ralph Waldo, xi, 20, 24, 59–60, 158, 184, 195
enthusiasm, ix, xiii, 23, 84, 114, 115, 117, 129–30, 143, 155, 159, 190
epic, 90, 93, 146, 150, 152, 153

fabrics, 17, 18, 20, 23–24, 40, 154–55, 158–59, 165, 194, 195

feminine, the, x, 9, 14, 27, 30, 37, 41, 46, 60, 63, 69–70, 90, 92, 102, 120, 155, 183
feminine speech, 8, 10, 12, 23, 40, 41, 47, 65, 78, 102
feminist criticism, x, 177, 182
Florimell, 69–72, 77
Foucault, Michel, 37, 174, 187
Fraser, Kathleen, x, xi, 11, 90, 114
freedom, xii, 5, 7, 10, 12, 15–16, 40, 45, 69, 80–81, 85, 97, 103, 107, 111, 124, 129
French and Indian War, 110, 183
Freud, Sigmund, 33, 58, 97, 98, 108–109, 120, 122, 123, 185
Frost, Elisabeth, 10, 80, 181

Golding, Alan, 2
grace, xii, xiii, 50, 82–84, 119, 125, 128, 147, 155, 190
Green, Fiona, 29, 168, 172
grids, 4, 5, 11–12, 28, 106, 114, 141, 142
Grubbs, David, 99, 184, 195

hallucination, 26, 72–74, 77, 124, 129
Hamilton Finlay, Ian, x, 48–49, 186
Harris, Kaplan, 49, 113
Hart, Kevin, 46, 176
Hawthorne, Nathaniel, 35, 103, 118–19, 121, 122, 173
Hedvig, 13, 16, 149, 170, 171
Hejinian, Lyn, ix, x, 9, 18, 45, 47, 55, 56, 139, 167, 176, 177, 178
hesitancy, 3, 50, 85, 90, 93, 96–97, 126, 129, 140, 148
history, x, xii, xiii, xiv, xvi, 6, 10, 15, 16, 32, 36, 40, 41, 47, 56, 61, 65, 66, 68, 70, 79–98, 100, 103, 110, 111, 113, 114, 122, 137, 147, 150, 155, 164, 173, 181, 182–83, 184
Holmes, Oliver Wendell, 28, 29

Homer, 134–35, 150, 152, 165, 191, 192
Howe, Fanny, xviii
Howe, Mark DeWolfe, xi–xii, xvii–xviii, 1, 6, 12, 16, 27–29, 33, 34, 46, 58, 69, 171, 172, 173, 187, 190
Howe, Mary Manning, xi, 1, 3–4, 5, 6, 13–14, 17, 18, 21, 24, 25, 69, 71, 179, 187, 190
Hutchinson, Anne, 44, 46, 82–85, 97, 128–29, 181

immediacy, xii–xiii, 44, 51, 80–84, 93, 105, 109, 114–15, 117, 119, 125, 129–30, 132, 137, 163
insubstantiality, 12, 27, 65, 67, 69, 72, 73–74, 77, 180
interleaf, the, 18–20, 24
Irish cultural nationalism, 118, 121, 129, 182
itinerancy, *see* wandering

James, Henry, xi, 135, 158, 162, 163, 166, 187
James, William, xi, 135, 156–57, 158, 160, 194, 195
Jesus Christ, xvi, 28, 42, 44–46, 47, 49, 50–51, 52, 53, 149, 172
Johnson, Esther ('Stella'), 4, 6, 7, 9–10, 11, 13, 14, 15
Johnson, Samuel, 2–3
Johnson, Sir William, 58, 100, 105, 109, 110, 183, 186
Jones, Inigo, 68, 72–75, 77
Jonson, Ben, 56, 68, 72–75, 77, 180
Joyce, James, 5, 8, 9, 118, 121, 122, 124, 188, 189
Judd, Donald, 116, 187

Keller, Lynn, x, 1–2, 182
see also Keller interview in index of works
King Philip's War, xix, 86

Krauss, Rosalind, 113, 141, 192

Lacan, Jacques, 128, 186
language writing, ix, 28, 55–57, 145, 176, 187, 194
Laplanche, Jean, 122–23, 125, 188
law, 4, 10, 12, 14, 27, 29, 30, 33, 34–35, 82, 83, 92, 93, 95, 97, 117, 128–30, 149, 173, 189
Lyotard, Jean-François, 32–33, 36–37, 105–6
lyric, ix, xiv, xv, 6, 16, 17, 18, 27–28, 43, 55–56, 57, 58–59, 63, 64, 66, 70, 71, 131, 145–66

Mangan, James Clarence, xiii, 117–21, 122, 124, 126, 129–30, 132, 188, 189
Manifest Destiny, 88, 96
Martin, Agnes, xi, 12, 114, 132, 141–42, 143, 192
Mary Magdalene, 41, 44–47, 49, 53, 149, 175
masques, 34, 39, 56, 68, 69, 72–77, 162, 174, 179, 180, 196
materiality, 17, 18, 21, 23, 43, 53, 67, 114–17, 130, 137, 142, 143, 154, 155, 158, 159, 160, 187, 192
maternal, the, 1–26, 27, 90, 149, 154, 171, 182
Melville, Herman, xi, xvi, 51–52, 59, 61, 91–92, 93, 94, 97, 103, 117–22, 124, 125–30, 140, 171, 176, 177, 182–83, 188, 189, 190, 194
Meredith, George, 131, 135
Metamorphoses (Ovid), 56–57, 59, 165, 178, 61–64, 69, 125, 165, 178
metamorphosis, 8, 15–16, 45, 56, 57, 59, 61–68, 77, 78, 125
Michaels, Walter Benn, 116, 187
Middleton, Peter, x, 92
Milton, John, xv, 18, 30–31, 37–41, 56, 61, 71, 78, 174

Minerva, 164–65
modernism, x, xx, 20, 63, 91, 93, 116, 132, 146, 150, 153, 178, 191
mourning, 29, 30, 131, 139, 148, 190, 193
mystic speech, 5, 34, 42, 47, 48, 53, 60, 83, 91, 161, 184

Native Americans, xix, 28, 77, 84, 86, 87, 88, 98, 101, 124, 158, 184
negative theology, 12, 37, 34, 35, 41–53, 60, 89
Nicholls, Peter, 10, 32, 33, 43, 89, 103, 130, 135, 188
Nietzsche, Friedrich, 46, 57, 173, 175, 178, 184

Olmsted, Frederick Law, 22, 24
Olson, Charles, x, xi, xxi, 11–12, 33, 35, 82, 88, 90–94, 98, 126, 140, 143, 173, 182–83
Ophelia, xx, 8, 16, 45, 57, 64–69, 78, 125, 149
Orgel, Stephen, 73, 77, 180

pastoral, 56, 60, 69, 75, 77
paternal, the, xvii, xviii, 10, 12–13, 16, 27–53, 58, 67, 79, 90, 171, 172, 173, 187
Peirce, C.S., x, xiii, 21, 105, 116, 117, 130–43, 150, 160, 191, 193, 195
Perloff, Marjorie, x, xix, 80, 167, 171
political, the, xiii, 29, 31, 32, 35, 36, 40, 41, 61, 72, 77, 82, 85, 87, 89, 96–98, 101, 102, 106, 116, 129, 191
potentiality, 125–26, 129, 152
Pound, Ezra, x, 11, 63, 88, 93, 178, 182
pragmatism, 56, 134, 146, 156, 158–59, 191
prophecy, 31, 34, 86–87
Prynne, J.H., 162–63, 196
psychoanalysis, 14, 18, 20, 35, 95, 97, 115, 117, 121–23, 188

Puritanism, 31, 72, 37, 38, 45, 46, 59, 81–83, 85, 87–91, 97, 102, 103, 107, 116, 156, 168, 175
Pythagoras, 56, 58–59, 62, 177, 179

Raleigh, Sir Walter, 70, 104, 172
Reed, Brian, x, 114, 116, 192
relational poetics, *see associative poetics*
religion, xiii, xiv, 2, 21, 23, 31, 30, 40–53, 60–61, 67, 82–83, 87–88, 95, 98, 114, 155, 159, 101, 165, 185
see also negative theology
Romanticism, 35, 106, 108, 115, 148, 150, 153, 184, 185, 189

Santayana, George, 156, 157, 195, 196
scattering, 35–37, 40, 95, 97, 100
Schlegel, Friedrich von, 152–53, 193
Schlegell, David von, 52, 130, 148, 154, 176, 190, 193
Schultz, Susan, x, 60, 80, 87, 103, 181
Second World War, xi, xvii, 5, 12, 46, 135
Serra, Richard, 142
Shakespeare, William, xv, 8, 19, 31, 36, 55–57, 59, 61, 64, 67–68, 74, 75, 77, 78, 93, 178, 180; *Hamlet*, 12, 19, 27, 31, 46, 57, 64–67 97, 170, 179; *King Lear*, 4, 8, 11, 13–15, 27; *Macbeth* 17, 19, 171; *Midsummer Night's Dream, A*, 71, 75
Shelley, Mary, 129
Shelley, Percy Bysshe 114, 117, 118, 120–22, 124, 129, 138, 188, 189, 191
Sidney, Sir Philip, 37, 40, 174, 179
silence, x, 8, 9, 10, 29, 37, 42, 43, 45, 46, 47, 58, 59–60, 64–66, 78, 84, 90, 114, 120, 127–28, 177
Silliman, Ron, ix, 27, 55, 58, 177
similitudes, xvi, xvii, xix, 167–68
see also associative poetics

Smithson, Robert, 116, 132, 142, 187
sound, 3, 11, 21–22, 30, 33, 43, 53, 67, 90, 94, 99–100, 114, 130, 134, 145–48, 153–54, 157, 165, 175, 193, 196
Spenser, Edmund, 56, 68–70, 72, 76, 78, 177, 179
Stevens, Wallace, xi, xiii, xv, 42, 53, 56, 62, 63, 88, 146–47, 158–66, 193, 194, 195, 196
Stevenson, Robert Louis, 18, 19, 24–25
stuttering, 92, 96, 98, 99, 126–27, 173
Swift, Jonathan, 4–13, 27, 46, 97, 169, 170
Swinburne, Algernon, 117, 131, 132, 138, 140, 141, 148, 149–50, 190, 192, 193
symbolic logic, 105, 133, 134, 136, 138

Taggart, John, x, 12, 13, 14, 15, 16, 27, 42, 61, 68, 88, 135, 173, 176, 180, 182
telepathy, xiii, xviii, xx, 119–20, 143, 188
temporality, xiii, 31, 86, 103, 107, 108, 109, 121–23, 128
theology, *see* negative theology

Todorov, Tzvetan, 100–1, 184, 185
transitional object, 18, 21, 155

Vietnam War, 63, 64, 88
violence, 15, 17, 28, 29, 30, 32, 33, 34, 39, 58, 62, 79, 92, 94, 95, 99, 101, 102, 106–7, 120, 123, 135, 136–37, 146, 150, 166, 168, 172, 174, 180, 186
visual poetics, x, 4, 5, 7, 11, 31, 36, 90, 91, 92, 99, 105, 111, 113–14, 117, 118, 130–43, 160

wandering, xv, 2 8, 23, 25, 44, 95, 96, 98, 105–6, 130, 160–61, 166
wilderness, 22, 23, 28, 44, 79, 87–88, 97, 101–4, 107–10, 119, 173
Wild Duck, The (Ibsen), 7, 13–17
Williams, Megan, 47, 115
Williams, William Carlos, xxi, 18, 56, 107, 191
Willis, Elizabeth, 145–46, 192
Winnicott, D.W., 18, 21

Yeats, W.B., xi, xv, 1, 2, 3, 8, 18, 21, 25, 56, 76 118, 129, 171, 179, 180, 187, 188

Index of Works by Susan Howe

Poems, books of poetry and prose texts published in books of poetry

118 Westerly Terrace, 160, 161, 164, 195

Arisbe, 134–37, 139, 142–43, 150, 152
Articulation of Sound Forms in Time, xiii, xv, xxii, 4, 34, 44, 70, 78, 80, 85–98, 100, 103, 122, 189

Bed Hangings, 18, 145, 154–60, 174
Bibliography of the King's Book, or Eikon Basilike, A, xiii, xvi, 30–41, 46, 73, 77, 90, 94, 97, 117, 132, 140, 160, 168, 170, 171, 172, 189, 193, 196

Cabbage Gardens, xxi, 2–3, 179, 182
Chanting at the Crystal Sea, xxi, 79

Defenestration of Prague, xxii, 4, 15, 30, 34, 38, 39, 55, 56–57, 68–78, 86, 94, 95, 151, 162, 171, 174, 177, 179, 183 193, 196

Errand (two parts), 160, 161
Europe of Trusts, The, 3, 4, 55, 56, 57, 58, 62, 66

Federalist 10, 181
Fragment of the Wedding Dress of Sarah Pierpont Edwards, 160, 195
Frame Structures: Early Poems 1974–1979, xxi

Frolic Architecture, 192

Heliopathy, 181
Hinge Picture, ix, xxi, 4, 113–14, 125

Kidnapped (the book), 171
Kidnapped (the poem), xxi, 18, 168

Leisure of the Theory Class, The, 130, 131, 137–38, 139, 143, 150, 154
Liberties, The, xi, xxii, 2, 3, 4–17, 27, 31, 55, 56, 57, 59, 97, 149, 169, 170, 172, 177, 185

Marginalia de Melville, 189
Melville's Marginalia, xvi, xxii, 18, 46, 59, 114, 115, 117–30, 137, 138, 181, 183, 189, 190
Midnight, The, xi, xxi, xxii, 2, 3, 6, 38, 59, 115, 116, 125, 156, 157, 159, 160, 167, 171, 187, 189, 190, 192, 194, 195

Nonconformist's Memorial, The (the book), xxi, 117, 129, 130, 190, 191
Nonconformist's Memorial, The (the poem), xvi, 30, 31, 34, 41–53, 97, 99, 125, 129, 149, 175, 176

Personal Narrative, 81, 160

Pierce-Arrow 13, 117, 130–43, 146, 148, 149, 150, 152, 153, 154, 160, 167, 187, 192, 193
Poems Found in a Pioneer Museum, 192
"Preface" to *Frame Structures*, xvi–xx, 6, 17, 58, 63, 131, 172, 173, 184, 192
Pythagorean Silence, xvii, xxii, 4, 10, 15, 27, 38, 55, 56, 57–68, 69, 70, 71, 78, 86, 89, 94, 125, 149, 165, 169, 177, 178, 179

Rückenfigur, xx, 130, 131, 138, 145, 148–54, 159, 192, 193

Scare Quotes, 17–26, 154, 155, 194
Scattering as Behavior towards Risk, xxi, 140, 168, 196
Secret History of the Dividing Line, xxi, 2, 19, 28, 31, 86
Singularities, x, xxi, 2, 31, 80, 81, 85, 86, 115
Silence Wager Stories, xxi
Souls of the Labadie Tract (the book), 160
Souls of the Labadie Tract (the poem), 145, 160–66, 196

"THERE ARE NOT LEAVES ENOUGH TO CROWN TO COVER TO CROWN TO COVER," xi–xv, xvi, xvii, xx–xxi, 3, 47, 57, 58, 62, 66, 135, 137, 152, 165
Thorow, ix, xiii, xv, xxii, 29, 34, 37, 44, 46, 70, 78, 86, 92, 98–111, 117, 132, 140, 145, 147, 155, 162, 173, 179, 181, 184, 186

Western Borders, The, xxi

Criticism and Prose
Birth-mark, The: Unsettling the Wilderness in American Literary History, x, xiv, xxi, xxii, 18, 19, 21, 29, 39, 40, 47, 52, 81, 82, 84, 103, 109, 114, 115, 116, 125, 138, 168, 169, 170, 172, 173, 174, 181, 182, 187, 190, 191, 192, 194
"Charles Olson: A Dialogue There Is," 183
"Choir Answers to Choir: Notes on Jonathan Edwards and Wallace Stevens," 147–48, 160, 165
"Encloser," 82, 181
"End of Art, The" 48–49, 114
"Ether Either," 6, 131, 171, 180, 190, 192
"Furious Calm," 156–58, 179, 180, 194, 195
"Leaf Flower in the Wind Falling Blue The Dark River," 141, 142
My Emily Dickinson, xi, xiii, xxi, 19, 20, 41, 43, 45, 81, 83, 89, 92 103–4, 119–20, 126, 135, 173, 174, 175, 180, 183, 195
"Sorting Facts: Or, Nineteen Ways of Looking at Marker," 131, 168, 170, 193
"*The Collected Poems*: The Next 50 Years," 156, 157
"Then *He* Is in Range," 184
"Where Should the Commander Be," 91–92

Interviews and published exchanges (listed by interlocutor)
Beckett, Tom, xvii, 43, 60, 68, 69, 70, 102, 177, 186
Bernstein, Charles, xviii, 41, 46, 47, 83, 125, 128–29
Creeley, Robert, 42–43
Falon, Janet Ruth, 9
Foster, Edward, v, 9, 29, 33, 37, 38–39, 51, 80, 126, 170, 171, 172, 173, 177

Heuving, Jean and Joan Jonas, 191
Keller, Lynn, 47, 48, 91, 113,
    116, 176, 183, 187, 188,
    190, 191, 192
Montgomery, Will, 130, 183, 193
Swensen, Cole, 93, 132, 135,
    180, 187, 191

Thompson, Jon, 18, 139, 190, 192

Audio Recordings
Souls of the Labadie Tract (with David
    Grubbs), 195
Thiefth (with David Grubbs), 99–100,
    107, 110, 111